Flo...

CW00376218

Acknowledgments

Ira
David
Maya
Sissy
Ed
Pamela
Roberta
Wayne
Frank
Mel
Jose
Steve
Barbara
Nan
Vadge
Mary Alice
Leonard
Mimi
Cookie
Ken
Bliem
Jan
Dianniese
Richard
Tina
William
Kim
Ellen
Nicholas
Gene Tierney
Mark

Bob
Doug
Steve
Edie
Martha
Spiro
Amanda
Cynthia
Harry
Dad
Lou
Ted
Mike
Suellen
Julian
Joe
Shirley
Sel
Mary
Eileen
Joanna
Tory
Tom
Larry
Susan
Neil
Jeff
Linda
Sheila
Tony
Ginny

Elizabeth
Lenore
Dahlia
Guy
Pat
Paul
Frannie
Mom
Debbi
The Texans
Muffy
Faith
Brian
Richard
Valerie
Craig
Rakesh
John
Karen
Darrell
Jack
my friend,
Donna
Cunningham
and *especially*
Cheryl Woodruff
who always kept
her eye on the
Light
May she be
blessed

Table of Contents

A Note from the Author

Dear Reader,

It's a subject everybody loves. Everybody wants to know how it's going to work out. Everybody wants to know what the future holds in relationships. So, after years of study and contemplation, I've come up with a recipe for the perfect relationship. And here it is:

Take a fingernail clipping from the one you love. In a saucepan place nails and two cups of water.

Boil briskly one hour, gradually replacing the liquid as it boils away so you have approximately two cups at all times.

Let stand until cool.

Drink while staring at the moon.

Now, you can do that and hope it works, or you can do what everybody else in the world does, and that's feel around in the dark and hope for the best. Maybe it's true that traditional relationships are going the way of blond coffee tables and 3-D glasses, crushed like a beer can in the fist of modern times. But we're all still driven by the urge to escape loneliness.

If you're warm and enthusiastic, rising joyfully to the challenge of being known and touched by another human being, then this book will help keep your relationships fresh and alive. If, on the other hand, you want only the ones you can't have and never want the ones you can have, then this material will give you some insights into some of the serious problems that often plague relationships.

For many people, both business and personal relationships can become *El Depressorama*. Oh, not when they're new, of course. When they're brand-new we run around the house, splashing on the cologne and singing. Ah, the ecstasy of those first moments, when you're a little tipsy on the hope that *this time*, things are going to be different.

Unfortunately, fantasies have a way of dissipating. And very soon a Frankenstein monster, your hidden relationship pattern, gets a jolt of juice and staggers forward to scare the daylights out of you and everyone around you.

I wish I had a buck for every time I've been asked by people, "Hey, what sign is best for Leo?" or "Is Aries really bad for Capricorn?" If there's only one thing you will learn from *Made in Heaven*, it will be that *it doesn't matter what sign you mate with*. If your head is on straight with respect to intimacy, sharing, and permanence, then any old sign will do. Some signs may be more stressful and others more harmonious, but the whole secret hinges not on what sign somebody else is but what your real requirements are when it comes to being with another person. And we all have requirements—whether we acknowledge them or not.

Do you die over blonds? Do you like serious business types, free spirits, homebodies? Why do we find ourselves attracted to the same types over and over again? In twenty-two years of astrological investigation, I've seen a lot of real-life soap operas. And I have found basic types, astrologically considered, that constitute our personal attractions. Whether it's a mother, father, lover, child, or boss, the people we are drawn to do indeed exhibit certain specific traits—things we always find, even when we don't think we're looking for them.

Every sign of the Zodiac has a complex relationship Rorschach. Everybody has a different set of drives and needs, based partially on the different positions of the stars and planets when we were born and partially on the fact that we've all been driven nuts by different parents in different ways. The more complex the celestial configurations found in your horoscope, the more complex your early family probably was—and, thus, the more difficult it may be to integrate all your conflicts and needs into one person.

But it must be said—I've seen charts where people have been orphaned at two and raised by wicked stepparents but who then went on to have well-adjusted, long, and happy marriages. So the first things to throw out of your mind are the Sign-to-Sign combination theories found in many books. While such analyses describe quite accurately the dynamics and interactions among the various archetypes, it's not really the place to start when making long-term transformations in your relationships.

Every person you attract, you attract to answer a specific need within yourself. Many times even without your conscious knowledge you'll conjure up a figure, or summon a type into your life to give you either pleasure or pain. Every relationship in your life reflects something deep inside you that you choose to act out through another; every relationship mirrors back to you another aspect of yourself.

In fact, if you know where and how to look, you can see your patterns in the very first encounter you have with any person at all. It's all there, the whole story, the whole secret, everything you need to know about what that person is doing in your life. Just take a second to think about the people in your life. Try to look back to the first moment you met. What were the conditions and circumstances of that first meeting? Where was it? Who introduced you? Who made the first move?

Remember that there are all kinds of relationships—parent-child, sibling, lover, friend, mate, business partner, teacher, student—and you'll find them all somewhere in these pages. It doesn't matter what gender you are or what your sexual preference is. Patterns are patterns. We're going to be making some pretty presumptuous statements along the way, but bear with my irreverence. When I tell you it doesn't matter what sign someone else is and that every relationship is actually a mirage conjured up by your own need to repeat a deeply buried pattern, I am definitely throwing down my glove and challenging you to look at some issues that may have been lying hidden in the trunk at the back of the cellar beneath Grandma's wedding veil for the last umpteen years.

Some of the conflicts, issues and relating styles described in the following pages may indicate patterns you exhibited at an earlier stage of your life. Don't be upset or make the mistake of thinking that I'm telling you you're absolutely still that way. What I am saying is that certain behavior is intrinsic to your sign and through growth, experience, and conscious effort, we change that experience.

When you've finished reading this book, not only will you have a healthier respect for the profound truth of astrology, but you'll carry away with you some tangible ways of dealing with your most compelling personal themes, such as why the very thing that's driving you crazy about someone in your life right this minute is the very thing that attracted you in the first place.

A note on agreement of pronouns and their antecedents to all you Websters, Oxford grads, nit-pickers and people with a loaded sixth house:

If you think it was easy to keep all the *your partners* and *your mates* in agreement with the his's, hers', him's and theirs', you're wrong. After a while I decided you'd just have to forgive me if I said a *someone* and followed it with a *their*. So I salute the grammarians, ask pardon and request that you read for the meaty context I think you'll find both fun and amusing.

Enjoy it!

Thank you for your indulgence,

Michael Lutin

Michael Lutin

INTRODUCTION

Pluto in Scorpio

What a strange era it is for relationships, although that could probably be said of any time in the history of human desire. We all need relationships, of course, always and forever, but as of this writing, people are exhibiting hair-trigger aggression more than ever before. Not like those beautiful days of the 1960s, when starlight glowed in everyone's eyes, or those rational seventies and early eighties, when *everything* was subjected to the scrutiny of sensible understanding.

Now, with the entrance of Pluto into the sign of Scorpio, people have retreated into their caves. And they may be there for the next ninety years. Each person stares out into the night suspiciously—listening for a hostile foot cracking a twig. These are dark times. The age of diplomacy is past. These days many people would really rather die than be taken advantage of. The terrorist consciousness we've all grown to dread is really no more than an extreme example of the rage many people feel toward those who have pushed them around.

Something has snapped within the hearts and souls of people. They're not eager to repeat a pattern that they view as, if not a fatal mistake, then at least a childish form of behavior they prefer to think they've outgrown. So these days, when you make what you think is one tiny little move that reminds somebody of his or her ex-wife or ex-husband, mother, father, boss or partner, you get hit with a frying pan or slapped with a pink slip.

The atmosphere for relationships is rough, and before we delve into the deeper relationship patterns formed by the various signs, we need to acknowledge this common social disposition pervading much of everyone's behavior today.

How long is it going to last? Well, if Pluto in Scorpio is any measure of it, then just think of how many babies are going to be born between now and 1995 with Pluto in Scorpio in their horoscopes and then calculate how long they'll all live and you'll get a rough idea.

We simply cannot talk astrology without confronting some pretty fundamental questions. If, as astrologers believe, one can accurately describe through the astrological charts and symbols the types of relationships a person will tend to form, and if we agree that our parents certainly influence our behavior in these relationships, then how do astrology, genetics, and environment fit together? How is it that your astrological chart, a map of the stars and planets at the time of birth, can describe both you and those parents who are going to influence you so stunningly, so tremendously? Is the time of birth already keyed in at the time of conception?

All living things respond to their environment—animals to danger, plants to light, etc. We interact with an environment the totality of which we are only dimly aware. The sun, moon, and planets are part of that environment. There's nothing spooky or mysterious about it. On sunny spring days you wake up often feeling quite different from the way you do on gloomy winter mornings. The planets of the solar system also create a kind of "weather," a much more subtle one that is registered only by the more subtle and sensitive areas of the mind.

The horoscope you are born with creates a deep and lasting impression on you. It is a picture of the cosmic weather pattern occurring when you chose to have your little picnic here on Earth. And because it is your first impression, it is your deepest and most lasting impression. Whether you think it's sunny or gloomy here depends a lot on that first, deep impression, which by the time you are an adult is lodged firmly in your unconscious mind.

As you probably know, your Birth Sign (or Sun Sign) is determined by the position of the Sun during the month of your birth. If we trace the journey of the Earth around the sun each year, we can study the repeated gravitational pushes and pulls made on our planet by the sun, moon, and planets as they move through their orbits. We divide the Earth's yearly path into twelve segments called Signs of the Zodiac, and from it we can observe various repeated characteristic effects each time the Earth passes along points on that path, relative to the changing positions of the other planets. The "Sign you were born under" is the Sign of the Zodiac the sun appeared to be occupying (from the Earth's point of view) during the month of your birth, and from it we can glean certain general trends concerning relationships.

For example, the signs *least* prone to divorce are Taurus, Scorpio, Cancer and Capricorn—that is, even when they *do* separate, they remain very much tied to their exes.

Now Libra, Gemini, Pisces, and Sagittarius—that's different. They are your Tommy Manvilles and Mickey Rooneys and Judy Garlands and Liz Taylors, Richard Pryorses, Bette Midlers, and Patty Hearsts. When they're with you, they're with you—but when they're gone, they're gone!

Aries, Aquarius, and Virgo—Leo, too, to some extent —even when they're married they're single. In fact, they are often closer to you when the tie isn't formal, for they often strain under contracts they themselves have sought to create. They always seem unattached.

Are Libra men like Chevy Chase or Ralph Lauren mad at their mothers but scared to show it? Do Tauruses like Barbra Streisand, Jack Nicholson, Al Pacino, and Rita Coolidge have an unusual investment in sex or power in a relationship?

General statements like these can be dangerous—because they are not true in every case, of course. But some patterns do occur and recur and consequently are worthy of being explored. But when dealing with astrology we have to be cautious. For astrology is subtle and deep and can easily be misused. It can help you to believe that although your patterns exist, they are justification for your actions.

They are not.

Everything is flowing, always moving, always changing. Each person is different and displays a different background, different motivations, and different compulsions.

Your Sun Sign, then, is just one factor. A huge one, but just the first of many. There's the moon and its path around the Earth. Then there's Venus, Mars, Jupiter, Saturn, Uranus, Neptune, and Pluto. And possibly more planets as yet undiscovered. Then, too, there's the tilt of the Earth with respect to the sun at the exact moment of your birth. All the distances of the planets to the Earth, to the sun, and to each other describe an impossibly complex set of reactions and responses that comprise our behavior.

All the planets, sun, and moon interact with force fields and cross currents against the backdrop of the stars. And whether we can grasp it or not, our actions can be accurately interpreted through astronomical symbols and astrological theories. Why or how, we can't exactly say until more scientific research is done, but we do indeed observe that our relationships correspond to astrological patterns visible in the chart from the moment of birth. The influence of your family is indelible, and the early stuff hardened you, but the astrological patterns were there from the start.

Made in Heaven will begin by telling you about you from the perspective of your Sun Sign. This book will provide you with endless food for thought, as well as some startling insights and practical solutions to long-term issues and problems in your relationships. Synthesizing all the combinations of mirages, monsters, and miracles, and making sense out of the contradictory questions, images, and conflicts that make up your particular pattern of relationships will present a most exciting challenge and lead you to a real sense of accomplishment with respect to understanding your relationships. Not to mention how you can check up on everybody you know and see what is making them tick and exactly how they tock in response to you.

If you don't know much about astrology, this book will still be of appreciable value to you. Simply omit the astrology from it if you like and refer to it by personality type, mirage, monster, or burning question presenting itself at any time.

We're not saying what's good, better, or best for you. We're simply observing the patterns that exist. Judge the rest for yourself. Insight is the first step toward permanent change.

HOW TO USE
THIS BOOK

Part One: The Twelve Signs

Every member of every sign of the Zodiac has a unique
pattern of relating to people. Specifics vary from person to
person, of course, but when you watch people closely, you
get to see some broad themes repeated over and over.
Maybe you're a fighter, go after money, act from your
heart, or play the therapist. Whatever your personal style,
we're going to analyze it first in simplest terms—according to your Sun Sign, by dividing all 12 signs into nine
sections.

1) The Mirage

In a room full of strangers, what draws you to that special person over there in the corner? What's that special
chemistry you feel toward a movie idol, or toward somebody at the office you just know you could have something
great going with? If you're single, let's face it—you're
shopping. And even if you're attached, you still have attractions outside the relationship. We're all in hot pursuit of
that elusive ideal. At the beginning of every relationship,
we all have a mirage we create and project onto the other
person, an idealized portrait of what the other person is,
based on what we *think* we want.

2) The Monster

After we get what we want, though, we tend to roll over
in bed, look at the prize, and scream, seeing for the first
time the Hyde that was hiding beneath the Jekyll of our

fantasies. Many relationships get wrecked when the monster appears.

3) The Real Thing

But the monster is only a mask, because when you're absolutely sure that you know exactly what you are doing in a relationship, be sure of one thing. You probably don't. Beneath it all, secret undercurrents are always at work; hidden games are being played. And to pass successfully through the monster phase, we have to probe beneath the surface of our attractions to learn what the real issues are and where we are really coming from.

4) The Burning Question

Every relationship poses its own questions, which must be answered if the people in it are going to grow and thrive. How can you be sensitive to another person and still retain your independence? How can one balance career and family, religious and cultural differences, deal with money and love? By examining our relating style, we can determine what our conflicts are likely to be.

5) Ultimate Challenge

To answer that burning question, each Sign must rise to a specific challenge, resolve a paradox, and meet another person in a real way, learning exactly *why* we draw certain people to us when we do.

6) The Miracle

Once one has blown the illusion of the ideal, grown through the monster phase, and erased the distortions, one is left with a whole, real person to relate to. It's at this point that each person makes the jump to reality, embraces another human being, and becomes whole, having learned what it was he or she was first attracted to, then fled from and finally has learned how to deal with. This is the miracle that each Sign discovers about itself through its relationships; through the miracle we discover why our partners are in our lives and why we're in theirs.

7) Working the Miracle

Now that we've gotten the meat off the bone with respect to relationship patterns and the Signs, we can start on the marrow and look at real ways real people can deal with real-life situations. We can't soak up an ocean of conflicts with one little sponge, but we do intend to discover some practical applications to all the theories raised, as well as present some possible solutions to issues that have come up.

8) Guardian Angels

Guardian angels are the symbolic representations of the types of attractions and relationships connected with the various Signs of the Zodiac. If you ever get confused or have doubts and problems about relationships, just visualize the guardian angels attached to your Sign. They will personify all the irony and humor you'll need to move you beyond the mirage-monster phase and into the miracle.

9) Celebrity Astro Games

Some fun and educational homework to test our theories.

Part Two: Theories and Practices

The Astrology Behind It All

Astrology can tell you much about your attractions and provide astounding insight into your choice of love object. But it's not as simple as saying Aries wants this, Taurus wants that. There's your Sun Sign to consider, Rising Sign, and lots of other little goodies called Venus and Mars, midpoints, planets opposing the sun and occupying the Seventh House, that will also hold one of the numbers on your combination lock. Because of all the various astrological factors at play, you're probably going to choose more than one ideal type. You could end up with four, five, or more, depending on what forces are at work. The more mirages you have, the more complex the personality of the individuals drawn to you will be. In this chapter we'll view some other possibilities and see how astrology tallies up with our personal choices.

Blame Your Mother!

Astrology is only part of the picture. What about that carnival we call family? Surely one's environment comes into play. We don't want Freud to turn completely over in his grave. So in this chapter we'll look at that eternal primordial triangle—your mother, father, and you—and see how your particular family environment relates to your astrological chart. Through this most vital connection we complete the transformation from the mirage of relationship reality.

Made in Heaven

This chapter presents a down-to-earth discussion of fate, free will, and how much we *can* change our patterns.

Part One

THE TWELVE SIGNS AND THEIR RELATIONSHIP PATTERNS

SUN SIGN RELATIONSHIP CHART

ARIES

THE MIRAGE: The Perfect Companion

Types you Arians love: shy, passive, congenial, polite, sensitive, responsive

THE MONSTER: The 98-lb. Weakling

Types you hate: weak-willed, lily-livered, indecisive, wimpy

THE REAL THING: Dominance and Submission

THE BURNING QUESTION: How Can Anyone Be there for Anyone Else and Not Be Turned into a Total Doormat?

ULTIMATE CHALLENGE: Identity vs. Merging

THE MIRACLE: Sensitivity to Others

WORKING THE MIRACLE: Listening

GUARDIAN ANGELS: The Bride and Groom

TAURUS

THE MIRAGE: An Irresistible Force

Types you Tauruses love: probing, intense, creative, sexy, spellbinding, powerful, magnetic

THE MONSTER: Dracula!

CANCER

THE MIRAGE: The Rock of Gibraltar

Types you Cancers love: successful, serious, businesslike, conservative, "older," "ambitious"

THE MONSTER: The Immovable Object

Types you hate: authoritarian, cold, troubled, world-weary, depressed

THE REAL THING: Recognition from the Boss

THE BURNING QUESTION: Who's the Child, and Who's the Parent?

ULTIMATE CHALLENGE: Personal Satisfaction vs. Worldly Success

THE MIRACLE: Depth of Commitment

WORKING THE MIRACLE: Dealing With Authority Figures

GUARDIAN ANGELS: The President and the First Lady

LEO

THE MIRAGE: A Flamingo among Ostriches

Types you Leos love: spontaneous, unusual, unconventional, inventive, offbeat

THE MONSTER: It Came from Outer Space!

Types you hate: weird, perverse, rebellious, erratic,

Types you hate: manipulative, controlling, jealous, draining, obsessive, sex-crazed

THE REAL THING: The Animal Within (The Dark Side of the Force)

THE BURNING QUESTION: Companionship and Sex: Can They Coexist?

ULTIMATE CHALLENGE: The Known vs. the Unknown

THE MIRACLE: Creativity

WORKING THE MIRACLE: Mystery

GUARDIAN ANGELS: The Magician and the Sorceress

GEMINI

THE MIRAGE: The Smiling Team Coach

Types you Geminis love: understanding, sporty, supportive, intelligent, generous

THE MONSTER: A Bloated, Self-indulgent Hypocrite

Types you hate: immoral, restless, lawless, self-indulgent, uncommitted

THE REAL THING: The Thirst for Experience

THE BURNING QUESTION: Is There a Line Between Healthy Optimism and Denial?

ULTIMATE CHALLENGE: Your Language or Your Partner's Language?

THE MIRACLE: The Raising of Consciousness

WORKING THE MIRACLE: Mature Communication

GUARDIAN ANGELS: Mr. and Mrs. Santa Claus

---

unreliable

THE REAL THING: Escape from a Controlling, Erratic Parent

THE BURNING QUESTION: How to Keep Giving If at Any Moment the Rug Could Be Pulled Right Out from Under?

ULTIMATE CHALLENGE: Security vs. Risk

THE MIRACLE: Friendship

WORKING THE MIRACLE: Granting Freedom

GUARDIAN ANGELS: The Munsters

VIRGO

THE MIRAGE: The Savior has Landed

Types you Virgos love: poetic, romantic, visionary, vague, unfocused, confused

THE MONSTER: Betrayer! Impostor! Fraud!

Types you hate: guilty, devious, deceitful, escapist, seductive, lazy

THE REAL THING: Fear of Making a Mistake

THE BURNING QUESTION: Is There Always a Good Guy and a Bad Guy?

ULTIMATE CHALLENGE: Order vs. Chaos

THE MIRACLE: Letting Go

WORKING WITH MIRACLE: Forgiveness

GUARDIAN ANGELS: Movie Stars

LIBRA

THE MIRAGE: World Champion of Everything
Types you Libras love: aggressive, decisive, pioneering, active, heroic, independent
THE MONSTER: Self-absorbed Egomaniacal Outlaw
Types you hate: angry, attacking, ruthless, selfish, unthinking
THE REAL THING: Powerlessness
THE BURNING QUESTION: How to Deal with Anger and *Not* Confuse It With Hate?
ULTIMATE CHALLENGE: Their Identity vs. Your Identity
THE MIRACLE: Self-esteem
WORKING THE MIRACLE: Open Confrontation
GUARDIAN ANGELS: Superman and Supergirl

CAPRICORN

THE MIRAGE: The Nursing Mother
Types you Capricorns love: nurturing, reclusive, ethnic, emotional, fertile, cuddly
THE MONSTER: The Yowling Brat
Types you hate: insecure, worried, changeable, babyish, needy
THE REAL THING: Giving In to Nature
THE BURNING QUESTION: Is It All Right to Feel?
ULTIMATE CHALLENGE: Office vs. Home
THE MIRACLE: Intimacy
WORKING THE MIRACLE: Bonding
GUARDIAN ANGELS: The Couple from *American Gothic*

SCORPIO

THE MIRAGE: The Rarest Emerald in the World
Types you Scorpios love: practical, pleasure-loving, loyal, commercial, acquisitive
THE MONSTER: A Green-Eyed Fiend of Jealousy and Greed
Types you hate: overpossessive, materialistic, selfish
THE REAL THING: The Nature of Desire
THE BURNING QUESTION: Does Money *Always* Have to Come into It?

AQUARIUS

THE MIRAGE: The Star
Types you Aquarians love: extroverted, ardent, demonstrative, warm, self-expressive, showy
THE MONSTER: NapoleonMussolini
Types you hate: bossy, egotistical, bratty, despotic, narcissistic
THE REAL THING: Direction
THE BURNING QUESTION: Love or Friendship?
ULTIMATE CHALLENGE: Distance vs. Closeness

18

ULTIMATE CHALLENGE: Attachment *vs.* Nonattachment **THE MIRACLE:** Manifestation **WORKING THE MIRACLE:** Cherishing Loyalty and Permanence **GUARDIAN ANGELS:** Elsie the Cow and Elmer the Bull	**THE MIRACLE:** Loving **WORKING THE MIRACLE:** Coping with Limerence **GUARDIAN ANGELS:** The King and Queen of Hearts

SAGITTARIUS

THE MIRAGE: A True Renaissance Person

Types you Sagittarians love: articulate, versatile, whimsical, dexterous

THE MONSTER: Schizo!

Types you hate: capricious, fragmented, split-off, ambivalent, nervous, superficial, lying

THE REAL THING: Restlessness

THE BURNING QUESTION: How Can/One Have a Relationship with Someone Who's Only Half There?

ULTIMATE CHALLENGE: Their Behavior vs. Your Sanity

THE MIRACLE: Communication

WORKING THE MIRACLE: Mental Flexibility

GUARDIAN ANGELS: A Team of Ape Language Researchers

PISCES

THE MIRAGE: Lighthouse in the Fog

Types you Pisceans love: hardworking, monastic, analytical, Spartan, pure

THE MONSTER: Parole Officer

Types you hate: suspicious, cynical, nervous, holier-than-thou, disciplinarians, unpleasable

THE REAL THING: Being Nailed Down

THE BURNING QUESTION: Why Work at Anything?,

ULTIMATE CHALLENGE: Reality vs. Romance

THE MIRACLE: Unfaltering Dedication

WORKING THE MIRACLE: Transformation by Example

GUARDIAN ANGELS: A Pair of Street Musicians

Chapter One

ARIES

The Mirage: The Perfect Companion

You Arians, when you first meet someone:

> "Wow! My soul mate at last! Someone who will be
> there for me and not hassle me every five minutes,
> the right glove to my left, the yin to my yang—all
> I've ever needed to feel complete."

You Arians don't really court; you campaign. You male
Arians are really funny—in your fantasies you play War-
ren Beatty and Captain Kirk of the starship *Enterprise*—
big-time prime-time tough guys with a string of girlfriends
they had to leave because they were really lone wolves at
heart. In real life, though, you often sit there holding the
yarn while your girlfriends knit. You female Arians take
long baths in Doris Day perfume but often run over your
husbands in the driveway. Men and women alike, you see
life as a hockey game, so your mates have to develop some
pretty swift responses if they don't want a puck in the
mouth.

You are definitely the most challenging sign to have a
relationship with. People have to be able to run fast to keep
up with you, but stop on a dime when you want a cup of

coffee. Your mates have got to be positively psychic to know what you mean when you say, "Honey, do me a favor and run and get my *stuff* over on the *thing*." And they must be able to execute such a garbled command instantly before you lose your temper.

But what draws you to your partners in the first place? You are all like uncut diamonds in that you need beveling and polishing off. You often see partners as a cool drink that will lower your temperature, because you are usually mad at somebody, and with Aries the scent of war is often in the air.

If your mate isn't the type to check collars for lipstick or listen in on phone conversations, you will prove remarkably loyal. At the beginning of your relationship with someone, you see him or her as gossamer rainbow-colored chiffon, as soft as mist, as fruitful and mature as a harvest of apples. You're drawn to the other's ease, and you actually believe your people can calm your angry seas with a wave of their hand. Their powers are so great, you believe, that they could have actually just walked right into the U.N., taken that shoe out of Khrushchev's hand, and said, "Now, Nikita, baby, what seems to be the trouble, hon?"

Though you're drawn to peacemaking powers, you love it when others fan the flames of *your* rage at someone else, murmuring, "Yes, dear. Of course, dear. I think you were absolutely right, dear."

You attribute to others all the powers you lack—to be able to deal consistently well with human beings. To talk to the neighbors without alienating the whole block, to get the phone company to come out in a storm to fix the line— simple things like communicating.

You admire (and envy) your mates' talent to bake the cake, decorate it, and then be civil to the person they did it for. Others seem to you to have a skill for guiding their ship through the mined waters of life—without major blowups. In your lifetime drama, you want someone as your co-star to give the piece polish and gentility and re-spectability. You'll supply the living room—they'll supply the taste. You usually hope to acquire not status through relationships but civility, because when you are with someone you can move about in society like a normal person and not have to shoot your way into or out of town.

I'm not saying that respectability is the only reason Diana Ross or Elton John got married. You are always romantic and always do it for love. And it's not exactly respectability that I mean. But there is a certain sense of wanting to belong to society that draws you to your mate. Because of the apparent ease with which others handle themselves, you believe that you can be taught breeding. Though you affect good manners, you are rough inside and look upon your partner as your charm-school teacher.

Who chases whom? It's never clear, but your partners often coach from the backseat. That's because Arians like to act single in public even when they're deeply and happily married.

To you Arians, your mates are the adjective that modifies the proper noun that is *you*. You see them as pure as the driven snow, fresh as this morning's donuts, and most egotistically yours. You have the most romantic picture of them as your soul mate, your cosmic complement. Someone to challenge and support you, fill you out, add to your life, fill in the blank spaces, cover your bases, be at your elbow for the 2001 little things you've neglected to take care of.

In return for their docility you'll bring out the best in them. You'll demand that they live up to themselves and meet your expectations of them. Fiery hoops they may once have feared, they jump through with gusto, thanks to you. They'll raft down a treacherous river and fill out every potential they have—all just for hanging out with an Arian.

Your mirage is the perfect mate who will love, honor, and cherish you, obey you for better or worse, in sickness and health, for richer or poorer, till death do you part.

The Monster: The 98-lb. Weakling

You Arians when you're sick of your mate:

> "This wimp is driving me crazy—can't make a move
> without being tailed by my shadow! And what a jerk
> this shadow is—so dependent, can't make a decision
> without whimpering and whining, afraid to take a
> chance on anything—in short, a ninety-eight-pound
> weakling!

BUT... Even though you'll periodically give them a
good stiff whack and then sincerely apologize, Aries hates
weakness in others. It scares you. Nothing nauseates you
more, and no matter how much you demand others' alle-
giance, what turns you off is their inability to stand up for
themselves. It's a paradox, of course, because when people
do stand up to you, you either crumble or try to crush
them. But basically you respect them for it.

You find it hard, however, to respect a wobbling, spine-
less jellyfish. And it horrifies you to discover that your
partner has allowed you to turn him or her into a human
glove into which you insert your iron fist. For you, the
monster is weakness, and it does not impress you if *people
you love* don't really exist on their own, that somehow
their identity is tied up to who *you* are, even if you thought
you wanted them to decorate you. Though you demand
submissiveness to a certain degree, you hold people in
contempt if they can't make any real decisions without
your help. You know such vacillation exists inside yourself, and when you see it in others, you throw up and
scream.

You Aries types are so scared of becoming weak that
you get the willies to behold it in others. So when others
whine, wobble, or snivel, you'll sometimes jump on their
chest and bang their head on the floor. You are always
striving for fresh outlets of self-assertion and hostility, but
ironically, if people try to speak out on their own behalf,
they'd better use diplomacy. You can usually dish it out all

right, but when it comes to taking it . . .

For you Arians, the monster is weakness. When you find out that your mate is really not the perfect complement after all, you're terribly disappointed. What you thought were thoughtfulness and consideration were not thoughtfulness and consideration at all. Those closest to you were just too frightened to say what they really thought. This you find too much to take.

Beneath your bravado is a tremendous fear of rejection, and when you are forced to look at it head-on in others, you run for the door. It terrifies you to see someone lacking in self-confidence, afraid to go after what he or she really wants. You are constantly fighting a fear of inadequacy, so you must stamp it out when you see it in others.

People who can't act overtly or make decisions for themselves were sometimes raised by parents who asserted themselves too much over them as children and made a personal battle out of the parent-child relationship. Soon the child became afraid to win and grew up on an endless cycle of self-assertion and self-punishment. The child grew into adulthood lacking in direction or confidence, fearing confrontation, or real communication, never daring to face an opponent openly and having to resort to sabotage and sneaky tactics.

This is the sick part of any relationship with an Aries— that the mates must resort to passive-aggressive acting-out, consistently weakening themselves, letting you think that you're so strong that they can't possibly exist without you. They go on perpetuating the illusion of their paralysis, until you can't even bear the sight of them.

In a relationship with an Aries, weakness could be a repeating pattern for the mates, and even though you Arians may do things to foster it, you don't approve of weakness. And if the mates repeat the experience often enough, they actually believe in their inferiority, incompetence, ineptitude, and impotence—and, strangely, enough, they lose the relationship with you.

What creates the illusion that people cannot live their lives without dependence on a strong figure? Why do we so often believe that there are circumstances outside ourselves that control us? Why do some of us arrange our lives so we are not free to make our own choices? Why do we feel unable to commit ourselves to a simple *yes* or *no* without checking with some authority figure first?

In the cosmic game plan, maybe there are some people whose task is to learn a lesson of dependence and sensitivity from other people. Maybe there are some unfortunate people whose parents broke their legs, then sold them the only pair of crutches in town.

But for all you Arians and all people in relationships with you, independence is always a key issue in the early background. Sometimes one or both of your parents may have instilled in you the belief that marriage was a threat to personal integrity and strength. So when people find you acting out against them just because they need you or because you're trying to prove you're not really dependent on them, they have to understand that you may have been conditioned to maintain your autonomy at all costs. Mixed messages undermine relationships. The mate is supposed to be the dependent one, but you Arians find it cloying. You want others to be pledged totally to you, but you still want to make decisions without consulting them. So your mates shouldn't be surprised to come home some night to find out you're moving to Phoenix tomorrow. You'll want them to go along with it all right, but if they're too docile and obedient, you'll squash them like a roach. You want their loyalty, but not their weakness. It reminds you too much of one of your parents.

The Real Thing: Dominance and Submission

You certainly don't want others to lead you, but you can't really stand a follower. You must be kept stimulated at every moment. At no time must you be allowed to rest. Your mate has to be there to give you a drink of water when you slow down around the turn, but you do *not* wish to be hassled by his or her needs. This, too, is a paradox, because when people you love are in *real* trouble, you don't walk; you fly to their side. If they're ever dying in a hospital, one can be sure it will be you who rushes past the nurses and the No Visitors sign, pulls out all the tubes, plants a kiss on their cheek, and commands them to live. And guess what—they will live.

But you don't want to be bothered with petty stuff. When you see someone whining or tugging at the line, getting pushy just for the sake of it, nagging you for attention or scared of their own shadow, you'll react by hitting them over the head.

Is Loretta Lynn, the country singer, working out her special issues of dominance and submission, strength and weakness, by maintaining her long-standing relationship with a very dependent but controlling man? One look at the commercials they do together on TV and you know she's stared down that monster a thousand times.

In fact, very often Arians seem to be selling out to losers. But others can't really know what's going on in a relationship unless they're in it. You Arians often hook up with people who seem a little less than you, less motivated, less famous, less confident, less something. Just the kinds of things in-laws love to wag tongues about over coffee. "What's she doing with him?" "What's he doing with her?"

You think you're so special that you usually have to have a relationship to find out that if you were totally perfect, you wouldn't need anyone at all.

You need people. But because your independence is a big deal, you often choose people who are more openly dependent. You Aries women, more than once, have undermined their own freedom by hooking into a macho pig to cater to. You're often so uncomfortable openly being the L.A. Rams tackle you truly are that you become the submissive partner you actually would like your partner to be and let the male express all the dominance you feel within yourself. This makes you so unhappy that at some point you force yourselves out of the relationship. You don't really want to be supported in the traditional way. Oh, you'll gladly take the alimony check, but basically you like to be able to say that you have cut through the jungle of life with your own machete. Do a little checking on Billie Holiday and you'll get the picture.

And you Aries men are just as uncomfortable with your female side as the women, but you, strangely enough, often attract aggressive women who try to boss you around. It's hard to imagine Pete Rose, Walt Frazier, or Omar Sharif struggling over who's going to wear the pants, but it is probably true nonetheless.

For Arians of both sexes the issue is always who comes first. And it's not as simple as saying *Aries* always comes first. Wrong. Of all the signs, you Arians are the most chivalrous. You don't want to be thought of as thoughtless, and even if it's killing you inside, you will often pass the food to someone else first.

The real issue is male dominance, and the monster is "female submissiveness." We say *male* and *female* because traditionally speaking men were always thought of as the bosses and women took orders.

Supremacy is an issue with you Arians. Who's on top? Who got there first? God is probably an Aries, so that should tell you something about how you feel about supremacy. In some way, you have to assert your dominance. When you have serious problems with self-image, you'll marry a pushy loudmouth as if to acquire courage by osmosis, because you can never be happy until your "maleness" is expressed. Again, we use the term maleness because self-assertiveness is commonly associated with having balls. Aries and testosterone go together like bagels and cream cheese. Not that you women aren't feminine or anything. You love silk and all that, but there's a primitive life instinct that has always been linked in our caveman history to dominant males.

No matter how idealistic and romantic the mates want to be, in this type of relationship they must see that they're playing games of sexual roles. You Arian men are trying to preserve your masculinity and prove your potency, and you women are waging a war on male chauvinism. These games can be either ferociously castrating and humiliating or loving and healthily competitive.

Male or female, you organize much of your behavior around issues of dominance, very often disguised behind a mask of politeness and caring. But beneath it all are issues often called male-female issues. Man or woman, you Arians will somehow gain the position of leader of the relationship. Not to degrade or humiliate the mate but simply to feel comfortable within yourselves—even though that position will always cause some guilt or discomfort. Our labels of male-female are inaccurate, really, because Arians of both sexes have to become the "man," as it were. You women have a tougher juggling act, of course, because you are striving for healthy self-assertion and independence while trying not to lose yourselves as women or be branded "unwomanly" by men who are threatened by your strength. You men struggle, too, in your own way, because you often have to act more macho than you really are. What's Eddie Murphy really like? Few people probably know.

It might be a good idea to check the dictionary yourself at this point for the terms *male* and *female*, *dominance* and *submission*. That way you'll be perfectly clear on your own without any sexual bias from me on the subject before you go on.

Just remember that you need the challenge of a challenger, but you really want to lead. When you win, you gain respect for yourselves, so others shouldn't expect you to throw the fight to make them feel good. You are masters at being masters. When the wagon train pulls out for the West, an Aries has to be at the front. You may make others the star of the movie, but you will always have to direct, no matter what else seems to be happening.

The Burning Question: How Can Anyone Be There for Anyone Else and Not Be Turned into a Total Doormat?

Let's not think that Aries relationships are a case of the Christians vs. the lions. In fact, the opposite is most often true. You are not in a relationship to weaken other people. Just the contrary. You come into their lives when a building is burning and they're asleep on the second floor. You always inject strength and vitality and freshness into a situation. You always bring strength to others. In fact, you are so ardent and sensitive to others that relationships are most exhausting to you. It hurts to find out that their sun does not rise and set around you.

You are not usually into sadism in relationships. You are ambivalent about your partner's strength. But you are into loving, passionate involvement and pleasing the object of your affections; being, doing, providing, and creating whatever they need. So you are truly the number one catch of the astrological sea. Maybe you women are screamers, and maybe you men have a new job every two years, but you are *prime* as prime can be.

Every relationship you have poses you the same question: How can you be there and be sensitive to another person and still retain a shred of yourselves and not be a doormat? You always go beyond the call of duty, turn into pretzels, and wind up behind the eight ball. You'll always go out on a limb for others, because that's who you are, but when that limb snaps, you're out there by yourselves, and that's a tough lesson to learn.

You want to be heroes, and in return you expect certain responses. But people cannot follow perfectly the choreography as determined by you Arians, and it's often hard for you to allow others to start taking their own cues. So you're often caught between doing too much and not doing enough. There's often a point in every Arian relationship when you pass by the mirror while *you* are carrying all the suitcases and say, "Hey, wait a minute. There's supposed to be two people here."

Then you have to separate yourselves from your mythic mission and see that you do not, indeed, hail from the planet Krypton. So ardently have you been taking on the relationship that you have become the only member of it. And your mates have grown so accustomed to the chivalry of it all that they enjoy riding through the relationship on a rickshaw pulled by you Arians.

True, you love it. For a while. Then you see what's going on, and there's a sickness or an explosion, a separation, or murder. Of course, it's your own damn fault. Your superhuman efforts tend to vegetabilize your mates. You finally realize they've gotten you to think less of yourselves, and you not only cater to their every whim but take out the garbage as well.

You are ever striving to find a balance between making too many demands and not making enough. You can be ridiculously demanding (I wouldn't want to be Debbie Reynolds's hairdresser or Gary Carter's accountant). But you are always trying to keep from exploding with anger. Because you know what pains you can be, you often try extra-hard to talk softly and be nice.

Yes, one has to watch out for you. In those dark games of master and slave, you know how to get the slaves to dance, but your burning question always keeps you hopping. You're always keenly aware of the balance of power, who's forming policy, deciding whether tonight you eat Chinese or Italian. You're positive controllers in the sense that you surround the relationship with your superb capabilities, and your burning question gets answered only as you decide whether you want to be thought of as heroes or humans.

It's a question we all ask ourselves at some point or other in our relationships, no matter what our sign. How can any of us develop the sensitivity for a partner, be there for someone else totally, retain our selfhood, and not become a total doormat?

Ultimate Challenge: Identity vs. Merging

You do want to share your food, money, pleasures, and love. But you need to guard against engulfment by your own need to merge with another person. You men often have serious issues of dominance, especially with other men in authority positions. Marvin Gaye was an extreme example. But it is both sexes in the Aries tribe who must develop a balance between maintaining personal integrity and joining with another person. You're all warm and generous, but you are still resolving big dependency issues. You men know well what happens to those who can't control their women, and you women know only too well what happens to submissive females who fall under the control of dominant men. Much of your sexual identification depends on your battle to free yourselves from the historical positions of your own sexual role model. You don't want to be your mothers or fathers. You want to be yourselves. You hate history and laugh at Freud. And yet there isn't an Aries alive who has not had to deal with the compulsion to recreate the drama of parents, those homey scenes we all remember in dreams and nightmares. Your analysts often end up taking Valium, because at the heart of every Aries lies the profound dedication not to change, because to change what is already perfect would be a crime against nature.

Those of you who can't get the balance together cannot get along with anybody. Your life is your war. Everybody's a threat to your precious integrity. You have a new job every five minutes because every boss is a moron. You scream, "Shaddap!" and grab the credit and push people off their crutches to get on the bus ahead of them.

The evolved Arian is a different story. You know who you are. And while you may still push ahead in line, you'll turn around, extend a hand, and help the person behind you on the bus.

If you do seem pushy, selfish, egocentric or dominating, others should understand that you are fighting your own tendency to go to the other extreme and become their personal doormat. Those of you who have resolved some of these issues do not boss others around indiscriminately or involve yourselves in control battles, putting a twig in the spokes of their bicycle so they'll remember you're there.

You are directive by nature. Even when you beg for peace and tranquility, you do best handling emergency room procedures in a hospital. When you're highly evolved you can allow others their independence while keeping your own. You have your sphere of direction, and you don't horn in on others. You can be there for them without either running them over with a truck or utterly disintegrating under their manipulation. You confront the challenge of another person's reality not with the primitive instinct to crush the opponent, not be melting into them, but by unified separateness.

It's a wrestling match for you, but as much with yourselves as with others. If the old push comes to shove, you do tend to pin them to the mat, but remember that your cosmic responsibility is to develop *your* strength, not theirs, and to create a spirit of healthy competition in which it is okay to win and come out on top.

Others have to be able to take a few bumps and a couple of dozen knocks when they're running alongside an Aries. There is no way their life can be boring. You Arians are fighting to keep a shred of yourselves against your own desire to melt into your companions.

The Miracle: Sensitivity to Others

While you Arians are afraid of being compromised by sharing control and are often on a mad crusade to prove potency, like everyone else in the world, you do want companionship, and sooner or later you're willing to come to the bargaining table. It's at that point that Arians open up to sensitivity to others. Never when you think others are trying to "get" you.

You have to go to others because you think they have something you want or need to share. And it's only then that others can work a deal and negotiate some kind of relationship.

Okay, so what if sometimes you're not the most giving or sharing individuals in the whole world? If other people had to survive on their own from a very early age or compete with ferocious siblings or even with a parent, chances are they wouldn't turn into Mother Theresa either.

The roots of rage and aggression are usually pretty deep, and every Aries is on his or her own path, each at a different step in the evolution of personal relationships. Aries with highly developed relationship patterns are still self-directed, to be sure, but you can be responsive and sensitive to the needs of other people without being threatened.

Naturally people can't be taught to care about others if they basically don't. To kill the monster of weakness and the fear of dependence, you Aries have to learn to share, and accept the validity of other people's viewpoints.

Successful relationships require that people forget themselves, and this unusual event, miraculously enough, happens quite often for Arians. That's why you rush into burning buildings and drag people out of car wrecks.

A rare occurrence is that moment of self-obliteration, an overwhelming experience not of slamming doors to get attention but of totally loving or existing to support another individual. It can't be bought or sold or practiced. It has to come from the core of being. And the Aries monster is destroyed always by dedication to somebody else.

If people believe down deep that it's dangerous to give themselves to somebody else, then they will always find ways to be proven right. Of course, the only danger is fear—fear that someone may be cruel, leave you, or die. But you Arians have the tools of self-reliance and the smart among you aren't scared it will go away. When you evolve, your relationships reflect a power that makes others' jaws drop. Under those conditions others thrive just by knowing you. Not only will you be finely tuned to the needs and wishes of your loved ones, but you will be able to throw them out of a moving car, if need be, to stimulate them to greater action, action that will get them closer to their real goal of personal fulfillment.

You people are alive like nobody else in the world. In fact, what you can do with a flick of your little pinky, most people can't do in a lifetime. One must put up with a lot when one is involved with an Aries—the selfishness is going to be hurtful, and the thoughtlessness will sting.

But the miracle finally happens for you when you figure out, either by instinctual human longing or practical necessity, that you don't want to be alone. This major decision, of course, changes five hundred times a season, but once you really and truly do decide you need someone, you're faster than a speeding laser ray and more powerful than a booster rocket when it comes to winning them over.

But winning someone over is not your miracle. That you can do with less energy than it takes to strike a match. Getting a relationship isn't the real feat; keeping one is. Once you've swept them off their feet or gotten them to give your company the contract, maintaining the relationship comes up as the biggest problem of all. And that's where you need your miracle.

We know you hate weakness and are threatened by strength, so you have to find a balance between your obnoxious aggressiveness and your intimidation by others, which you blow all our of proportion. You can only find that balance when you relate to your mate not with disdain or defensiveness but on a person-to-person level. To develop sensitivity and a spirit of cooperation, you Aries fireballs need to learn how to listen, discuss, negotiate, compromise, and share.

You evolved types don't just turn your heads off while a partner is in the middle of a sentence, just because he or she is going to have a need that inconveniences you. You'll still push people, but your pushing will know its limits. You have to be able to discuss things with them, not just blare at them or crumble and disappear when they have a gripe. You evolved Arians look at honest communication as an exciting and stimulating challenge, not an aggravating exercise in will-bending. Once you learn how to listen without being enraged by another's point of view, then you can discuss issues fully.

Although you'll probably always think a lot of talking wastes precious time, it leads you closer to your miracle of sensitivity—cooperation and the companionship you seek. Above all, you have to overcome your fear of hearing what you might not want to hear.

At that point you can develop the art of true negotiation. A successful lover or executive knows the art of graceful self-restraint. If you are hell-bent to prove yourself as a petty tyrant, you can go around blurting orders to inferiors. You get away with this during crises, of course, so some of you unevolved Arians will create a crisis as a way of showing your rage without being taken to task for it.

You wise Arians don't simply say, "I'll expect this on my desk by February second. Period!" That only creates hostility on another person's part toward you, and even if other people are not in a position to act out openly, passive-aggressive retaliation only undermines the success of the relationship.

So you successful Arians, knowing full well you are in at least partial control, discuss feasibility and tactical alternatives, curbing impatience and rage all the while, in an effort to preserve a relationship you fought to get in the first place.

This leads to compromise. Compromise is not just the crushing of someone else's will or being crushed by it. It is the greatest leap toward your miracle, because it shows willingness to participate in the give-and-take that is relationship.

Once you are there, sharing is all that's left to open you to the full power of the miracle. It's hard for you, though, because as generous as you are, you're often jealous of the strengths your mates do have, and it's hard for you *not* to exert force, bend them to the breaking point, before you realize that both parties are bringing something powerful to the relationship, and sharing these strengths is the joy of the bond. Sharing strengths, weaknesses, assets, and liabilities brings you close to achieving that miracle of jumping out of yourself, even for an instant to touch, know and, bring new life to a relationship.

Working the Miracle: Listening

Every Aries has that miraculous power to form and maintain a lasting and intimate bond, *can* leave himself or herself—jump away from self-involvement, self-aggrandizement, self-improvement, self-anything, and *be* there, truly, totally, and with a loving heart, for another person. Can overcome all issues and accept others' intuitions, hear their advice, abide by their decisions, embrace their needs without rancor or bitterness (no punitive action), and give wholehearted support for whatever others have chosen to do.

This is not a fairy tale. You Arians do indeed have the power to be sensitive to other people. How limited is this power? Every Aries is different. But a lasting relationship is always possible, depending on Arian willingness to *listen*. This is the Aries point of connection. Listening is the key to sensitivity and the path to your miracle. As you learn to listen fully and deeply (without interrupting every two seconds or contradicting silently), the door opens—listening without fighting, listening without defense, hearing not only the words someone is using but the tone, hearing everything that is *unsaid*, comprehending all the unspoken messages that are forever being communicated. Noticing everything, observing, taking in the total picture, grasping the hidden agenda. This is the secret clue to the Arian miracle of your sensitivity to others.

First of all, Aries, you have to want it, of course—*it* meaning a relationship with another healthy human being. And there's quite a difference between saying you want something and wanting it. There are twenty million single people out there who say they'd like to find and be with somebody, when what they really want is a faceless person to keep them company while they go around and do what they want when they want. But if they think they want it and don't have it, then there are a few glitches in their unconscious minds that are not permitting the development of enough sensitivity toward others to create, nurture, and promote a long-term commitment, business or personal.

Some people are profoundly more interested in themselves than in other people. It's no sin; it's the way they are. And while they will often *try* to talk to someone they don't care to talk to and are no longer interested in, after a short while, it simply *ain't* there, and the relationship dries up and blows away.

So, Aries, developing sensitivity to other people is predicated upon the simple premise that you give a damn about somebody else. If an individual is dedicated to his or her own development (and, again, it's no sin), then naturally he or she still has to have relationships—family, business, love, etc.— but at the push-shove point, their priorities surface and the card that comes up is #1.

But if you want to hear someone, really hear them, you have the power to do so. Besides the fact that they might actually have a good idea once in a while, nobody is boring. Even the most boring individuals are communicating a wealth of information, about their inner life, and most of the time they're often not even aware of what they're doing. So when you turn yourself toward listening, really listening, to others' stories, complaints, and demands, you will get a library of input that will help you to deal much more successfully with them. In addition, the things that matter to them, problems they're solving, questions they're raising, issues they're wrestling, all in some strange way mirror your life and mind.

So by learning how to listen, you Arians can have a fabulous revelation about your own inner lives. We are all drawn to people, and they are drawn to us for specific learning lessons. It's a wondrous system. You could be going crazy from listening to someone ramble on about their grandmother or the rude guy in the drug store, when suddenly, just by opening up that "third ear," everything becomes clear.

While they're droning on about meaningless trivia no one in their right mind could possibly care about, there are unexpressed wishes people are transmitting to you, their listener, about their relationship with you. All proving, of course, how enriching it can be to be present in a relationship.

While no Aries on Earth will get an A in paying attention every single semester, it is the key to success in relationships.

Gift Ideas for Arians

Here are a few gift suggestions to help you Arians along this path:

- Large rubber ear. This can be found in any novelty store and makes a nice big hint to remind you to listen more fully.
- Note pad with stamped envelopes. This will help you validate others' communications, respond to their letters, and recognize their requests a little better than you often do.
- Answering machine. This allows you to come and go as you please but to have no real excuse when you fail to answer calls.

Reading Material for Advanced Arians

The Listening Process, Robert Langs, M.D., Aronson Publishing. A book of 655 pages. When you get through reading it, you will be completely and totally evolved.

Guardian Angels: The Bride and Groom

The Bride and Groom watch over Arian relationships, because together they symbolize a perfect union of opposites, yin and yang, masculine and feminine, active and passive, dominant and submissive, taking and giving. These symbols have nothing whatever to do with the gender or sexual preference of the Aries in question.

The Bride and Groom together stand for a newness of commitment shared by two people, a freshness in a relationship that is achieved by uniting a constant thirst for change with a pledge to remain bonded together. They represent the overcoming of resistance to sharing, and God knows that you Arians often suffer from a defense against giving over too much of your lives to somebody else.

There's always the danger of getting knee-deep in wedding cake or having the relationship turn into quicksand, but the Bride and Groom preside over relationships with Aries to preserve the freshness and to guard against stagnation.

In fact, it's probably a good idea for people involved in a relationship with an Aries to have a renewable option put into the marriage contract. If I were married to an Aries, every year on our anniversary, I'd get married all over again—probably with a different ceremony in a different city.

Others should not throw the marriage vows or business contract up to an Aries. You will not be moved by those guilt tactics and will tend to tear up the paper and throw it in their face.

When trouble brews in an Aries relationship, one should remember that success means a harmonious blend of ego demand and compromise. Besides keeping the novelty going, negotiation is the key to longevity, and the Bride and Groom denote two consenting adults committing themselves publicly to an agreement both will honor.

Celebrity Astro Game

You'd be surprised how many ways people reveal themselves in everything they say and do. To sharpen your sensitivity to other people and to learn more about the ways renowned Arians handle their deepest relationship issues, look over the following list and pick out the people who interest you most.

Do a little sleuthing about their lives. Observe their actions; listen to what they say in public. The songs they sing, the roles they play, the particular contributions they make, will enlighten you about the relationship patterns of this sign.

William Shatner
Eddie Murphy
Ron Jaworski
Steve McQueen
Anita Bryant
Gloria Steinem
Erica Jong
Diana Ross

Betty Ford
Aretha Franklin
Hugh Hefner
David Letterman
Dudley Moore
Ed Marinaro
Walt Frazier

Chapter Two

TAURUS

The Mirage: An Irresistible Force

You Taureans, when you see someone across a crowded room:

> "Oh, my God! Who *is* that? I've never seen eyes like
> that in my life. They go right through me. Now, *that*
> is an attractive person. What's happening to me? I
> feel as if I'm being dragged across the room by those
> eyes. Wow, this is great!"

When a magician needs a body to saw in half up on the
stage, it's a Taurean in the audience who volunteers. You
Tauruses love to be drawn into a relationship by mysterious
figures who never reveal all their tricks.

You love to cuddle and be cozy and close but what
really draws you in is remoteness. You are aware of that
stranger at the back of the bus, the guy or gal who lives
just beyond the bus line, way over at the other side of
River Road. It's not exactly the social outcast that attracts
you but you are truly intrigued with the misfits who dwell
far away from the other villagers, the shamans and spirit
watchers who mix their dark potions far from the camp-
fire's light.

Did Candice Bergen fall in love with Louis Malle's power and mystery? Was Mikhail Baryshnikov perhaps not mysterious enough for Jessica Lange? Will it be different with Sam Shepard, though? If part of him is truly unhavable, ungettable, is that going to change her?

Tauruses love mystery. Just think of Shirley MacLaine's fascination with the beyond.

In fact, you will build a mystery around a partner even if it isn't there. To keep a Taurean interested, your mates should never tell you what they do on their way home from work and, when they get home, they should be so terribly amorous that you will be sure they're guilty and hiding something.

Your ideal mate is the wizard, the alchemist, and you will attribute to him or her the most medieval of powers. You approach relationships with the excitement and terror of Mickey Mouse as the Sorcerer's Apprentice, and you love to feel that these powerful figures willed you to take off your clothes just with the sheer force of their eyebrows. You give them power that is positively nuclear in its awesome potential. And because you think it's there, when others are with you, their chest does in fact swell, and they do get the hormone rush of an elk in mating season.

You like your partners to be above the rat race of Wall Street and to exist for art's sake while they prepare their magic potions, paint their pictures, and turn water into wine. You are forever people, and like palm trees in a hurricane, you bend only when you absolutely have to, but once you're planted in a person's life, you almost never uproot. In fact, after a storm hits Tallahassee and the flood waters recede, there you are, Mr. or Ms. Taurean, still poised over the hibachi, and all you have to do is flip the burgers. You're permanent people who base your relationships on a trust any bank could bet on.

But you see your mates as more withholding, secretive, unable or unwilling to share the darker parts of themselves. You are indeed very sexual beings, but your upbringing and values demand that you seek much more out of life than a roll in the hay. So while you insist that sex is not number one on your list of priorities, you often choose people for whom sex does play a greater role and who act out sexually more overtly than you do.

You Tauruses are sensual, earthy beings who enjoy the pleasures and delights of this fleshly world. But your appetites often rule you, and you find much trouble regulating your desires and needs. As a result, you find yourselves often overactively involved with your sexual attraction for other people; or when you go too far in the other direction and abstain totally, you are drawn to seductive individuals who sexualize too much. You balanced Tauruses conquer this problem and find yourselves drawn to powerful, magnetic artists and healers.

You like the benefits of power without getting sullied in the dirtiness of politics. You want the pleasures of the flesh without being drowned in the preoccupation with those pleasures. And you usually find seductive figures to promise you both.

There are many kinds of seductiveness, we should add, many ways of manipulating people, leading them in one direction or another, distorting their views and subtly altering their perceptions, indirectly evoking looked-for responses.

You have to be on the lookout for this type of seductiveness. Power figures drive you wild. You love to be moved by some giant force of magnetism and destiny. You love to be lifted up and taken from your armchairs into the unknown. So, naturally, you go like a sleepwalker into the arms of hypnotists, magicians, and those men and women who can exert the greatest power in the most subtle ways.

The Monster: Dracula!

You Tauruses, when you find out what someone is really like:

"How could you? How could you carry on like that behind my back? Don't you have any self-respect?

Don't you have any respect for me? And to think I
left my mother for you!"

But ... when you Tauruses start feeling as if you're
being drained by someone, you clasp your necks and
scream, "Oh, my God—Dracula!"—draining your blood
banks, emptying your bank accounts. Here you thought
you were getting a life companion and your partner was
practicing prostitution! O black day! To have invited such a
faithless fiend into the house!

There's nothing frivolous about you people, and you
don't appreciate a misuse of power on a mate's part. You
are offended down at the base of you if he or she takes
advantage of your generosity. So when you see and feel
people who are sucking you dry, emotionally or financially,
naturally you struggle to get free. It horrifies you to see
that other people's seductiveness and salesmanship did not
have the sincerity, intimacy, and personal involvement with
which you approached the relationship. You perceive them
then, as charlatans, prostitutes, purveyors of cheap tricks.
They've posed as suave and debonair when actually
they're merely creatures of the night with dark habits and
unfathomable obsessions. What you first thought to be intense and creative in them turns out to be a compulsive and
impersonal restiveness, and you are crushed to see that
they fly like a mosquito from neck to neck to get their
sustenance.

You loved their subtlety, their magnetic attractiveness.
You were turned on by their powerful being and the way
everyone just seemed so naturally drawn to them. But now
you see the cruel manipulation and it scares you. They
want to turn everyone, you believe, including *you,* into a
puppet attached to the strings of their desires. They scheme
and plot, skilled in political game-playing and revenge, as
organized as an army general, as oriented toward their own
survival as an insect.

And what frightens you most is how secretly self-destructive they turn out to be. What you at first considered
their bold daring is only their ghoulish attraction for dark-

ness and danger. Their hysterical need to exist close to the edge threatens your security, wrecks your nerves. Although you Tauruses loved them because they brought you a little closer to that edge, you hate disruption and sudden change. What once seemed like bold self-expressiveness soon seems antisocial and vulgar, and when you behold conduct you deem downright ungodly, you are tempted to grab a silver crucifix and wooden stake to see if they flinch.

Did Cher like Sonny because he was tough and savvy —knew how to handle agents and press people and get them to say and do things without even their knowledge they were being manipulated, knew when to advance, when to retreat? I'd sure like to have been a fly on the wall if Cher ever began to feel her flesh turning into wood in a weird reverse-Pinocchio process that would eventually lead to Sonny's having all the creative control while she, the real dough, was baking all the bread.

That is an inevitable dark moment in Taurean relationships, when the other person finally draws the bottom line and says to you, "Okay, say whatever you want to me or about me, but give me the money." It titillates you to believe that some Force Majeure drew you into their arms, you are horrified to find out that they were the Force Majeure and that they had resorted to sorcerer's manipulation, just because they wanted something you had.

You want to be wanted by a figure you consider sexy, remote, and ungettable. You love your partner's insatiable-desire nature. You Tauruses play the kid from a good family who is fatally attracted to the riverboat gambler, or "black bra and panties" type. But when their seductiveness continues and is directed toward others, you crack. For nothing fractures you more than to be lured into a spider's sexual web.

You, do, however, titter excitedly when you disobey a No Trespassing sign, so while you say you are definitely not a gambler and are practically attached to your Limoges teacups or gun collection and don't really cotton much to change, still you pick people you know will demand a complete and total change in your life.

If you have any interest in mythology, this is the place to pause and do a little extracurricular reading on the Pluto-Persephone myth. It's the basis of Taurean relationships, where the Taurean (male and female) enacts the role of Persephone, who is taken from her mother, Demeter, and carried underground by Pluto who probably looked as Italian as De Niro or Loren.

There are many variations of that great myth, but here's one of them:

Pluto, god of the underworld, came above ground and saw Persephone and went wild for her. Who hooked whom is not clear—whether it was a mutual wink or a first-class rape and kidnapping. In any case, off went Pluto to the underworld with Persephone either over his shoulder or on his arm.

Demeter, Persephone's mother and goddess of green plants, cereals, and grains, was fit to be tied when her daughter missed curfew. The gods from Mount Olympus went downstairs to intercede for Demeter, and finally Pluto let Persephone go.

One hitch: She had eaten six pomegranate seeds over the weekend she was with Pluto, and for some reason that meant she had to spend six months out of every year down in the underworld with him.

Demeter then decided that for six months out of every year there would be snow, ice, and no green plants, cereals, or grains.

Besides the fact that it drives up the prices of produce and Caribbean cruises, this myth has great impact on the sign of Taurus. You Tauruses always seem to have to find a powerful person to seduce you away from your mothers so you can carry on shamelessly for a while. Symbolically you relive this myth by finding someone who can take you away from everything that is known and carry you into an experience with the unknown.

When they do actually introduce you to your new life, you are as hard to move as a piano. Did Judy Carne really write all those terrible things about how Burt Reynolds had abused her? Hey, we can't say that you Tauruses are into the real kinky stuff, no matter what Cher's body-building commercials on TV seem to imply, but it's important to set the record straight about one thing. What you first perceive as an exciting temptation you sometimes later interpret as abuse—not that victims of abuse who happen to be Tauruses are asking for it. We're simply stating that you Tauruses and the other astrological combinations who fall into this category are drawn to powerful, mysterious, controlling, potentially dangerous figures.

You often come from families where one of the members was perceived as sexually hyperactive or deeply manipulative in a seductive way. There's a fabulous Italian movie starring Silvana Mangano, one of Earth's most gorgeous Taurean women; the movie is called *Anna,* and it's a perfect tale of Taurean obsessiveness in relationships. Mangano is sexually hypnotized by a powerful man (Vittorio Gassman) who's got such a hold over her that all he has to do is ring her phone in the middle of the night and she gets out of bed and drives over to his place.

You Tauruses are sexually vulnerable. Once others abuse their power over you and reveal to you your monster, it's hard for you to open up again.

You are peaceful people but should not be pushed too far. Some Tauruses have been known to shoot their lovers.

The Real Thing: The Animal Within (The Dark Side of the Force)

You love biologists, detectives, fearless explorers of the South Pole, and anybody who lives on the edge. You can forgive others for being furtive, prurient, or genitally fixated. That's part of what drew you in the first place. But once you allow yourselves to be known, opened up, penetrated, once that gland of appetite gets stimulated, you are all like hungry little birds with their beaks turned up waiting for a big, fat, juicy worm. You are creatures of appetite and, thus, usually struggling against one temptation or another.

You are not sex fiends. You like to spend time polishing the furniture and nailing it to the floor. You all clip coupons and watch for bargains. I'll bet when she's reading the London paper even Queen Elizabeth gets turned on when she sees a sale at Harrod's. You are respectable people who don't want to cause talk in the neighborhood. In fact, you aspire to *be* the very Joneses everyone else is trying to keep up with. You believe in loyalty, trust, stability—everything the First National Bank promises to give. You will provide the land, the house, the bed, and the sheets, but it's going to be up to your mate to provide the rest. You are the producer and they are the performer, as in Isabella and Columbus.

Taurus is the bank, the keeper of the "eggs." In that sense, it is feminine and needs to be "fertilized" by a "male." This symbolic union has nothing to do with physical gender or sexual preference. Although the heterosexual human female fits most readily into this archetype, the symbol of the egg being fertilized applies to both genders. Taurus is all about a long-term monogamous relationship from which there is always issue. It's about planting in fertile soil and nourishing the growth of crops.

So you are the stable one. You're the plant that needs watering, the cat that has to be fed regularly. You Tauruses stand for all the permanence that keeps this old world turning.

Even though you have this unshakable need to have a job and know the car payments are being made on time, and you put away savings for the tuition you'll need in the year 2026, it doesn't prevent you from having creative aspirations or craving excitement.

Au contraire.

Nothing can be manifested here on Earth without being nourished by the unseen forces at work in the universe and you Tauruses know that better than anyone else. Though you are always making long-term contributions to society, ever trying to follow a civilized form of morality, you are always aware of the dark power that lies deep within us all, a power that turns us all on like light bulbs, quickens our souls to life, turns the planet Earth, and moves the galaxy through space.

It is an unnamed and unnameable force, something raw and atavistic that responds only to its need to survive and keep going; a primitive, instinctual drive that is the animal, the reptile, the amoeba, within us all. It is this animal drive that is at the core of Taurean attraction.

You Tauruses are in love with it. But you sure aren't comfortable with it. It can't be bought at Brooks Brothers or Neiman-Marcus, and you know it. It is sheer creative power, natural magnetism, a fearsome force within some people that allows them to confront the unknown, penetrate the unknown, and return to the land of the living to tell about it.

Tauruses are passionately mad for it. But it's scary, because it often surfaces as compelling sexual attractions.

Some of you Taurean men use your sexual positions to control your women. You think that just because you have that equipment between your legs, you have to hit a woman over the head with it every five minutes or she'll chop it off. But some of you Taurean women, too, can be sexually threatening and use your powers of allure and attraction to keep your men in line.

Many Tauruses were involved with parents who (always very appropriately, of course) may have been subtly controlling and seductive at the same time. But your present relationships are certainly more than your partner's merely being manipulated by their reactions to your past.

As a result of your Taurean values and your upbringing, your success in relationships depends on your ability to discern appropriate sexual behavior and how to deal with the many elemental forces of the invisible world that are beyond your control. You must learn to grapple with things you cannot see.

It's the achievement of a nonjudgmental balance between your simple Taurean material goals and the complex creative and antisocial behavior of the people you find most attractive that gives you everything you really want. And in gratitude you'll not only pick up the check but give others the world. All they have to give you is the power to experience the pleasure of a starry night.

The Burning Question: Companionship and Sex: Can They Coexist?

You not only bring your partners an appreciation of long-term loyalty and deep emotional commitment, but you contribute a wholesome light to a relationship. You'll keep your partners rooted, make sure they stay on track and in sight of their goals, and help them develop their resources so they have something tangible and lasting to show for all their sweat, toil, and anguish over their hopes and dreams. So you help them to push out of the darkness and up into the light.

In business relationships you take delight in marketing creative imaginations. You always know deep down that even though you may jiggle the purse strings, they are a powerfully controlling force in everything you hope to do. You require them to keep their distance, and even though it angers you to show them all *your* books, you unconsciously like it when they retain their air of secrecy.

How does one balance honesty, sincerity, and trust with remoteness and secretiveness? Nobody knows that except you and your mate.

In a personal relationship it's an even greater question, because while you need your mate to help free your passions and ardor, you are also guarding against your own emotional obsessiveness. And while you seek greater familiarity, it's still the thrill of the unknown that keeps your passions aroused. Can deep, long-lasting, intimate, familiar companionship coexist with the uncertainty, spontaneity, needed for sexual tension?

Sex therapists and Tantric Yogis say yes, but in order for that to be achieved, your partner's excitement has to come from the union, and not vice versa.

And anyway, how exciting is it when one has seen somebody in their pajamas, brushing their teeth with one hand and scratching their bottom with the other? If sex is the only thing a couple has going, after about two-and-a-half years of living together, there's going to be a lot of fighting about money, who's giving more to the relationship, and who's not getting what out of it.

It's a little hard for you Tauruses to accept just how important the sex factor actually is. You'll admit it's important but insist that loyalty and deep caring are far more vital. If, however, your partner's sexual attention should stray from you for one second, watch out. You'll admire mysterious people, then get on their case because they're too secretive, and when you find out just how sneaky they are, you freak.

And yet, to keep you interested, they've got to keep up the mystery. And that's a paradox.

If you're going to have a life companion, he or she can't always be on, always fetching and staring down a cigarette holder over two champagne glasses. Besides, you Tauruses like to get past that part so you can just sit around and have the relationship and play Scrabble and not have to worry about being exciting. But . . . when the relationship jettisons the mystery, is it in danger of collapsing?

So how can someone be close to you, relax, and be natural without losing the magic? Trust has to sleep next to doubt, and that's all there is to it. Delaying the sexual revelation is certainly one way to keep up the mystery, but since you Tauruses ultimately demand physical contact, that's only a temporary solution.

Mrs. Bluebeard was probably a Taurean, because she was married to a guy who kept one room locked, and that's a good idea when someone is with a Taurus—at least one dresser drawer the Taurus in question is not allowed to penetrate.

If we could solve the question of sex and companionship, we could end forever all the little intrigues between executives and their secretaries, ladies and their hairdressers. This world is full of people beating their heads against the wall, hoping the answer will come into their brains. There isn't a person alive who doesn't want that luxurious feeling of crawling into a bed on a freezing night into a familiar set of welcoming arms, even if you've seen the person who belongs to those arms with their teeth in a glass of water beside the bed.

On the other hand, you Tauruses, as well as the members of the other eleven signs, also have a little bugger called a libido who lives somewhere down where your legs meet the rest of you. This little creature is not stimulated by familiarity, consistency, and respectability. Those qualities are great for getting mortgages—lousy for foreplay. And when you know exactly what move the other person is going to make, which will induce a certain known response in you, which will trigger your next move, excitement is often diminished. The thrill you get from giving pleasure has to lead you to experimentation with the unknown realms of your partner's hidden desires.

You Tauruses, therefore, should try not to scream and throw up when you find out all the hidden drives of your partner, because when they feel judged by you they hide their drives and act them out elsewhere.

But there are people who can develop trust while respecting privacy. Beyond the fleeting fads of sexual mores and practices, is there anything unchanging about the sexual needs of people and how they define them? No matter what period you're born in, you Tauruses strive to build a relationship that includes sex but does not organize itself only around physical attraction.

Isn't it strange, that right there in the marriage ceremony itself, where they talk about honoring and cherishing, there is no mention made in front of God and all the in-laws about the sexual commitment to satisfy the partner's earthly appetites?

This is an issue that the mates of all you Tauruses need to talk about with you.

Of course, it's not just sex we are talking about. We're using sex to symbolize the power you always ascribe to your mates. It's this power that draws you into the relationship in the first place but poses you the greatest questions. If you give in to it, you could be devoured by it. If you resist it, you risk forfeiting growth. And you're constantly asking yourselves how you can blend your sincerity of commitment with the excitement your mystery fantasy engenders within you.

How can you be expected to open up and be close to a figure who is remote and unreachable? And why should you open up to one who won't do the same for you?

But if your mates do show you all the tricks and how all those tricks are done, if they reveal their vulnerabilities, present themselves as flawed and human, does your image of them as an irresistible force go *poof*?

Ultimate Challenge: The Known vs. the Unknown

You must rise to the challenge of dealing with your own hidden drives, often acted out by the persons to whom you are attracted. The most successful Tauruses relate fearlessly to the primitive functions of their partners. It's hard to imagine Elizabeth and Philip having frank bedroom discussions, but surely the Queen has had a lot of serious facing up to do, even though it's not openly discussed in Parliament.

You must face the terror of the unknown, and it's the happy Taurean who recognizes that beneath the wall-to-wall carpeting there is the dark void of empty space. You hip Tauruses know that you do not relate well to that dark place. You know good food, good wine, where clothes are cheaper, but the vast swirling underworld that governs our passions and unconscious drives is not your terrain.

But that's where your mates come in. People are there to take you where you have never been before. They shouldn't scare the hell out of you while they're doing it. You have relationships so you can challenge the very secure little material world you've built for yourselves.

You're trusting partners with your greatest fear—the unknown, so they shouldn't just drop you off in the Twilight Zone and say, "Have a good time. I'll pick you up at six." Your partners introduce you bulls to your own animal desires and, of course, to see how much you're willing to kick in for it.

You will seek out others because you want them to prick a hole in your material balloon, but you will try like hell to put a patch wherever they have pricked a hole.

This challenge extends to every other realm of your life. A partner enters the sphere of a Taurean because, ironically, he or she may know that money isn't everything—even though you enter people's lives to awaken them to the fact that maybe it is.

They're there to challenge your hold on your position, to be the tidal wave that forces you out of your beach chair, to help you to accept a whole underside to your life you find it difficult to cope with and acknowledge as your own.

Tauruses are engaged in a dynamic struggle between practicality and emotional honesty. You are trying to live normal, healthy, regular, dependable, productive, moral everyday lives—while inserting some excitement into your existence and not destroying it in the process. You're searching for a sane balance between a hard-headed business attitude that's ever nosing its way like a bloodhound toward an ultimate bottom line of what the relationship will cost you and what you're getting in return—and the irresistible attraction to the sheer force of creativity. You adore art and artistry and always encourage those you love to open up and be more creative, not worry about money, and just concentrate on creativity.

Yet when your partners do toss caution to the winds and live *ars gratia artis*, you'll be right there to remind them of realities like rent, food, and electricity. Still, you are inexorably drawn to the creative life. So if the individuals in your life are totally dedicated to what they do, whether it's painting or marine biology, you will respect them, because you love the wildly insatiable, compulsive, obsessive personalities of people who make an art out of anything they do.

But Taurean relationships get into the worst trouble when the sexual balance is lost, when sexuality is either overvalued or undervalued by one or both of the parties involved—even in a business context.

You Taurean types want to be wanted by magical, magnetic, sensual, and seductive individuals, but want to be pillars of society, drive your children to private school in a lovely car, and be admired and envied by everyone in town. To achieve those goals, you have to be savvy, cool, keep your wits about you and your clothes on, and not run off with your hairdresser or secretary the way some people do. You like to keep to business, live steady, live right, day to day to day.

But here's the challenge: To fulfill yourselves in relationships, you have to blow off steam, let go, experience the ultimate. It takes tremendous courage for you to open up, share your most intimate drives and needs, be known and vulnerable, surrender to the power of emotion. You are challenged, by every major relationship you have, to leave terra firma, walk off into a sunset with a dark stranger, headed straight for the unknown, to give up your familiar territory—whether it's your favorite TV show or native land—be totally impractical, go where it's unsafe, to sail with another in uncharted waters.

In your relationships, you are all groping through the blackest night for something real and tangible to hold on to. The world of passion is a terrifying realm to creatures who know only too well the meaning of the term *addictive personality*. You know how easy it is to get hooked on the sweet taste of anything—and when that anything is love, you know you'd better be damned careful.

And although you are tuned in to the dangers of mixing business with pleasure and your personal life, you usually do it—as if emotional security could ever really be bought. So while we acknowledge that you Taurean types are built brick by brick on values of trust and loyalty and mutual credit card rights, still we must state that when you do reach out in any meaningful way, you want and need to be taken away from the safe world you've constructed. This surrender is best symbolized by total union, because by exposing yourselves completely, you are being known deeply, truly, and taking the greatest risk of all.

The Miracle: Creativity

Despite all the defensive postures you take, you are really the most open to being penetrated, accepting intimacy, and being known by another person.

For all your self-righteous positions, your staunchness notwithstanding, of all the signs, you alone have the greatest flexibility and will go the furthest out on a limb for someone you love. You need to be carried off kicking and screaming from your mother maybe, but the miracle is creative transformation. You choose the mates you choose only because you know thay are strong enough to move you. And in the process, of course, it will be they who will be transformed because they will be called upon to dredge down into their deepest selves to first face their own goblins, demons, and obsessions. Then, with the changes they make in themselves, you will be similarly changed.

You want prenuptial guarantees signed in blood of your mate's undying loyalty, but ironically you will take the biggest risks of anyone, whether they give you the goddamn guarantee or not. Even though you rarely get your partners to prove their loyalty to your lawyer's satisfaction, the very fact that you allow them to penetrate you as deeply as you do says it all.

Despite the stink you will always make about having things your way, you are happiest when you let someone move you.

You need someone to pollinate you. Like Virgo and Capricorn, the other two Earth Signs, you Tauruses are drawn to people who will undermine your rigid position. You all feel you can use a little jazzing up; you're too dry and need someone to "lubricate" you. You are all, however, afraid of drowning.

It is only when you give in to the forces of the universe that you experience the renewal of rebirth through the relationship. Only when you surrender and allow someone to cause the death of your position, open up to penetration of the alien's power, is the life-giving force injected into you.

As long as a partner guards against offending your dignity or putting you into a humiliating position, you will respect his or her privacy and allow intrigues that keep the relationship alive and glowing.

The miracle of your transformation means your mates eventually change you by changing themselves. What you love is the creative challenge. You don't want to be thought of as a commercial sellout to capitalist pigs with no taste for anything but whipped cream or tequila. You crave a creative relationship. This is the miracle your relationships achieve for you. Through your partner you are awakened to creativity. Not that you're not creative on your own—just think of da Vinci, Jasper Johns, Barbra Streisand, Bing Crosby, Ella Fitzgerald, Stevie Wonder, Zubin Mehta, and thousands of other Tauruses. But it's your contact with other human beings that not only evokes creativity in you but awakens it in others as well.

You have no time for trivial relationships. You want it all, the whole package, now and forever, kit and kaboodle, tied up with a big red ribbon. You want to connect on the deepest possible level. When you do, something inside you explodes, pervades your whole being, and something of the other person is inside you forever. They leave upon you an indelible mark and you are changed.

When you get past the horror-movie phase, you come to understand that it is your own animal within that terrifies you. You are seeking to know someone who won't permit you to enter their life completely, and that both frustrates and excites you.

No matter what you think of your own strategic capabilities, you Tauruses are not as good at playing games as the people you attract. And because of that, you are sometimes

at a great disadvantage. The only weapons you have are
honesty, loyalty, candor, and a trust fund, which means you
are going to be duped by schemes.

You have creative longings and are often willing to support projects financially if your creative input is welcomed.
Many of you Tauruses have been led down the tubes by
phony artists and charlatans. You pride yourself on your
hard-headed practicality and down-to-earth realism, but
more than one grieving Taurean in this world has written
out a check to a Ouija board medium who claimed to be in
direct communication with the other side.

You must learn to play games.

You need to rise above your own curiosity, resist the
urge to pry, let those who wish to sneak around back doors
sneak around back doors. You must overcome the copycat
game of retaliation.

Ironically, though, if you want to achieve the miracle of
creativity, you must learn to manipulate and play games
and be ever more conscious of the games people play. The
more you grasp the nature of those games, the more successful you will be with the Olympic-scale game players
you always choose. In fact, the Taurean game is to pick
game players, and you can't get to your miracle without
knowing that.

You yourselves are not comfortable with intrigue, and
you look ridiculous on a streetcorner in a trench coat with a
hat pulled down over your eyes. But you have to learn how
to deal with intrigue.

You attract subtle, seductive, utterly sophisticated
human beings, masters of suggestion and manipulation. If
you want to achieve your miracle, you have to revel in
your love of controlling figures. You often feel you're too
stuck in practicalities and are hoping someone will drag
you away from yourself. When it happens, you fight it
with all your might, but are inexorably drawn to earth-
moving magical powers in others. You love the probing,
penetrating, snooping mentality, one that threatens to dis-
turb your cozy little nest and change forever the rigid
structures you create and hang on to for dear life.

You have to open up in every sense of the word. In business you'll be forced to share your resources and give up control to someone who can add that magic spark and connect you with the public in a big way—or else crush you like a bug under a fist.

This is hard for you to accept, because you'd like to be able to keep a tiger in a matchbox, but no dice. You have to open your wallet as well as your soul if you want success, and let danger enter.

Personal relationships can awaken your hearts, bodies, and minds. But again, you have to open up. A sexual-emotional transformation is promised if you can allow this dark force of passion to penetrate you, rip you away from your inhibitions and values, and fling you onto the shore of a new life, borne on the wave of your thundering sexuality.

Finally you have to accept the biggest threat of all—change. "Arrrggghh!" scream all the Tauruses in the world at once. The magic of creativity lies in the acceptance of all the principles of alchemy. The desire to change the state and nature of your life draws you to people. The more total the change, the more enlivened you are, the more vitality you'll have, the more creative you'll be.

Working the Miracle: Mystery

Allowing a person to wander alone to that edge to relight the magic fire encourages creativity.

And this is what you Tauruses wish to accomplish in your relationships. You'll get mad, of course, because you'll feel you are being more open than your partner is. Even if this is not true, you Tauruses will often perceive it that way. You'll often think your partner is holding back, holding out. You'll see the mate as having a much more sophisticated and Byzantine set of rules to play by. And while you often strive to maintain a financially controlling position, you'll often be at a loss when it comes to knowing what other people are *really* up to when they're not with you or at work.

In fact, it's that torturous uncertainty that keeps your fascination for them alive. You'll scream for them to be more open and honest with you, but they shouldn't do it. No matter how much of themselves they reveal, you'll be titillated no end by all the stuff they *didn't* say.

A magician would be a fool if at the end of the act he showed the audience exactly where the rabbits came from, how the roses got up his sleeve, and why the lady didn't actually die when he sawed her in half.

So to keep you turned on a mate should confess his or her deepest, darkest secrets just as a blaring fire engine is going by or a jet is flying low over the house. Under no circumstances do the Tauruses really want to see backstage or the strings on the puppet.

It's a hell of a thing to achieve, all right. To build a real, live, ongoing productive, fruitful relationship, there has to be trust. Nothing will grow in the soil of suspicion. Loyalty is fertility for you Tauruses, and you can't open up if you think someone is just messing around with your head or heart.

It's that hint of doubt, though, that tiny grain of sand in the Vaseline, that causes you a delicious amount of ecstatic pain.

You should never be exactly sure how your mate knew that the three of diamonds was your card. You should not be specifically told what goes on in the booth when the curtains are drawn. Your partners should probably take a lifetime to reveal it all.

The creative impulse is the link between the known world and the unknown world, the invisible, unconscious realm and the everyday, known, tangible existence we all lead from dawn to dusk. To be truly creative, one must cross over, let go of the known, and touch that which is usually unseen, unheard, untasted, untouched, unsmelled by the everyday mind.

You Tauruses need a push off the bank into the dark waters of the unknown. In the dangerous passage between Wall Street and Heaven, the miracle of creativity takes place, transformation occurs, and you are forever changed by the experience.

Gift Ideas for Taureans

You need help to let go and jump into that abyss. This is where magic and mystery are crucial. So when your mates are shopping for you, after they bought you everything in all the catalogues, they might try these gift suggestions to help them develop your capacity to enjoy mystery and the dark side with a minimum of nail-biting and gnashing of teeth. And in this instance, it's therapeutic if they get you to pay for the gifts.

- A matched set (studded in jewels or plain) of a blindfold, earplugs, and clothespin for the nose to remind you to quit snooping and just look within.
- A key to their private strongbox or vault and tell you you must never use it without their knowledge or permission. The suspense will drive you deliciously mad.
- A three-month subscription to one of the more raunchy X-rated magazines, just to expose you to how the other half lives and help you go through a stage of revulsion and disgust at pure prurience.
- A trip with just three hitches:
  a) you pay
  b) they get to choose where
  c) you never know the destination till you get there (this should be repeated yearly)
- Copies of the following books: *My Secret Life*, *The Secret Life of Plants*

Reading Material for Advanced Tauruses

The Secret Doctrine, H. P. Blavatsky
The Godfather, Mario Puzo

The Guardian Angels: The Magician and the Sorceress

 The Magician and the Sorceress guard your relationships, not, as some might think, because these two figures symbolize deception, trickery, and deceit on the part of shysters, but because they represent the power of the invisible world, a realm you need to be initiated into.

The rabbits that come out of the magician's hat stand for the constantly living, changing, growing, creative force emerging from a seemingly inert object. This transformation is the essence of what you Tauruses desire in your relationships.

Through relationships you are being initiated into sorcery. Obsessive-compulsive, self-destructive, manipulative, abusive, mafia-esque relationships are the black magic kind, but you are protected by your guardian angels, who symbolize an alchemical healing process that can be the nature of the Taurean bond.

The Magician and the Sorceress gaze into your soul with their penetrating eyes. They seem to see all, know all, force you to a kind of openness and honesty you've never known before. Your desire to be opened up, known deeply, totally, and completely is described by the Magician's trick of sawing the lady in half. That act symbolizes your trust that someone of great power can enter your being, sever your connection with your past and with what you considered to be reality, and put you back together again. The Magician and the Sorceress help you to see into yourselves, expand your perceptions inward, free you from repression in a rare confrontation with your raw unconscious.

Such a confrontation transforms you, liberates you from your own life. As the Magician and the Sorceress always bring the audience back to reality, so the true Taurean relationship promises to carry you through the ordeal of initiation, past the "surgery," transport you to the edge, but always bring you back safely.

Celebrity Astro Game

You'd be surprised how many ways people reveal themselves in everything they say and do. To sharpen your sensitivity to other people and to learn more about the ways renowned Tauruses handle their deepest relationship issues, look over the following list and pick out the people who interest you most.

Do a little sleuthing about their lives. Observe their actions; listen to what they say in public. The songs they sing, the roles they play, the particular contributions they make, will enlighten you about the relationship patterns of this sign.

Queen Elizabeth II
Judy Carne
Candice Bergen
Fred Astaire
Cher
Jean Harris
Al Pacino

Jill Clayburgh
Reggie Jackson
Shirley MacLaine
Barbra Streisand
Silvana Mangano
Grace Jones
Stevie Wonder

Chapter Three

GEMINI

The Mirage: The Smiling Team Coach

You Geminis, when you meet someone at a party:

> "You know, this is really nice. Here we've been talk-
> ing only five minutes and I feel like I've known you
> all my life. This is fabulous. We're on the same
> wavelength and that's important. It really is. You are
> really an interesting person, you know that? Really
> interesting."

Who knows? Maybe it's just their wonderful smile, their
hearty laugh, the twinkle in their eyes and glow in their
cheeks. But even though simple good-naturedness will
hook you every time, you are actually looking to plug into
intelligence. The socket you seek is the brighter side of
other people's brains.

What makes you follow them home in the first place is
their bigness—you Geminis like people either taller or
smarter than you are. They have to have a scope and perspective you don't have. They have to be able to see over
trees and forgive sins. And you'll love them when within
five minutes they can tune in to you, talk to you, know
what you're about.

It thrills you if they open up your head in ways other

64

people haven't been able to do. And it doesn't put you off if they're foreign or were born into a different cultural or religious or racial background. *Au contraire*, Jewish Geminis love Gentiles, and vice versa, and you positively glow if passports are needed for dating.

You are looking for a mind-expanding experience, no question about it. In seconds you'll sniff out raw intelligence, whether they've got a Ph.D. in philosophy or dropped out of school in the eighth grade. You'll roar at their jokes and be mad about them if they're upbeat. If they agree with you, sympathize with your position, indulge you a little, you'll be theirs. They've got to be the cheerleader that gets you to make it down those last ninety-five yards to the goal.

To attract a Gemini, one has to be interesting. If partners tickle one brain cell that hasn't been tickled before, they get on the A list of that Gemini's busy address book. Partners' minds have to be far out—is that what Gene Wilder loved about Gilda Radner?

When you talk about your partners to people in your other life, the one they're not part of, you will describe them with a big broad stroke, tell all their best qualities and are always taken with their optimism and good sportsmanship. You hear them recounting how after the pie, they wiped the whipped cream off their face, laughing, and you think, Now there's somebody interesting.

You Geminis are terminally naughty, so you love to be scolded soundly, but you want to find the keys to the new sports car hung on the Christmas tree anyway. You've got to see your partners as Olympian, bigger than life, gods who take the slings and arrows with utter resiliency. So when they move all their chips into the red and lose, they've got to take a swig of brandy and scream with delight. And if after the horse throws them today, they ride tomorrow, they've got a Gemini for life.

You Geminis like Hollywood types, so the more outrageous their fish story, the more you love them. If partners are not afraid to be a little loud or outspoken while doing it, you're putty in their hand. You adore hyperbole.

No matter what your mates are really like, you'll see them as huge and generous as a big plate of spaghetti, and in the beginning you will be elated by all the space they seem to need. You'll tell them what a wonderful smile and laugh they have, because that's all you'll want to see. You go for the type who can stretch the truth like a rubber band, because you do, too. You'll love them if they act like a permissive parent and lie for you once in a while or make it through a yellow light right in front of a policeman's nose.

You are looking for a merry old soul to commune with —somebody who doesn't sit around biting fingernails but is exploring the world from Disneyland to Africa. You want them to be Auntie Mame and Uncle Remus—witty, wise, worldly, and casual—no hangups. And if there's a difference of opinion occasionally, no big deal: You've got to be able to take off for a day or two, cool it for a while, till the difference of opinion blows over and both people are in a better mood, and then just pick up where you left off, no big deal, no World War III. It's probably why Jessica Tandy and Hume Cronyn have made it past the thirty-year anniversary.

If you think you've found someone who doesn't mind cheating a few routines, you've got your hero or heroine, an easygoing Southerner who isn't impressed by all this formal Boston stuff. Even if you're wildly attracted to someone, it's not going to last if he or she has an IQ of 58, because what dazzles you is the offbeat mind—the humor and intelligence, which you will see at the beginning as shining, thrilling, and blissful. All Geminis would like to keep a relationship at this high pitch. The fun starts, of course, when the high wears off.

The Monster: A Bloated, Self-Indulgent Hypocrite

You Geminis when you want a break:

> "We're just not on the same wavelength anymore. We're just not."

BUT... When restlessness overtakes you, you spot the clay feet you never saw before, then blame this figure for allowing your self-indulgence and do whatever you can to flee this smiling hypocrite. You demand that someone adjust, be versatile and completely solicitous of your mercurial changes of mood, and certainly forgive all your little sins. If you feel like acting as flaky as a pastry puff or turning out as many selves as Sybil, you want only that certain somebody who can roll with the punches. But there's an inevitable point in all your major relationships when you try to jump ship and go looking for someone who *really* understands. Your perception of that bright, witty, good-natured team coach sours rapidly. That wonderfully refreshing view of life you thought they had now seems remarkably flawed, full of its own rigidity and prejudice.

You Geminis have just as many needs for long-term relationships as anyone you might meet at Club Med. But ... there's an inevitable point in every relationship where you maybe could go deeper, but for some reason you take a sharp left at the last minute. Maybe you've already dived once too often into the shallow end of the pool, but you Geminis will always keep one twin free of the relationship at all times.

When you get bored, your perception of an individual as that bright, witty, good-natured parent figure gets a little distorted. You will find out his or her good-naturedness has just been an excuse for self-indulgence or substance abuse.

The jolly old soul you loved just a short time ago is worse than any character out of Hawthorne. This hypocrite in front of you actually kicks little dogs. Your Olympian vision is destroyed, the walls of the temple come crashing down and the icons are dragged into the street.

Like inflatable clown toys that keep popping up smiling, after a while you see people as false and empty. You may have liked them because they let you get away with murder, but then you'll have to pull away because they didn't set limits. You'll blame them for aiding your fragmented incompleteness. Though you demanded their permissiveness, you actually believe it fosters your irresponsibility, prohibits your commitments from maturing, and leads you further and further away from fulfillment. You'll make it hard for your mates to set up anything consistent, but then—guess what—you'll blame them for the chaos that results in your life style.

If someone tries punitive action with one of you Geminis, you'll bolt—so that doesn't work either. If they threaten to take away your T-bird, you'll start thumbing madly through your address book for that person you met down the street who *really* understands you.

It dawns on you after a while that your partners allowed you unbridled freedom, even encouraged your childish conduct, because they actually wanted support for their own caprice; that they're not really so wise at all, just shrewd rationalizers. When you feel frustrated from your lack of grounding, you often place the onus on the relationship, believing that if you could get to another place, relate to another person, "everything would be better." You are great ones for weekends off in the country or at the sanatorium as an antidote for the times when the relationship is making you sick to your stomach.

When you feel like withdrawing, there's little anyone can do. You're looking for the father confessor, guru, teacher, shrink, holder of the key to great wisdom and experience. But there's a point where every one of you looks upon every teacher as a dictator to be overthrown. The teacher doesn't know everything, the shrink is controlling, the priest is a fraud . . . At this point you usually split. If we could figure out why you need to split periodically, we would have a clue to your restlessness and the problems you encounter and create in relationships. Maybe we could find out why JFK couldn't be true to Jackie or why Stacy Keach really went to jail.

The Real Thing: The Thirst for Experience

You don't like problems. Problems make you nervous by hanging on too long. Besides, you know that when you get close to people, problems start surfacing. People expect to have the relationship solve their problems for them. They expect too much, they make judgments about behavior, and try to tailor others to their specifications. Well, you hate all that.

When you start to hear lectures, you fall asleep. As much as you're fascinated with others' perspective on you at first, you believe that psychology does have its inherent limitations. So even though you like someone to sit around and discuss the big picture, you don't want them looking deeper into your life. You believe there is nothing to see there. You don't believe that your reluctance to put down roots or get serious is pathological in any way. *Au contraire*, you see it as healthy. You require an upbeat mental stimulation. Your philosophy of relationships is, "Keep it light and it can go on forever."

Many of you Geminis were raised by two mothers or got shipped out to your aunt's every time there was a meal to be cooked or in some way had two homes very early on. You've been juggling forever, and you know how to bounce from one figure to another. Because you were moved around like a checker on a board, you're forever balancing loyalties, playing options, and keeping everyone happy.

You've often been fed a set of inconsistent or opposing

philosophies, and your relationships always reflect an agile balancing of moral positions, as well as an ambivalence about the kinds of support and encouragement you require from people. Because you're always shifting positions, you are always slightly apart and watching it all on television, even while you participate fully in the relationships.

You are looking for someone to help you solve the splits you experienced in early childhood. For that you need your mate's intelligence and support. But until you learn that the healing comes from within, it is always an endless search for the next wonderful thing that comes along.

From a very early age you learn how to juggle people and allegiances, how to be agreeable, pleasant, and keep from getting hit by becoming a moving target.

You Geminis are the bon vivants of the world. Rock star Prince, fashion designer John Weitz, Bob Dylan, Isadora Duncan, Joe Namath—all Geminis. You're the great communicators and artists of your age: Gladys Knight, Miles Davis, John Cheever, Herman Wouk, Henry Kissinger— all members of this mental sign. You've all been up before issues of religion, race, or morality with the parent of the opposite sex, and you've learned how to look the other way, let things go in one ear and out the other, do what you damn well please and then confess it to the good-natured guru who won't scold you too severely.

You all have that special someone in your life—a grandfather, great-aunt, or neighbor who sees the better side of you, whom you show a better face to, who you can talk to because this special person can get you to see other sides of issues without making you feel small or wrong.

So you always live in a foster home one way or the other. Right from the first, you are more comfortable upstairs, next door, or down the block. So in adult life your pattern in relationships is to set up a home base from which you can wander upstairs, next door, or down the block. Even Queen Victoria had her palace to go to when she wanted to get away from Prince Albert.

Why you look for a haven outside your home (it could

even be the park where you walk your dog) varies from Gemini to Gemini. You can be sure that Barry Manilow, Lionel Richie, and Brooke Shields all have their home away from home. Many of you love your families and adore the coziness of your happy home. But coziness is only half your story. You always need someone to talk to —within that ten-block radius, of course, and always *outside* the set of intimacies you've established.

You turn on to a person in the beginning maybe because they offer you a place to be other than where you are. Exactly why you have to keep one hand free depends on your personal situation and the extent of how crazy your early environment was. From childhood, you're all a bunch of thirsty, curious souls, and you all develop a sixth sense very early on about keeping your escape routes open. When you walk into a room, the first thing you do is check the exits. You want options, not necessarily because you are pathologically afraid of commitment but because you have naturally healthy, curious minds and a natural tendency to connect with people in any level of society with equal ease. When someone needs a plumber or a musician or a computer programmer, a Gemini can whip out the appropriate phone number in two seconds flat. True, you often use your contacts to distract yourselves from doing whatever you're supposed to be doing. But you're good companions in the sense that you like to be cheerful and will always help others do whatever it is they want to do.

But it cannot be full-time, twenty-four hours a day, seven days a week, from here to eternity. Your lives are usually divided, halved, and halved again, every step leading away from your original destination, ever spreading yourselves thinner and thinner, until often all others can get of you is five minutes a month.

Your lives are a series of seemingly unconnected anecdotes, short poems, and scribbled notes and lyrics. You need breaks from everything in your unceasing flight from boredom. For you, existence is a series of interruptions; it's all so choppy, you can't seem to keep your mind in one place. (Does even Dick Clark get nervous and jumpy and have trouble staying focused?) Why do you Geminis look for people to indulge your caprice and then be angry that their lack of discipline has turned you into a superficial dilettante? You often spend thousands in therapy trying to find out why you have to leave something in order to come back to it and why you have a teensy problem running from third base to home, and it sometimes turns out to be because people have not demanded enough of you.

The simplest truth is that periodically your pencil leaves the paper and that's the end of the message until it begins again. You can be tied to the kitchen table or chained to the couch, but it won't do any good. Others have to accept at some point that psychologizing won't change your basic trait of restiveness. Therapy is not going to turn a Gemini into a Capricorn. You have an unceasing thirst for new experience, and you'll turn on to anybody or anything that strikes a new chord. You don't have to be promiscuous necessarily, but you always lead at least two lives—either simultaneously or consecutively. So you're really better mates when you've gotten the first marriage out of your system. Ask Artie Shaw why he married so many times, why Dashiell Hammit and Lillian Hellman had so many off and on dramas, why Gauguin took off to take up with the natives. Though it conflicts with your very traditional need for Christmas trees and picket fences, you detest dreary sameness.

The disparity is most perfectly described in the idyllic family scene from "Meet Me in St. Louis" where Judy Garland sings "Have Yourself a Merry Little Christmas," and the actual way she probably spent that holiday with Vincent Minnelli—her husband at the time and director of the film.

You Geminis security-oriented but hungry for change. You've all got a wonderful sense of being able to pick up the afghan you were knitting last fall and continue it for a stitch or two—until the phone rings. Nothing is uninteresting to you except repetition. If one flies Gemini, one has to accept that fact.

The Burning Question: Is There a Line Between Healthy Optimism and Denial?

You Geminis are fun because you like to enjoy yourselves in a relationship, and you don't make a federal case out of every indiscretion. A partner will definitely have to play shrink and put your little wheels back on track when your engine derails from time to time. But others can't come down on you like the Vatican. They need a sense of humor.

Even if you can't be there all the time for your mates, you want to keep them happy and do not like the relationship as a backdrop for any dark forces swirling about inside you. You'd rather act out the negative stuff away from your partner.

Because you don't like problems, you avoid them, and you often help others avoid theirs with a pretty empty jolliness. After a while, people start to feel they're being lied to, that things are going on behind their back, which is sometimes true. You see a mate as a bright new penny you would not want to tarnish by showing the reality of your split-off side, so you often act it out elsewhere.

We can't say where that thin line is between keeping someone happy and keeping them blind. You will always try to see the best in others. That's what makes you great partners, but you are reluctant to deal with stress or conflict, so your partner could be a thief or an addict, and you might not notice for a long time.

The secret to success lies in how your mate presents information to you. You Geminis believe you are truly spontaneous and that you do not have any compulsions. You get a kick out of it when others get you to stretch your brains, but you hate to be analyzed and observed like a little mouse.

You love the good-natured priest who chuckles behind the confessional as he grants pardon, the permissive parent you can collude with, the casual California shrinks who do their thing right in the hot tub.

You evolved Geminis are not threatened by truthful confrontation. On the contrary, you welcome it. You know that to be a whole person, you need the perspective of how others see you, as well as the awareness of your effect on other people. But it's all in how somebody handles you. If one wants to present a problem to a Gemini, one shouldn't drape it in black. You'll just block it. But if one can offer it in sit-com form, one will get better results.

So how to tell the difference between thinking and acting positively, and simple denial of truth? In a relationship with any Gemini, there's always got to be a touch of Christian Science.

If people are too serious and come on like Puritan ministers, you'll aim your pea shooter at them and shoot them out of your life. They've got to be up and bright and ready to hit the road at a moment's notice. Exactly how to create that balance between casual spontaneity and irresponsibility is what keeps them on their toes and their mind active.

That's what they'll be doing when they're traveling with you—trading ideas, sharing disparate life styles, cultural backgrounds, and upbringings, while spurring you on to new heights of understanding and experience.

Ultimate Challenge: Your Language or Your Partner's Language?

Any major relationship involving Geminis usually hauls in religious, cultural, ethnic, or civil rights issues. You can't help it. You just love foreigners and anyone else who speaks a totally different language. We can but dimly imagine that historic first meeting between Paul McCartney's Liverpudlian family and Linda Eastman's fancy New York parents.

Geminis, you will keep others jumping with what we will kindly call your spontaneous mind. Success for you comes always through the challenge of belief systems. Which means your partners have to show you that they know something by forcing the blood vessels around your brain to pump a little harder. You don't like to have to think before you act. You want to be moved by the particular zeitgeist of this millisecond. If you feel like doing something, you want to do it; see something you want, take it.

Successful relationships help you to exercise higher thinking functions. And while it usually cramps your style, you definitely want others to offer consequences to your actions. Without a strong relationship, you Geminis sometimes lack morality, because it is the very crisis of morality presented by a relationship that develops you best. Your partner's function in your life is to help you set up a code of ethics, raise your consciousness, expand your horizons, help you see life from a totally different perspective, add depth to your perceptions, and make you pay your parking tickets.

Your versatility makes you a great sex partner. But it's hard for your mates to face that they're never really the only person in your life. Oh, you're interested in them, and you can be good listeners, but basically, if they end the relationship tomorrow, you're sure to meet somebody attractive by Saturday night. It's a healthy attitude you've got, that life goes on—those widowed grandmothers who get married at seventy-three, those old geezers who start new careers at eighty—they're all Geminis.

No matter how old you are or what the situation, for someone to keep you interested, he or she has to be very different from you culturally, socially, ethnically, racially, religiously, economically, or politically. You need the challenge of opposing views to develop any sane ethical sense. A Gemini child of Orthodox Jewish parents will find a hot-blooded Spanish, black, Italian, or Irish intellectual. The Cuban exile will go for a Brooklyn woman.

If you know anything about the fabulous love life of

Libby Holman, or the stormy marriages of Marilyn Monroe and Joe DiMaggio, or MM and Arthur Miller, you'll see the wide gulf that exists for you Geminis in the personal choices you make. It's almost as if you think you can buy another nationality, merge with a whole other culture, just by choosing a mate. You love to marry across boundaries.

This is the challenge for every Gemini—to communicate with someone who speaks a totally different language. Once you've gotten over the novelty, you need to develop the skill to speak with them on a level deeper than a Berlitz guide book provides for. You seek out a relationship because your differences pose a chance for you to grow mentally. Reaching out and touching another mind often requires a depth and a patience you lack.

You know how hard it is, how much effort it takes, to actually communicate with another human being. First of all, nobody listens to anybody. So few people actually respond to what others say. They merely recite a story relating back to themselves, a story that was suggested by whatever was said.

You evolved Geminis have no fear of that point where discussion of real problems is the next logical step. But you can't take it without a break, so you require the mate to be gone part of the time. In order to have a relationship with you a mate must leave periodically. This will free you to relate to other people (even if you spend the whole time talking about your partner).

Your partner's allowing you to relate freely to other people helps you communicate with him or her because it releases you from having to deal with anyone on a full-time basis, which for you is a strain.

You have a resistance to sameness such that if you can't get away for part of the time, you will clam up and have nothing to say. Once you discover the hole in your partner's ideologies and prejudices, you get threatened and will go through the challenge of either throwing off the relationship or learning to make major adjustments in your thinking. At first, these compromises are more than you can bear. But in time you realize that sometimes a real breakthrough in consciousness is not achieved by that thrill-seeking high in five minutes of conversation but by a long-term communication with someone whose customs and behavior are hard to understand.

You love to talk, and when communication is deep, you're ecstatic. To achieve it, you have to learn your mate's language.

You evolved Geminis know how to do that. To speak, to listen, to respond. Gena Rowlands has been married to John Cassavetes for countless years. Now, we know these two have a fantastic communication. You Geminis can't just bite a bullet and go through life like zombies. For a relationship to withstand the ravages of boredom, there's got to be a true meeting of minds.

The Miracle: The Raising of Consciousness

You Geminis get the worst reputation for being ditzy and schitzy, when actually you have the greatest ability of all to make that flying leap across the canyon to understand and accept concepts and ideas people of normal intelligence could never grasp. It is this very leap across the gulf of socioeconomic, ethnic, religious, or racial barriers that keeps the Gemini mind stimulated and elevates your consciousness. Real relationships expose you to challenging beliefs and moralities and demand higher understanding on your part. Through these real relationships, you Geminis are led to an appreciation of how much other people have to offer, as well as an understanding of the difference between blind support and true wisdom.

It is through your connection with people that you actually complete your thoughts and communicate with the world in a language the world can understand. When you

are face to face with belief systems and moral structures
that are alien to you, many of you tend either to laugh it off
and reject the relationship or to make a serious effort to
learn about and grasp how some people can believe some
of the things they believe. Opening up to such possibilities
moves you forward along the road of consciousness, and
while you may not ultimately accept or incorporate these
belief systems into your life, you get closer to people not
by writing off codes of ethics as ridiculous and absurd but
by examining the lives of the people you like, to see how
these systems actually work.

You don't have to become Italian if you marry an Italian
or be a psychiatrist just because you're involved with one.
You are not obliged to subsume the whole thinking process
of your partner. But you need to gain an appreciation of
other value systems and how they work.

This demands greater maturity on your part. You love
expanding your awareness, and the more honestly and
deeply you're able to look at issues with intelligence and
perspective, the less infantile will be the behavioral response. Communication is a volley that never ends. It's a
trade of ideas, revolving around a simple theme, maybe,
but proliferating outward in all directions, led by both parties, developed by two people in the eternal attempt to link
minds together in a mutually nourishing way.

When you connect with a real mind, you gain an appreciation of the vast resources other people have to offer you.
For some reason, you are often lucky enough to find generous individuals who are willing to share what they have
and lend support and enthusiasm for your projects. While
this can breed a pattern of endless opportunism, your for-
tune is to gain tremendous momentum through contact with
people. In some way your relationships spark your consciousness, fuel you, allow you to move, grow, travel, and
experience the world. You mature and conscious Geminis
have a total appreciation for this resource and always value
it.

Real support, though, from a real relationship, is not

merely blind and enthusiastic cheering for every notion that pops into your Gemini head. Wisdom is more than indulgence. No Gemini wants to get a lecture from holier-than-thou fools who can't keep their own lives together. But when you reach out, you want not just a green light but sagacity and judgment and a deeper dimension to your thinking. That's why your choice of partner is crucial— you can go after lazy, lawless slobs or wise and talented successes. Whom you choose reflects the level of your own consciousness.

Having grasped the true nature of support, you are led straight to your miracle, the permanent change of perspective and raising of consciousness. You value the education real relationships give you, because no matter how much you resist, you are searching to learn from the people you admire and look up to. Connecting with real people gives you the zest to complete projects, follow through with your ideas, and thus communicate with the world.

The raising of consciousness means that you are then able to give more at the moment, be more present, and thus be able to complete and accomplish what you set out to do. Above all, a real relationship helps you to see your forest above the trees, gives you a perspective on your behavior and insight into your patterns, which gives you what you long for most—the power to change and grow.

Working the Miracle: Mature Communication

You Geminis will shake up others' value systems, as well as their morals. For every square inch of Gemini in a relationship, at least two tons of compassion are needed. You challenge others' level of tolerance and understanding and make them redefine terms of mental health. You are attracted to people who will help you get a grasp on your actions and expand your mind.

But your mate can expect a barrage of defenses and a resistance stronger than the French Underground. You are devoted to attaching a brain to body, and that's why you reach out to others.

You Geminis are not really two people or split personalities at all. Each Gemini is only one person with one brain. You happen to enjoy developing parallel interests simultaneously. If there is any "split-off" side, it's an alienating withdrawal from communication that should be avoided at all costs.

So others should avoid pointing out to you how many of the Ten Commandments you've broken this week, or you will withdraw. But the alternative is denial—and they can't just cheerfully drive the getaway car during the jewel heist. You all want some moral order brought to your hooligan's consciousness, but also, you are a free spirit who has to be allowed to do your thing.

What you want from your mate is an alternative point of view, one that points out new long-range possibilities and healthy options. You don't want them to be the parole officer or AA sponsor.

The way to work this miracle is through the open mind. The search for truth, knowledge, and understanding is the point of greatest sharing in this relationship. The open mind does not condone criminal action just to prove itself. You will often flout the law just to test to see where your mate fits between Moses' rules and those of the IRS. You test to see if they'll turn you in to the church or state or if they'll go smiling down to the station when they get booked as an accessory.

When one is in a relationship with a Gemini, one is in an active mental dialogue about personal freedom and morality. You want your partners to play devil's advocate, not get up on a soap box and start preaching. If they do, you'll throw a cup of sacramental wine right in their face.

To help you raise your consciousness, your partners should follow their own moral path, stick to their own code without judging. You Geminis are watching to see if they are using true wisdom, which does not condemn wrongdoing but rather frees people from enslavement from their own actions.

So you don't want a missionary for a mate. You want them to set an example of how much fun it is to lead a happy, productive life based on a shared desire to look for truth and meaning. Not by pointing to the Bible but by becoming a living example of how their own set of ideologies works for them. You'll be so impressed with them you'll probably rush into the conversion chamber and be devout for five minutes, but it probably won't stick, and soon you'll have to revert back to who you really are.

Nonetheless, you gain much stability from a relationship with someone who is following a path of self-knowledge and enlightenment, has a belief system and moral code.

You will never fail to challenge your mate's moral position, force them to grow in understanding by making them accept behavior they once shunned. They're only asking for trouble when they get on a high horse around you, because you are always looking for the hole in the priest's garment.

By handing your mate impossible moral problems to deal with, you challenge their sincerity and force them to test their own theories in practice. Despite your resistance, their conduct rubs off on you, and thanks to them you understand yourself a little better.

You can scan a French phrase book and fool a Parisian, read a simplified text book and snow a physicist. But to get you to think beyond today, your mates need that miracle of higher consciousness. You Geminis will put them through a million changes in the course of a relationship. They'll no sooner get the last shutter painted on the upstairs window that they'll be told to pack up the van for a trip across the desert. You'll have them coming, and you'll have them going, and you won't be sure yourself whether you want them to sit there and feed you with a teaspoon or go off by themselves to Africa to fight apartheid. You'll get mad at them and stop talking to them for days, weeks, or months on end. Then you'll forget what made you angry and cook them a Thanksgiving dinner, complete with all the trimmings, just to show them there's no hard feelings—even in the middle of July. You'll fly off the handle, swerve off the track, and periodically wobble right out of orbit. And your mate has to be there to restore the perspective.

You are not going to be stable 365 days out of the year for the next fifty years. What you need from your mates is wisdom and understanding. If they play shrink or priest to your amoral sociopath you'll fight them, but if they can bring you back through nonthreatening communication, you'll love them again. If they can reach you when you're at your worst, you will indeed return. They can't judge you too harshly, because you want a cool, reassuring hand on that fevered brow of yours, beneath which a brain is often buzzing out of control.

And if *they* stray off course, you will go even further off the deep end, as if to shock them back to sanity, to force them by mirroring their horrendous behavior, to start thinking about what it is they are doing. And it's that thinking process that elevates the whole relationship, and together you fly from childish acting-out to mature communication.

Gift Ideas for Geminis

- A complete college education. A must on the gift list for you Geminis. An ideal mate has to give you the opportunity not only to flirt with attractive teachers, but to expand your education.
- A Doctorate of Thinkology, similar to the one the Wizard of Oz gave to the scarecrow, which will remind you that every fleeting impulse you have need not be acted upon instantly, that nothing exists within the human mind that can't be understood and worked out by rational thought.
- A new car (with phone) is another great gift for a Gemini.
- An unlimited credit card with the international airline that has the most varied routes. This will give you the

unlimited mobility you demand, and provide you with the one thing you always need—escape.

Reading Material for Advanced Geminis

The Koran, in original Arabic

Guardian Angels: Mr. and Mrs. Santa Claus

Mr. and Mrs. Santa Claus guard Gemini relationships because they symbolize the eternal and renewing optimism that children express from generation to generation. Optimism is the primary element in a healthy Gemini relationship. There are Mr. and Mrs. Santa Claus, eternally turning out gifts for good little boys and girls, because we all know that all little boys and girls are good little boys and girls, no matter what they do. If they're bad or spill their milk or refuse to go to bed or do their homework or if they tell white lies, their parents still love them. Their parents still know that deep down they're good little boys and girls. And when Christmas Eve comes, all is forgiven.

This pair represents a totally benevolent attitude, one that needs to persist in a Gemini relationship, one that you Geminis require. An attitude that overlooks petty crimes— indeed, sees all crimes as petty and believes in rewarding loved ones to help them grow to be fuller people.

Santa's bag of toys suggests the countless ways of enjoyment and diversion, limitless possibilities and endless opportunities that a relationship with Gemini will bring to anyone's life.

The reindeer and sleigh flying over the rooftops describe the constant motion, mental and geographical, that you create in every relationship.

The Clauses represent a united cause of enjoyment and pleasure, and the fact that they symbolize a lay image of Christmas, as opposed to a religious one, suggests that you

Geminis create a spirit that crosses all religious boundaries. You are more interested in giving than in really judging the behavior of the children.

Celebrity Astro Game

You'd be surprised how many people reveal themselves in everything they say and do. To sharpen your sensitivity to other people and to learn more about the ways renowned Geminis handle their deepest relationship issues, look over the following list and pick out the people who interest you most.

Do a little sleuthing about their lives. Observe their actions; listen to what they say in public. The songs they sing, the roles they play, the particular contributions they make, will enlighten you about the relationship patterns of this sign.

Marilyn Monroe	Queen Victoria
Joe Namath	Dashiell Hammett
Joan Collins	John F. Kennedy
Stacy Keach	Brooke Shields
Paul McCartney	Prince
Jessica Tandy	Joan Van Ark
Judy Garland	Lionel Richie
Gene Wilder	Bruce Dern
Rosemary Clooney	Joan Rivers

Chapter Four

CANCER

The Mirage: The Rock of Gibraltar

You Cancers, as you crawl toward another person:

"At last! Somebody sane!"

You Cancers take one look at another person and see the Chief Justice of the Supreme Court of the Universe, maybe a little gray at the temples, but exuding stability, balance, and equanimity.

You are struck to have come upon someone who listens to you. Someone who listens and hears, who listens, hears, and, above all, understands. O joy! To enter the eye of the hurricane at last. It's such a pleasure for you to encounter someone who will say, "There! There!" and mean it. You are always drawn to figures displaying the prudence of an old soul, something in an ancient Greek, perhaps. Maturity in a person turns you on, somebody who's not wringing their hands and going to the window every five minutes to see if the bomb has fallen.

You adore stature in a mate and are restored to calm by that beautiful rational mind, a calm that comes from the tranquil voice of the president coming over the air waves in a time of national turmoil—something somber, yet reassuring and deliberate, in a tone that lets you know that all is well, all is under control. (Is that what drew Nancy Reagan to Ronnie?)

You Cancers need it, love it, when somebody is cool. So, naturally, you're at home with an "older" man or woman. That slightly stuffy, at-home-with-an-escargotfork, successful, established professional businessperson or artist. You are excited by discipline, polish, and the seriousness with which others approach their goals, how big their offices are. You think executives are nice, too, the way they take charge and say exactly what has to be done. You like authorities and top specialists, because what you see at the beginning of your relationship is the consummate capability with which your partner attacks life. Rather than fancy good looks or frivolous glamour, you see him or her as a class act, a creature of breeding who knows things and has been places, who's aware of what "black tie" means and who doesn't think that the term "romanesque" refers to kitchen floor tile. Is that why Ginger Rogers danced right up to Fred Astaire? Your mirage is your partner's protective sobriety. He or she is the consummate cool cat with the experience of Marcus Welby, the suaveness of Cary Grant, and the class of Dietrich, whether they're a man or a woman.

You are drawn toward the successful people in this world and to those who *promise* to be successful. George Lucas's success didn't exactly turn Linda Ronstadt off. You Cancers are always attracted to those masters of the physical world who might help you realize your ambitions, so you like stable, serious business types who are as faithful as the pyramids. In fact, you get about two thousand volts when you approach the bench of that Supreme Judge —All Good, All Knowing, Wise Heal-A-Booboo Mother-Father.

The Monster: The Immovable Object

You on a bad day:

> "There's no sense discussing it. It's the same old story. And don't tell me all I have to do is walk out to make it better, because if you say that, then you don't understand. Where would I go that this thing wouldn't be right in front of me every minute?"

BUT... You Cancers don't deal well with authority. You hate it. You marry so that your spouses can handle all that stuff. Then, before they know it, you've turned them into the authority figure you hate!

It's a law of physics. If one moves toward a rock, one bumps one's little head. When you Cancers find out you've actually married the great-grandchild of Cinderella's stepmother or Ebenezer Scrooge, you cringe. You do get depressed when you find out they can take you or leave you, and mostly leave you. What sends you to the doctor is their coldness and silence, that they don't even know, or care, that you are there and hurting. *Brrr!* And what a disappointment you experience when you need to be deeply embraced and all you get is a dutiful cadaver's kiss on the cheek. It is sheer horror for you idealistic children to be faced with a scheming, Machiavellian, controlling, guarded individual who remains concealed behind a wall while you poor Cancers lay yourselves open.

You're crushed by that cruel-minded Dr. Moriarty who never stops playing chess, every move calculated two jumps ahead of you so you're always in check, at a slight disadvantage. When the monster appears, you Cancers see your partner putting up obstacles and barriers, and you feel like Edmund Hillary the first time he saw Everest. And punitive! Every time you forget to genuflect, your mate has you eating scraps in the doghouse for a month. Even if this is not really the case at all, this is what you see: a person who claims to be logical and rational but who is actually unreasonable, as rigid as a steel bar, and as impassive as the IRS's computer, with little or no real sensitivity to the tides and eddies of your inner being, yet who goes on demanding and demanding, holding up that infernal contract in your face and pointing to the fine print.

What happened to that highly developed understanding mind? you wonder. How could it have gone from pure logic to pure cement? What you considered to be a deep thinker turns out to be a narrow-minded, cynical, tit-for-tat parent exercising their muscle of authority at every possible moment, observing every flutter of your tender Cancer heart as coldly as an EKG, measuring and judging your behavior as if he or she had seen it all before in a maze with a mouse.

You thought you'd met someone with unique and insightful talents, and then they've turned out to be a doctor who will not be disputed.

You Cancers worry that if your partners get depressed over their own limitations, the mistakes they've made, the issues they have about self-image or success, they'll lay their problems on you. This scares you. You fear they will actually stand in the way of your success, actually get jealous when you are moving ahead, getting over hangups and obstacles, stretching an invisible string across your path so you're sure to stumble.

The monster vision of a relationship through your eyes is one of a supremely calculating and depressed sadist. You fear that people will make you choose between *them* and success in some punitive way but will organize *their* life so they don't have to do the same for you and will be able to put you second in their life without your being able to do a damned thing about it. And while they will get away with being too busy for you with complete impunity, they'll still be in a position to scream orders to you from their wheelchair.

Where do these wicked-stepmother fantasies come from?

The Real Thing: Recognition from the Boss

Many of you Cancers come from homes where at least one parent was much too busy for you or failed to see, hear, or understand you. Maybe that's true for just about everybody, but you Cancers are especially sensitive about not being taken seriously. This is tricky, because while you often think you are looking for someone to recognize you, you are often subtly and unconsciously involved with people who *make* you want to try to get recognized—in other words, you are drawn to the obstacle. Part of the pattern is to seek recognition from one who is strict and unfeeling or absent and disinterested. This can't be true for every Cancer, of course. We all know the institution that is Steve Lawrence and Eydie Gorme.

Your tendency is always to form permanent, lasting marriages, but there is always an issue of sympathies and lack of it. Often when you think you are being drawn to qualities you like, you are actually also being attracted to a feeling of frustration and coldness.

Depressorama! This is not always a pleasant prospect. There is one aspect of your sign that's a yowling baby, being silenced by a disapproving parent who expects you to grow up immediately and shut up while you're still lying in the crib. The baby within every Cancer needs to be exposed to what is commonly referred to as the *cold, cruel world*. That is where your partner comes in. Though it sours your stomach from time to time, you are drawn to and need the sophistication that contact with other people will offer you. You're in their life to soften their views and do for them what Anna did for the King of Siam, but you love them best when they fight the erosion. Political struggles and dynamics terrify you, and yet in the light of truth, you Cancers go for the biggest politician of them all. Yet can't really compete with a cool thinker.

The parent whose approval you wanted (but didn't always get), whose absence left you frustrated, or who was too busy or preoccupied sometimes sends you searching for the opposite type—the easygoing, lackadaisical, hang-around-the-house type, just because you want to make sure somebody will be there. But you lose respect quickly for that sort of person, because above all, you Cancers like success in your mates.

The alternative, of course, is to go after the high achiever and then play second fiddle to somebody's goal-oriented life. In either case worldly success becomes an issue always, as does the question of who is the head of the household. It's hard to imagine that Mel Brooks would feel abandoned when Anne Bancroft was shooting a picture and not broiling his chops, but astrology is true, and these dynamics have to exist somewhere in the heart of these relationships.

Looking for a present, actively understanding parent figure can be frustrating for the Cancer sometimes, because the rational individual eventually gets sick to death of catering to your moods. A mature person comes to see that you Cancers, left to your own devices, would be in an eternal state of emotional flux and that limits have to be set for you by people on the outside. If your partners want merely to placate you, they should indulge you. To satisfy you, they must truly give you a red flag once in a while. That way they'll never go wrong. You want them to say no, create boundaries, make rules.

The more resolved about your attitudes toward authority figures, the better defined your relationships will be. You evolved Cancers draw people who are also clear on these issues. You have few or no problems with integrating yourselves into society and often have thriving long-term bonds with career and bosses. Unevolved Cancers stay in the house and eat donuts, venturing out only to go to the doctor.

In every one of your major relationships, issues of success, recognition, and status will always arise.

The Burning Question: Who's the Child, and Who's the Parent?

You Cancers want to be grown-up. Look how macho Sylvester Stallone acts in all his movies. But never rely on outer appearances, because you never know who wears the pants in the crucial moments of a Cancerian relationship.

Back in the old days, roles were clearly defined. Dad earned the bread, and Mom baked it. But today we're more open to the inner reality of people, and men and women are beginning to flourish in the light of their true selves, whether they're shy and retiring or worldly and aggressive.

Male and female, you are struggling to mature into adults while always being drawn to relationships where you are "protected" from the big bad world under a big eagle's wing. But the weakened state you find yourselves in when you yield to a paralyzing dependence leads you ironically to having to protect yourselves from your protector, who early in the relationship takes on all the forbidding attributes of the big bad world he or she was supposed to be protecting you from.

You and your mate often take turns being grownup, but it's rare when you both get out of the bed on the grown-up side on the same morning. One day you want your partner to be the goal-oriented success story while you hide under the covers. The next thing you know, you will be roaring around, dealing with a full time job and administering tea and honey to him or her through a straw.

Mothering is a giant issue for you, and—guess what—it is for anyone near you as well. If you could decide once and for all which side of your mother's womb you wanted to be living on, you'd make everybody's life easier.

Your relationships permit you (sometimes force you) to wake up and deal with your life today, here and now. Many of you are lost in a reverie, dreaming of a happy past that never really happened, and you expect someone to rescue you from a childhood that was insensitive to your greatness. You expect the other person to be the parent who either frustrated or ignored you, except for one major rewrite of the script.

He or she is supposed to indulge you, recognize you, coddle you in ways that parent failed to.

Just one hitch. That's not what you really want at all. You have to *become* the ideal parent, modeling yourselves after the parent whose methods you criticize more.

Oh, it's all so complicated that one could spend a lifetime on the couch, sorting out complexes that come from the mad, mad, mad world of family.

When you read all the traditional astrological stuff about how sensitive and caring you Cancers are supposed to be and how "family-oriented" you all are, try to remember you often have more sympathy for yourselves than for others. You want your mates to be strong and stable, and you don't like to see them cry at the movies (even though you're dying to see a crack in their armor).

You Cancers are playing out a subtle remake of the movie of your parents' marriage. It's often hidden, but you are in a huge turmoil about the unfeeling way your father treated your mother (sometimes it's the reverse).

You unconsciously, then, move toward cold figures to repeat this pattern. But you will test the partners to see if they'll be different, to see if they'll pick up the baby when it cries.

You overwhelmingly responsive by the way. And no matter how much you fight the "female" role, you usually end up needing about a thousand nipples to feed all the people who need feeding. You can't resist repeating a child-parent stance in every relationship you form.

Of course, your individual family determines a lot. If you come from a happy, well-adjusted home, you'll probably be in much better shape in your attempt at adult life. Your relationship with your mother is crucial in determining how you relate to your partner. How much you identify with her, what ideas or attitudes she communicated to you, how you saw her, how she bonded with you, your attachment for her, all will develop your patterns in later life.

Of course, we could say this about everybody. All our relationships are influenced by our relationships with our mothers. But you Cancers personify this issue and carry it to the nth degree. You *always* create some kind of family scene and child-parent dependency wherever you go. You'll mother your partner, but in return someone will have to play big daddy to your whining child.

The brand of nurturing varies, of course. There are the Mamma Mia types, those of you who can just feel a moussaka coming on; and the throw-a-frozen-vegetable-into-a-pot types, those of you who think you've fussed for a mate's birthday dinner if you phone for a pizza with everything. You whine and moan about the pressure put on you just by existing, but deep down you know you have to take care of your partner forever. As you're being carried out in the ambulance, you'll call out that there's meat loaf in the freezer.

Cancers are wrestling all the time with Mom-Dad, parent-child issues. You get someone into a relationship and before long they'll be asking the same question:

Hey, who's the parent, and who's the child?

Ultimate Challenge: Personal Satisfaction vs. Worldly Success

You're trying to live in the present and not in some lilac-scented dream of the happy summer you were nine or in a neurotic fantasy of a future date when everything will be straightened out and you feel better. But most of you Cancers consider the present day to be just about two centuries too crass. The moment of awakening is painful for you tender souls who could easily retreat into a plate of pasta and TV, surrounded by your plants on a soft and private moon where you wouldn't even skin your knees.

You're simple country folk at heart who need the challenge of a big city's filth, noise, and corruption. You need people's critical feedback, their cool scrutiny. You need their scientific dissection of your idealistic schemes. You are the philosophers of the world and call on your partners to challenge your speculative creative musings with a rational approach. Can your theories be observed in fact? Your hypotheses tested? Will the damn thing sell?

Left to your own devices, you'll sometimes keep your dreams under the pillow like a pulled tooth the tooth fairy is supposed to trade for some hard cash. But you need others to yank you into reality, to pull you out of your retreat with the forceps of reason. Life is as hard and shocking for you as a baby's first glimpse of a delivery room.

Your mate symbolizes for you everything that is too real, too tangible, inexorable, destined to block your path. He or she becomes your symbol of social acceptance, something you fight against but ultimately have to accept about yourselves. You are a goal-oriented individual who needs the recognition in this cold, mechanical, robotized machine called society. You want someone to sympathize with your disdain for what people think, but you can't accept anyone if he or she rebels and strays too far from social convention.

Your ultimate challenge, through your relationships is to integrate your natural barefoot-in-the-woods mentality with the image of success in a tailored suit behind a desk with a big-city skyline behind.

Much of your challenge stems from your deeply buried attitudes toward your father's success or failure in career and the burden that placed on your mother.

This theme runs through everything you Cancers think, say, and do. So creating an acceptable balance between your role as emotional nurturer and economic provider not only grants you success in a relationship but helps remove much of the residue of early conflict as well.

It's your relationship with your mates, with all its pressures, demands, and problems, that creates a dynamic equilibrium between your need to withdraw and your urge to achieve success. You'll think they expect much too much of you, and you'll complain, because if it weren't for their problems, you'd have a more peaceful, personally fulfilled life, but ironically, it's precisely because of their problems and limitations and the pressures they put on you that you eventually rise in life.

So whatever they do, they shouldn't worry about making it too easy for you. In fact, when you need it, they might give you a good spanking.

The Miracle: Depth of Commitment

For all the whining and wiggling you do, nobody sees things through like a Cancer. You'll sit by the bed, listening for labored breathing, sponging that brow till the doctor comes in and covers the patient's face with a sheet. Maybe it's because you take pain so well without screaming, but when you're a Cancer, you develop commitment because your task is to learn it.

To achieve your miracle, the first thing you have to do is acknowledge your involvement with the world. The hermit stuff we read about you Cancers is only half the story. You are only semi-dedicated to hiding down in the rec room with a box of oreos. You're people-oriented, always searching to connect and be seen, touched, and recognized. Acknowledging this fact starts you on your path toward achieving success through a strong commitment.

You have to recognize also the need for limits. Without limits, you would be all over the place like spilled floor wax. Limits help you to flow through definite channels, like a river through its bed. Adhering to limits sets a course and allows goals to come to fruition, commitments to be fulfilled, whether it's to a person or a creative idea.

Since you are looking for people to direct, protect, and develop you, you've got to accept your attraction to those individuals who set up limits. At first it's easy. You will bow and curtsy and polish up the apple, but oh, do you resist control, and oh, do you fight those limits. Your patience will be tried ten thousand times, until you realize that you've got to stick to the deals you make. You tend to hold other people to the letter of the law but squirm when similar guidelines are set for you. Accepting the cold, withdrawn, withholding types you seek opens the door.

You need to expose the roots of your dependence and embrace rather than reject the very people you need to accomplish your miracle and your goals. You need to involve yourselves deeply in the problems of others, in fact make it part of your career in solving problems *without being engulfed by them*.

By moving slowly into a relationship, carefully defining goals and duties, you reduce the risk of disappointment and enhance your chances for long-term success. You need to understand the fact that people have a history and psychology that will sometimes exclude you. You need to understand your own ambivalence about your responsibilities to your partners. Though you'll often complain about the burdens your mates' existence puts on you, if they close the door on you, you'll crawl through the keyhole to be near them. You must see that if you want your partners to be tops in their field, you yourself will not be at the top of their priority list. And above all, once you see clearly that solving problems is your task, the totality of your commitment to a relationship can be assured.

At that point you can be devoted without being engulfed, dedicated to helping solve problems without being threatened with abandonment once the problems are solved. When you see something through to its complete solution, without fear of the abandonment that may follow, all problems are solved.

The miracle for you Cancers is success through depth of commitment. A collaborative effort between two people brings that Oscar, the Emmy, the real estate prize. You fight against success sometimes, because it reminds you of insensitive, grasping people, takes you back to when you had to show your report card to someone who refused to acknowledge the A's—only noticed the C's.

Once you've overcome that old resentment, when you've stopped confusing your mates with the Immovable Object from your childhood, when you cease to perceive them as the red light in life that never turns green, then you can see them for who they really are.

At that point you let go of your resistance. You quit trying to merge completely with them and your frustration vanishes. You become aware that they have their own history, one you'll never be part of. You don't hate them for their dedication to a life outside of you. As you begin to see their issues and blocks more clearly, less personally, you no longer use them as an excuse for your lack of motivation.

On the contrary. As the picture clears, you see exactly why they have been "brought" to you. You see how deeply their blocks or demands reflect your own most cogent issues, and to help them with their blocks and issues miraculously solves your own.

You no longer feel ignored or used or frustrated, because their preoccupations put you lower on their list of priorities. You confront their problems without taking them personally. Their needs no longer hold you back but become the food of your own advancement.

The shared experiences of the problem eliminates the separation. You don't have to try to get away from them anymore. You see that a greater sensitivity to their problem not only will win their loyalty and support (which it will), but it becomes their medium for success.

You deal in problems. All you have to do is face it. And that's the secret of success.

Working the Miracle: Dealing With Authority Figures

Understanding the defenses of another person without getting all tangled up in them—that's the secret for your success. It's easy to say, but when you are deeply involved with people, their problems do indeed rub off on you.

Working this miracle means accepting some pretty heavy facts about your life, about the influence your family has on your relationships, about the consequences of your commitments.

Working this miracle takes patience. On good days, that seems relatively easy—you feel enthusiastic, accepting. But on bad days you feel sickened by people's interminable problems. These problems provide structure to your life, walls that limit your freedom and flow but always ensure depth of commitment. You need that structure, although you'll try like mad to erode it.

Your relationships are in your life to say no to you, to make you reason and impose order on your unconscious urges and instincts.

There's no free ride here on earth. A tick goes where the dog goes, and you Cancers just can't burrow into your mates for protection without having to accept them fully and really. You've chosen them because you want to go deeper, to know a real person, and that means problems.

You've sought them out to help you mature, to help you develop as a man or woman, to help you conquer the world. First you have to get over your negative identification with them as the bad parent. Male or female, you need to accept and respect the authority and direction of another human being. No matter how manipulative and cute you are, your maturity is dependent upon your ability to share control without acting out childishly. You pick your partner because you are unconsciously drawn to controlling parent figures, and your success depends on your capacity to accept that fact as your relationships deepen.

You do not want to have to become other people's psychiatrist, nor should you be enslaved by their endless needs as they play on your guilt till the end of time.

But you have to look truthfully at what drew you into a relationship with them in the first place. Some deep-seated problem they have fitted neatly into the Cancer scheme of escapism, jibed perfectly with your father problem. If they're closed off and you feel shut out, it may have been this very attribute that drew you together in the first place. And the relationship soon becomes a battle for their attention, your need to melt their iceberg.

But if you are turned on by coldness, will you lose interest if the object of your affection finally responds, needs you, ceases to play the critical, distant parent? What would happen if he or she were to become warm, caring, and ardent? Do you then create distance, throw up obstacles, somehow build up a wall you were always trying to tear down? Do you actually require that other people hold·up a stop sign? Are you asking them to be the authority, set the parameters of the relationship, make rules, and set limits?

And if you are drawn to your mates because they're professionals but are ambivalent within yourselves about worldly motivation, then you'll resent their dedication and try to undermine their success.

But when you wake up to the truth of your attractions, when you learn how to work with them, you're no longer insulted by their self-absorption, and you're the most supportive partners in the world. Lady Macbeth herself was probably a Cancer.

Maintaining your separateness is something you have to grapple with. But when you're with people, you've got to be attentive and follow the direction you've sought them out to give you. When you're not in the mood to make love, you'll get the proverbial headache, and when you feel you're getting a raw deal in business (which you often feel even when you've agreed on the terms), you'll shrink away, be passively aggressive, and fight the very conditions you accepted, because you think you were coerced into them.

Your partners have to be clear, specific, and essentially unbending. The reason you agree to terms that put you at a disadvantage could vary from Cancer to Cancer. Often, though, you get caught up in your fantasy of your mates as figures whose approval you want to win. You're half expecting them to reject you, laugh at you, turn you down. So you're so wound up with their acceptance that you don't dare make demands or set up terms that are truly agreeable to you. You even forget to check *their* credentials or appropriateness, so intent are you on being accepted by them.

When it finally dawns on you that they were much

cooler about the whole thing from the outset and knew exactly what they were getting and what they'd have to give, you get angry and you balk. But of course, it's much too late, because once a Cancer is in, the Cancer is *in*.

If they can stand tall and *not* yield to crocodile tears or complaints of a tummyache the night before exams, and hold you firmly in place in those shaky moments when commitments tend to wobble, success is inevitable.

You want shape; you don't want shape. You want to make something out of yourself; you don't. Your mates can't hope to resolve single-handedly your ambivalence. They can't make somebody grow up who has thirty or forty years of resistance or resentment built up toward authority figures. They can help you by responding logically and objectively.

It will drive you crazy, but in the end you'll thank them for not letting go.

Gift Ideas for Cancers

- A genuine antique ball and chain used to keep prisoners. Not only do Cancers appreciate the value of priceless old things, but the message will be loud and clear.
- A copy of a standard house or apartment lease, which can be purchased at stationary stores. All the details have probably been left blank, but that doesn't matter. A fountain pen and a bottle of permanent ink can go with it. This will symbolize the binding power of agreements (Cancers *love* those formal ceremonies) and still convey the message that even permanence is temporary.
- A bag of cement. Any hardware store can supply it. Have it gift-wrapped and include a card that says, "Just add water and stir. When the stuff starts to set, think of me."

Reading Material for Advanced Cancers Only

The biography of Eleanor Roosevelt.

Guardian Angels: The President and the First Lady

 The President and the First Lady symbolize the ascent from a childhood fantasy to a top position in the real world. We could just as well have considered the image of a woman president and her husband, and however we choose to think of it, it should be as a traditional male-female couple.

No matter what the true psychosexual dynamics of this couple's relationship might be, on the outside, at least, they have their roles clearly and traditionally defined. In reality it's never simple, of course, but Cancer's guardian angels are the President and First Lady because they denote the potential heights such a relationship can reach when the participating partners have adjusted to the pressures and expectations of society, can cooperate with each other, and create a healthy environment in which their family can thrive.

The family can be a nation, company, or houseful of children, but the integrity of the household depends on the stability and clarity of definition of the role-playing. Granted, many zoos have been created by parents who looked perfectly normal on the outside, and the public aspect of this symbolic relationship makes it impossible for us to see what's going on beneath the surface—who's the controlling one, who's the boss, who's the parent, who's the child.

We see them smiling and waving in front of their White House, so we infer that whatever the inner dynamics might be, the relationship is strong, cooperation is total, and together they are fulfilling their duties and responsibilities to society as a whole.

These guardian angels suggest for Cancer a bond between two people, possibly taking turns privately fulfilling role of nurturer or disciplinarian, but in the eyes of the world they carry on a socially accepted tradition of parental roles.

Celebrity Astro Game

You'd be surprised how many ways people reveal themselves in everything they say and do. To sharpen your sensitivity to other people and to learn more about the ways renowned Cancers handle their deepest relationship issues, look over the following list and pick out the people who interest you most.

Do a little sleuthing about their lives. Observe their actions; listen to what they say in public. The songs they sing, the roles they play, the particular contributions they make, will enlighten you about the relationship patterns of this sign.

Bill Cosby	Gilda Radner
Phyllis Diller	George Steinbrenner
Anne Morrow Lindbergh	Dianne Feinstein
Jane Russell	Meryl Streep
Helen Keller	Jimmy Walker
Henry VIII	O.J. Simpson
Ann Landers	Cheryl Ladd
Mel Brooks	Linda Ronstadt
Sylvester Stallone	Kris Kristofferson
Dan Ackroyd	Harrison Ford

Chapter Five

LEO

The Mirage: A Flamingo among Ostriches

You Leos, when you see someone coming down the beach on horseback:

> "Now, here's somebody who doesn't give a damn what anybody thinks, and that's a rare quality today."

If someone falls out a window and lands on a Leo, they'll be married before the week is out. You Leos always get hit with a bolt from the blue—that's how you know you've met your soul mate. In fact, you like your relationships to make the society pages *and* the Richter scale. You stumble on your mates, get zapped by their oddball spontaneity, and think it will free you from your insufferable self-consciousness. You're big on shock value, so in the high school pregnancy department, there have to be a lot of Leos. You're always looking for an unexpected adventure, so the odder someone is, the more you think, now, here's a really unusual person. The more people freak you out, the better you love it. You love it when they tell you to meet them on the corner at four P.M. but don't tell you if it's

New York or California time. You love it when they drop a bomb on your complacency. When you get too pushy, they should just write *shove it* on the mirror (that's the one place Leos are sure to look). Isn't that what Madonna saw in Sean Penn way back when?

Even if your mates are truly conservative, you will create a myth about their nonconformity. Even though you'd never be caught dead wearing the getups they'll put on, you'll consider it refreshing if they can throw an outfit together at the last minute, hold it on with safety pins, and come off smashing, mainly because many of you Leos are hooked into *GQ* and *Vogue*. And if their home is furnished like a prehistoric cave or pasha's den, you will glow. The more bizarre, the better. You're thoroughly bored by a house done by a decorator from *Apartment Life*.

If it's one thing you admire, it's originality and daring. You adore someone who can actually fart while speaking to the Queen and giggle, "Excuse me, Your Majesty," and just continue talking as if nothing had happened. Just think of Gloria Bunker's attraction for Meathead, and you'll see how Leos get excited by someone who tocks when every other zombie in America is ticking, a wild and crazy rebel who won't get a green mohawk or crew cut just because everybody else does.

What strikes you deepest is a gutsy, ballsy, frenetic electricity, and strangely enough, whether your mate is like that or not, being around you brings it out. You see him or her as the wild free-thinker who's going to smash the mirror, shatter the pattern, catapult you into Dimension X.

The Monster: It Came from Outer Space

You Leos, when you get over the shock of who your partner really is:

"I won't let this throw me.
I won't let this throw me.
I won't let this throw me."

BUT . . . when the diet pill wears off, what you once found kooky and whimsical turns out to be disruptive and perverse. You loved them for their thousand and one eccentricities, and soon after the relationship gets going, you devote all your energy toward eradicating their idiosyncracies and teaching them how to spit-shine your shoes. When you wake up one morning to see them sticking their finger into the light socket to get recharged, you know they're from Uranus.

So many of you Leos panic and lay down the law.

Bad move.

You often find that the more tightly you squeeze the controls, the more ingeniously your mate will drive you out of your mind. Sooner or later it dawns on you that you have a real problem about being bossy—one that now and then will interfere with closeness and intimacy between you. Again calling to mind Gloria Bunker as an example of Leos' fatal attraction to meatheads and oddballs, you'll soon find that your mate's disrespect for tyranny, which at first you thought quite refreshing, affects his or her attitude toward you as well. Teaching the boss a lesson may well have been what Josephine was doing when she told Napoleon she had a headache.

You Leos don't really want to succeed in domesticating your mates, but you have to try. It is difficult for you to accept not only that you have on your hands a person who's got a dozen pushable buttons, but that the combinations keep changing. So he or she might reward you for a certain behavior on Sunday, turn around and zap you for it on Monday. You are frizzed out by this monster of unexpected reversal.

You get jealous of other people's freedom and try to crush it. You take their nonchalance as a personal insult, and what you once admired as spirit and freshness, you perceive as insolent insubordination or a deliberate effort on their part to upset you. Many of you Leos were raised by a parent with a wacky thyroid gland, and when you start to feel those gyrations from eccentric behavior, it knocks you for a loop.

You're full of swaggering bravado, but inside, you're actually scared of being blown away by someone else's hurricane. It's already happened to you before. People have dropped into your life suddenly, turned you on, and then woosh! down through a trap door and out with no warning.

For you Leos, the monster is that unexpected dropout, that curve ball coming out of nowhere. You love it, of course, but you hate it, too.

It's impossible for you to cope with the fact that by giving in and trusting, your whole life could be put on an electrified grid and at any moment the juice could be turned on. All you can trust in then is the unexpected.

Arnold Schwarzenegger married late, but he'll find it out. Madonna's already learned it. Many of you Leos almost don't dare bring anyone home for dinner, because at any time a bomb could go off somewhere between the soup and the nuts. At monster moments you Leos find yourselves in the suicide seat while your mate has grabbed the wheel, high as a kite and screaming, "Whee!" as the vehicle jumps the curb. No matter how much promise you have, no matter how stable and dependable you try to be, when it comes to relationships, one can't bet money on what you will do.

You invariably invest your emotional well-being in proud rebels who either up and disappear, shock you without warning, or turn out to be totally nuts. Just look at all the weirdos in Andy Warhol's life.

The Real Thing: Escape from a Seductive, Controlling, Erratic Parent

Though you think you'd like to live and die behind that white picket fence, in reality you like rebels. You express your rebellion in the choice of mate, insuring yourselves against a boring bourgeois life. But once you've married the alien from Uranus, you spend your lives trying to hide the antennae under a hat and make your mate conform.

Exactly why you have such a complex attraction-repulsion for the bonds of family life is hard to say, because it varies from Leo to Leo. Many of you have close and loving relationships with parents, but often this closeness chokes you, and you are all, males and females, profoundly determined to be free of family domination. So whether or not there's a history of sexual abuse at home, you're all running away from a seductive but unpredictable mommy or daddy.

You idealize uninhibited behavior and seem to thrive on a relationship with someone who will throw a live radio into the bathtub while you are splashing around with your rubber duck. Many of you were caught in the grip of a fanatically controlling parent and so wait for a bird of paradise to fly by and yank you out of the parental grasp. But because you don't deal easily with separation from the love affair with this dragon parent, you often will try to achieve it over and over through shocking methods. Many of you marry out of your religion or social station for this very reason. Did Princess Margaret herself wish to freak out the Royal Family when she married Anthony Armstrong-Jones?

Glamorous and exotic as she is, in her inner life Jacqueline Kennedy Onassis was probably horrified at the thought of repeating her parents' lives and made many of her moves in relationships because of this.

. You Leos look upon your homes as both a cozy hideaway nest and a prison you've got to escape from. At the deepest possible level, many of you were involved in unconscious seductions (most of the time unconsummated), with one of your parents. And not seldom do you repeat the pattern when you create triangles in relationships as if to make the parent jealous of your "infidelity." Because you are held in the talons of a powerfully dependent relationship with a seductive but erratic parent, this pattern gets repeated in adulthood. The unrequited seduction is often unresolved, so you make the mate the parent and then have to have extramarital affairs to keep the whole conundrum going. If one meets a Leo man at a party, he'll probably act as single as hell, but one must make sure one asks where his wife is. The women, too, probably have some guy safely tucked thirty miles away.

You Leos try to work out an ambivalent feeling about being intimate by picking slightly unreliable partners. You yourselves are magnetized by a compelling need for closeness, but just to ensure that it doesn't happen, you pick weird people. So then it becomes the mate who pulls away, withdraws, rejects the closeness you think you are seeking, flees from the control and manipulation you exercise. So just as one of you is getting totally cozy, the other one has to get up and go to the john.

The Burning Question: How to Keep Giving If at Any Moment the Rug Could Be Pulled Right Out from Under?

But all that psychology stuff is for the birds, most of you Leos think. You've got little time to get stuck in the swamp called the past. Besides, all that Freud stuff about what happened to you twenty, thirty, or fifty years ago can't be as important as what a person does with their life right now. You Leos feel that if you're positive and productive, that's all that counts, and when you're in a relationship with someone, they're either there for you or they're not.

Yes, you're all in training as Marine sergeants. But somebody's got to make the rules. You know only too well about anarchy in relationships. Yes, you do have a little trouble keeping from whacking your mates over the head when they decide to do something on their own without kissing your ring first and getting your seal of approval. But you love them when they give you the finger, because if they're wimps you'll eat them for breakfast. You respect them if they disobey you. But it's hard for you too, because when you open up and show your vulnerability, lean a little on them, *wooop!* the trap door opens and down you go.

You are born leaders, and if your partners weren't followers, at least a tiny bit, they wouldn't come anywhere near you. But when they discover that you are truly dominant through and through, they jump three feet in the air and their hair gets all frizzed out. When you weaken and show your neediness, they often flee with no explanation. How then are you Leos supposed to conduct yourselves sanely?

There comes a point for you when the game gets tiresome; when the bump on your head and the egg on your face get a little hard to take. The disapproving parent-rebellious teenager game is one all you Leos have played. The emotional game of tag has to come from somewhere. You are asking yourselves over and over, "How can I keep giving if at any moment I'll be dropped on my head?" If every time a person walks into the room there's a pail of water over the doorway, a body is not going to feel comfortable just coming on through. So, after a while when you are not sure if you are going to be warmly embraced or zapped, you get a little jumpy. And when you start to notice somebody acting a little funny—cool, distant, weird—you think, "Oh, no, not again!" You interpret your mate's need for freedom as rejection—and just when you were getting comfortable! And that's where the fun starts. Because that not only upsets you, but it also turns you on.

In every relationship, you have to look at the issues of control, not blame the other person for being a flake, but realize you are attracted to unpredictable figures and then try to eliminate the eccentricities you first found attractive.

Ultimate Challenge: Security vs. Risk

Can you have it both ways? Can you have somebody there in the nest when you want them and be able to come and go as you please and not grant the other person the same freedom?

You want your own freedom and while you often *think* you want the other person to be equally freed, actually you are training a domesticated little mouse.

The gap often seems hard to bridge. It almost seems that the situation demands one mate for life and another for play. But how positively European even to suggest such a thing. But if there was ever a walking personification of the double standard, it's Leo. If the one who wants the security were the one to stay home all the time, then maybe you should take up knitting sweaters and stoking up the fire. Maybe you Leos should let *your* partners have all the freedom, take vacations alone, have affairs, jump out of planes, and there you would be when it was all over, arms outstretched and smiling say, "Land sakes, honey! You sure are a sight for sore eyes. Did'ja have fun? Hope so. Come on in and tell me all about it while I fix up some nice pea soup."

But that doesn't sound like you. Instead you always get someone else to play that role (even if it's your analyst).

You are utterly warm individuals with an ardor and sweetness that could make a nun forget the church. You know how to make others feel alive and important. There's no real way to resist or say no to you. You project such a force of stability you make others automatically want to fall in step with your parade. And your sheer power is so great that they will go along with almost anything. It's not that they don't dare oppose you. It's just that you don't exude democratic vibes. So they feel that whatever they want to do on their own they have to do in secret and be back by reveille.

You want others there when you want them there. But, you're often so absorbed in yourselves though, that you have trouble listening to the second half of their sentences. But you *can* still love and care for them in a very real way.

Your mates are not there just to mirror you, though. If they are going to have a relationship with you, you must recognize—they must make you recognize—that though they are attracted to fascism, they will never totally revolve around your orbit. And if you have to interpret that as insubordination, that's your problem.

You have your own personal work to do on yourself. Though you act like the big shot of the world, you're still a little mouth screaming for a nipple in many ways. You are haunted by feelings of abandonment the same as the rest of us, no matter how early you left home and started fending for yourselves. You still keep your hidden wireless umbilical cord with you and have to have somebody at the end of it. Then, too, you like the rest of the world to be able to drive by and see that picket fence and somebody out on the lawn raking leaves.

But you are all afraid of getting impaled on that picket fence. You are dedicated to the image of family and emotional security. You are always trying to recreate the Waltons, when you're really setting up the Munsters, because you still like everyone to see how liberal and unconventional you are in the person you have chosen for a mate. It's a paradox. You live vicariously through your mates, but if they ever surrender and hold out their hands for the handcuffs, they shouldn't count on when they'll see you again.

These are your paradoxes, and those involved with you are grappling with the same issues. They probably wouldn't be interested in you either, if you didn't try to tell them what to do.

You are happiest when you can resolve this paradox between your need to live under the fat part of the bell curve and the need to pair up with someone who cannot fit into formal shoes—or any shoes at all, for that matter.

The Miracle: Friendship

One should always remember how truly heroic you Leos are. Oh, you'll lie like rugs to make yourselves look good, and you'll turn on a maitre d's charm to hook someone. You women find it easy to be absolutely anything for your mate—except be just a woman, of course. And while you'll smile and say, "What do I know? I'm just a girl," you're the most competitive player on the squash court. You men have just as much trouble with your softer side as you women have showing your masculine natures. You guys will peel potatoes or carry up the laundry, but you usually have to make male grunting noises. Despite these idiosyncrasies, you're your mate's lifelong pal and protector. And if there's a bully scaring your loved one, you will beat 'em up in five seconds.

Above all, you want your mate to be your friend, and there is no dragon too scary for you, if it's threatening someone you care about. All you really want is friendship, and you'll do anything to prove yours. Friendship means freedom and freedom means separateness.

The Leo dance can go on forever if you dance apart. One of you must waltz while the other break dances. The rhythm must be hammered out, the tone must be cacophonous, and the result must be a dance that has never been danced before.

If you want to hold on to your mates, you must let them go. Not just as strategy, but you must learn to open the cage. Fulfilled Leo women know they can't control other people. The happiest Leo men have accepted women's liberation.

You have to learn how to open the cage and respect someone else's freedom, encourage their independence. You have to teach them to fly, then let them fly, not put a band around their leg or a leash around their neck.

The happiest Leos know that.

You love the wild bird, but you have to remember that a creature caught in the wild sometimes dies in captivity. If you want to be happy, hold that bird in your hands, point it toward Heaven, and let it go. Then put a cold compress on your ego and go about your business.

If you cripple your partners, they'll run away limping. If you free them they'll be your loyal servants forever. And you can't make them promise they won't sit on anyone else's window sill either, or when exactly they'll be back, but if you allow them their anomalies, there will be no separation.

But you do have to swallow a lot. You have to redefine the word loyalty. You can't just hand them a book and say, "Here. This is Hammurabi's Code of Ethics. Live by this standard and we've got a relationship."

You Leos cannot stand to be cuckolded or cheated on. But the Leo miracle is you *can* make a friend of your partner. In fact, that's the only kind of partner you really want.

That's what causes you to stray from the homestead in the first place. You don't want a usual kind of relationship. It has to be the special kind of thing that other people might be able to achieve somewhere around the year 2300.

You Leos have the capacity to maintain a closeness of communication that won't be harmed even if one of you is living on the moon—a perfect blend of intimacy and freedom, so that when you are together, you're utterly close, open, and strong. There's nothing you can't say to each other. But neither of you is locked into insecurity or mistrust. But the strength of the bond is tested by how much you encourage freedom and relate to your loved ones the way you would treat a friend.

You've got to be able to provide a warm and stable base for your mates, understand that it takes all kinds of crazy people to keep this crazy world turning and support, not undermine, their attempts at independence. Even if their rebelliousness smacks of adolescent acting out, you have to help them develop creative or personal freedom and in the process free yourselves of your neurotic fear of abandonment.

You have to be able to adjust to unexpected circumstances. There are unwritten agreements in contracts, scores of riders and contingency clauses put there in invisible ink. In fact, most of the agreement *is* between the lines. And the most successful of you Leos look there first. At any rate, the miracle can be achieved only through the development of emotional flexibility, because what will maintain the bond between you and another human being is the ability to make certain adaptations to rules that have been drastically changed at the last minute. You Leos have to learn not to do this to others but to be undaunted when it's done to you. Your task is loyalty to the rebels.

Your need to be able to support people's crazy schemes and counter their chaotic perversity with consistency, in the end accepting metabolisms that you can never outguess. You have to be there, warmly disapproving yet forgiving. Many of you Leos stray and act out childishly, defending yourselves more aggressively against abandonment, and keep your mates on tenterhooks, keep them guessing, never allowing *them* to play the wild wanderer. Life eventually teaches you, though, that you need to welcome your mate's return in a nonpunitive way and still be able to cheer their departure.

The miracle is achieved when you are able to pass the ultimate friendship test—to be able to hear who your mate slept with last night and think it's funny.

Working the Miracle: Granting Freedom

Had you been raised under the rule of a highly unpredictable parent, your relationships would show it all throughout your life, and you'd tend to set up your security base somewhere along the San Andreas fault.

Because your unconscious urges would drag you back time and again toward a repetition of those early, unstable conditions, you would create a shaky existence, living from hand to mouth, or somehow or other trembling in constant expectation of that thunderous event. You'd always live on the edge, either financially or emotionally.

Some parents create economic instability, while others are emotionally erratic. Sometimes they up and disappear altogether.

It's just this sort of behavior that you are rebelling against. You are often trying to overcome the aftereffects of the influence of a "crazy" parent neither you nor the other members of your childhood family could rely on for consistent support in one form or other. Even when you make a conscious effort to find someone stable and even-keeled, your *real* self, the urges buried deep down at the base of you, is searching for a scene where the partner is erratic, where it's more exciting, you are the stable and loyal one, sounder than a dollar, and more reliable than the sun in August. You find it hard to deal with erratic behavior, but you encounter it over and over.

You draw people who will mess you up, drive you nuts, upset your plans, flagrantly disobey your commands. Why are you so fascinated with unpredictable behavior?

You Leos need to understand that many people who seem crazy aren't really crazy after all. Many people are moved first and foremost by an impulse to rebel against any domination. If somebody has a "thing" about *not* being told what to do, then when you start telling that person what to do, it's going to push a hell of a button, and that person will certainly set out to teach you a lesson.

There are some people in this world whose personal task it is to blow up the principal's office. They will *not* be controlled. And if you want to have a relationship with those people—and Leos usually do—their freedom has to come first and foremost. Not only will such freedom have to be permitted; it will have to be encouraged.

You sometimes think you're encouraging your mates' freedom when you stand over them and smile. "That's wonderful, dear. Now tick. Excellent. Oh, I'm so proud of you. I knew you could do it. Now tock."

But if it's your compulsion to feel that rug being pulled out from under, then won't even the stablest and most loyal mates be pushed beyond their limit, constantly tested to see at what point they will snap? Won't you be just waiting for someone to flip out or fly away? Does there have to be that inevitable dropping shoe?

In fact, you grant freedom to your partner only when they take it—when you have to and because you have to. You'll wine and dine them and come to their window singing, but once you have them, it's Rapunzel City.

You love their free spirit, but you have to learn how to cherish that spirit. The only way to grant freedom is to let go, overcome your rage at their daring to follow their own eccentric orbit. You try so hard to win their attention, so they can't possibly have any needs outside you.

When it comes to providing for them, there's no better.

But you do wait for that other shoe to drop. And at some point they have to take for themselves the one thing it's hard for you to give them—their freedom.

Gift Ideas for Leos

- A can of trick peanut brittle, the kind that holds a snake that jumps out when it's opened.
- A lapel carnation that squirts water.
- A buzzer that fits in the palm of the hand and gives a little shock when one shakes hands.

    You Leos have to be reminded through relationships that life has many surprises, and you are not in control of any of them. When you remember this, your relationships revitalize you and the people you try to bring under your sway.
- A banana peel. To remind you to let go and overcome your natural urge to control. When Leo can learn to slip up and still laugh there are no limits to how far the relationship can go.

Reading Material for Advanced Leos Only

A Tale of Two Cities, Charles Dickens
The Dialectic of Materialism, Karl Marx

Guardian Angels: The Munsters

 The Munsters rule over your relationships as guardian angels, because they symbolize the incongruity of unique beings attempting to simulate normal life. With them, utterly weird creatures occupy a real and natural place in commonplace society, to all outward appearances traditional, and though they may be completely ludicrous in everyday roles placed against the conventional backdrop, nobody seems to notice.

The total effect of the Munsters is inappropriate, comical, and bizarre when measured against accepted standards, and yet they carry on as if they were as normal as apple pie. What's more, they get away with it! They represent a blending of an unlikely pair, the successful resolution of the seemingly impossible conflict between the search for a novel, even revolutionary identity and the need to fulfill purely commonplace roles.

The outside of the Munsters' home may be like every other house on the block, yet the minute one steps inside, one is confronted with steaming potions, trick corridors, cobwebs, and many other humorous caricatures and iconography from spookdom. Similarly, your relationships seek to hide a whole set of oddball and outlandish characteristics beneath a mask of normalcy, as you always attempt to fit progressive, far-thinking, even antisocial behavior into the mold of conformity.

Your relationships are never organized conventionally on the inside. The neighbors, relatives, and friends will often accept the charade and pretend not to notice, but under no circumstances will those family pictures on the mantle tell the real story of the wacky setup that truly exists.

This weird bunch symbolizes the Leo genius for concocting the most outrageous conditions and making them work. The Munsters portray originality and the imposition of spontaneity, humor, and bizarre charm on every mundane setting. They guard your relationships, keeping you from falling into mediocrity or stagnation, always making sure you don't stray too far from your vow of unpredictability in relationships. As long as you retain this fierce rebellious attitude and war on normalcy, the Munsters will protect you.

Celebrity Astro Game

You'd be surprised how many people reveal themselves in everything they say and do. To sharpen your sensitivity to other people and learn more about the ways renowned Leos handle their deepest relationship issues, look over the following list and pick out the people who interest you most.

Do a little sleuthing about their lives. Observe their actions; listen to what they say in public. The songs they sing, the roles they play, the particular contributions they make, will enlighten you about the relationship patterns of this sign.

Robert Redford	Vitas Gerulaitis
Mick Jagger	Norman Lear
Jackie Onassis	Evonne Goolagong
Arnold Schwarzenegger	James Baldwin
Lucille Ball	Keith Carradine
Andy Warhol	Robert DeNiro
Dustin Hoffman	Lynda Carter
Napoleon Bonaparte	Rex Humbard
Princess Margaret	Princess Anne
Don Drysdale	Jerry Falwell

Chapter Six

VIRGO

The Mirage: The Savior Has Landed!

You Virgos, seated with someone at a little table in the corner, when you've just had the first sip of your second martini:

> "I don't usually do this. I really don't. But I have a feeling about you. I felt it the first time I saw you. Something I can't explain, almost as if we've met before. A strong little voice inside me told me I should go out and have this drink with you. Almost like destiny or fate. Something wanted us to be together tonight."

It may be hard for people to accept, but when one meets a Virgo, one has come upon an honest-to-God saint. Saints are difficult to deal with, because they ask so little for themselves and hide their pain so well, one would think they didn't have any needs at all. Before leaving the house, they always dry their eyes and roll up their sleeves, just in case they come upon a fellow who needs help.

Because you Virgos lead guileless lives on your path to canonization, you lend yourselves beautifully to exploitation and must be ever on the lookout for unscrupulous scoundrels who offer you martinis.

Your love for all people is pure and simple. You're as shy as a sixth grader at a tea dance, so one really has to be gentle with you. There should probably be more people like you in the world. You'll venture out hatless into a blizzard to get someone orange juice when they have the sniffles (and be crushed when they're not willing to do the same for you).

Most of your relationships are happy ones, especially the nonsexual ones. You tend to be a little aloof and not always available, and your scoffing cynicism is a giant defense against your fatal flaw—your naivete. If anything, you believe too much in people.

The first second you Virgos lay eyes on someone, harps start playing in your ears. No matter who they really are or what they're really all about, you see their highest potential, and you'll often stumble home from a first encounter with them as if you've just emerged from the grotto at Fatima. Even if the first thing you noticed was the way they moved in their blue jeans, you do get that don't-bother-me-I'm-digesting-my-First-Communion look in your eyes.

Like Melanie Hamilton in *Gone With the Wind*, you see only the divinity in those you choose to love. You see a glow that others cannot see, a talent you might not even know they've got. Even if they think they're all thumbs and tone deaf, you will have them playing Chopin in no time.

When you meet someone, if you love them, a healing takes place deep within your own soul, as if a plant that had been dry and withering is at last being watered and becoming green again. You see them as a cosmic reward for your patience and goodness, a special order sent over from God's factory. Relief has arrived, ordeal over.

In short, you view your partner as a visitation of the divine kind, swathed in a magical, musical, mystical healing light, and only you can recognize them for the being they truly are—your celestial reward for being good.

The Monster: Betrayer! Impostor! Fraud!

You, when you're having coffee with a friend after you've sobered up and come to your senses:

> "And then to find out that I'd been so completely had. What a fool I made of myself. Boy, I won't do that again.
>
> "What a jerk. To believe all that stuff. God, I knew the whole thing was wrong from the beginning. The trouble with me is I'm too trusting. I'm too good."

BUT... Soon enough it turns out that your partners need the help, whether they've asked for it or not. For when they stray, sin, err, or otherwise fall from your grace, they must prepare their defense before the Burgundian Court. They shouldn't make the mistake of staggering toward you at a party, clad in a lampshade and apologizing through a champagne slur, for you're sure to give them that just-wait-till-I-get-you-home look.

When the harp music ceases and the haze lifts, you will find yourselves with the job of making sure they don't fall asleep with a lit cigarette in their hand or eliminating one or more of their favorite addictions. Before they know it they're in St. Virgo's hospital, and at that point, it's not clear who is the savior and who needs to be saved.

At first, though, you are delighted if your mates plays the madly creative but foggy artist-mystic who can't quite get it together. That way you can dust them off, get their inventions patented and put their name up in lights. You love the types who lie around on a couch, eating grapes and composing music. But you feel betrayed when you find out you're the one who has to write down the notes. It tickles you if they're completely uninterested in the details of living on the Earth, like tying their own shoelaces or standing in line at the bank, but after a while you interpret this lack of diligence as a personal insult.

You Virgos identify strongly with Mother Theresa and countless other weary, unappreciated saints. You get inspiration staying up late and watching old Claudette Colbert movies.

In fact, many of you Virgos identify with Claudette Colbert. You may remember that she was always falling in love with handsome soldiers and ending up cheerfully working in a factory. You can always also identify with librarians who are taken in by riverboat gamblers, or hard-working farmers who get rolled on Saturday night. It must be understood that you are not betrayed by romantic scoundrels, harlots, or shysters but by your own escapist fantasies.

No matter how bright the heavenly glow may have been at first, there's a point in all your relationships when you draw the card of disillusion. It is necessary for your spiritual growth.

Certainly Joan Kennedy must go at the top of our list of Virgo saints. She must have flipped out the first time Teddy asked her out on a date. No matter who you are, you'd have to get that F. Scott Fitzgerald feeling to be paid attention to by a Kennedy. It must have been like the Red Sea parting.

You Virgos are disillusioned because you see life too simply. You actually believe that one day a magic genie will come along and take you on a shopping spree for contact lenses and all your troubles will be over. Many of you see yourselves as marionettes, attached to life by the strings of working-class routines. So you wait for the one who will come along, cut the strings, and turn you into a "real" person. And in that way you are as naive as an aborigine who sees a jet plane as divine.

You do need someone to add color and music to the black-and-white documentary you see as life. But the shock of pleasure is often too much for you and many of you Virgos emerge from relationships sputtering as if you'd been dunked in a horse trough or forced to kiss a leper on the mouth. When you lose your way in the thick undergrowth of the emotional fray, you Virgos come limping out of the woods like violated campers, all stained and torn. All you wanted to do was pet the nice bear!

The Real Thing: Fear of Making a Mistake

Because you feel your pure love was misused in the past, you are ever watchful for deception, trickery, and deceit. When you are deceived or disappointed, that old button gets pushed, and you'll blow the little white violation way out of proportion, getting much more hurt than the situation warrants.

Because you make gods and goddesses out of everyone in the beginning, people usually do something to shatter your illusions and disappoint you. Maybe you imagine glamour and grandiosity in others because you feel drab and colorless on your own. Many of you were good little helpers to your parents, and so continue the pattern in adult life. So no matter how strong or capable people are, you find it hard to relate to them in any way other than as patient and therapist. So you actually look for something wrong with people you can fix. You can't just let your hair down and dance. It's more bearable for you to see yourself as duty-bound than to admit your full and conscious participation in what you consider a cardinal sin: fun.

You consider yourselves the lighthouse in a foggy sea of gasping and drowning human beings. You must remain alert, awake, ever on duty, lest you be dozing when needed. After a while, you start believing that you are healthy and others are sick. And before you know it, you relate only by scanning for other people's pathology.

At your best you will tune a partner's instrument so finely that his or her music plays perfectly, and you often act as the link between art and the human world. He or she may have a brilliant idea, but it takes a Virgo to make sure the application for the grant gets in on time.

You do often feel used, though. You set out supposedly

to "help" your mates. Actually, you want to be distracted from the humming little hive of industry that is your life. But you cry "Sabotage!" when they actually succeed in mussing up your hair, pulling off your glasses and kissing you.

You truly believe you are on Earth to make sure all the sinners stick to their diets. You get in trouble when you take on the role of guidance counselor for all of humanity, sitting there with your lips pursed, waiting for all illusions to come crashing down and champagne to go flat, so you can be right there with a cup of black coffee in your voice and silent judgment in your eyes.

You evolved Virgos are not forever screaming, "Look what you've gone and spilled all over my wings!" You take life's little disappointments with a smile on your lips. But you unevolved Virgos will tie your mates to a chariot and drag them around the Colosseum if they make you look foolish. You do so dread being hoodwinked and you are so susceptible to it.

Eddie Fisher, for example, was under a strong influence of Virgo when he fell for Elizabeth Taylor. "Now what would a goddess like her see in me?" he might have thought. I'm just a pipsqueak from Philadelphia. So he dumped his wife and went dancing with Liz. When Taylor streaked by in Burton's limo, did he imagine her shouting, "Ta-ta sucker! Sorry if I hurt ya"? It would indeed be hard to believe in romance after that.

You Virgos are on your guard against being fooled, when it's the very thing you have to let happen to you. You often see yourselves as innocent as Pinocchio on his way to school but it isn't true. The real issue behind the monster of betrayal is your deep fear of exposing your most primitive, chaotic needs in front of other people. One would have to check back to your toilet training to figure all that out.

You do feel that your purity has been abused, your good nature played on, so you sometimes cling to the isle of safety called the rational mind. Nevertheless, to have relationships, you have to learn to swim in the deep and dangerous sea called emotions. You have to learn when to throw away the book and rely not even on gut, but on the greater force in the universe that has created the gut, a bigger scheme of things that requires you to abandon your myopic perspective, let go of reason, and float in the current of trust.

And for cheerful factory workers, librarians, and hardworking farmers, that is scary.

The Burning Question: Is There Always a Good Guy and a Bad Guy?

Every one of you Virgos has to resolve the great debate between Lucifer and St. Michael, and if you finally understand the illusion of "right" and "wrong," you're a being who is a walking union of hard-headed pragmatism and infinite compassion.

There's a fuzzy line between good and bad, the seducer and the seducee, the sinner and the saint. When you feel cheated or undermined, you can summon up every misdemeanor your mates have committed, simply by referring to page 26,207 of the transcript of the relationship, where both *their* sins and *your* good deeds have been recorded. It's difficult for you to catch a glimpse of your complicity in the crimes perpetrated against you. You imagine yourself a devotee of humility and righteousness, spending every waking moment caring for the sick and throwing cold water on dogs in heat.

But those of you with vision who know there is no blame, those of you who pierce the illusions of right and wrong, see with blazing clarity. You will be a partner's path away from defeatism. You will spread your apron to catch the fruits of his or her creativity. With your almost mystical sensitivity to the links between psychic and physical health, you hold the key to functioning in the material world. You alone can bring something from the mind into being. You have what it takes to take a mental picture of an apple blossom and turn it into a quart of real cider.

You Virgos with the true vision of good and evil illuminate the way for everybody around you. You accept the vast inconsistencies in all human conduct—your own included—and you embrace with a slightly embarrassed good humor the naughtiness of the human condition. *The deepest changes you can make in relationships will always reflect a shift in attitude between who is the hero and who is the villain.*

Some Virgos truly believe that when the Apocalypse comes, the "good" guys will be lined up behind God, sticking their tongues out smugly as evildoers fall through the clouds. But mature Virgos recognize the amazing subtlety and intricacy with which people send one another signals and fulfill one another's secret wishes. Though you Virgos will shoot holes in others' fantasies, you're the ones to look for to restore a precious equilibrium between the ideal and the real.

Ultimate Challenge: Order vs. Chaos

It's never a clear-cut case with you who's the neatnik and who's the slob. What stimulates you most is the great challenge of your sense of order by the forces of the universe called chaos.

When one needs a paper clip and knows exactly which drawer to look in, that's order. Chaos, on the other hand, is that infernal tendency to run out of toilet paper a half hour after the last store has closed.

Ironically, the greatest success that you Virgos can achieve is to let go of your crumbling ledge of order when blown by the winds of chaos. Everybody knows that even a cactus needs rain, and to have the most successful relationships, you need to be able to take a sip of faith and learn to play the game of chaos that results whenever two people get together.

In fact, no other group of people has the powers that you have—to be able to relate to someone *without* melting into them like a lump of butter in rum. That's why you're a little aloof, slightly buttoned up, just a tad unmarried, no matter how committed you are.

You evolved Virgos have room in your closet for both the whalebone girdle and the South Sea sarong. You accept the four-legged paradox that is a human relationship. You know well how ridiculously inconsistent and ambivalent people are, and you accept it. You evolved Virgos know how your mates will pick out the one sin that's hardest for you to deal with, then commit it. You know how hard it is for them to face some problems head-on, so you can handle it when they take a thousand-mile detour around an issue. You successful Virgos completely understand why they might flee from their pain into drugs, sex, booze, TV.

But you know it's not your duty to turn up all the lights and make all people look in the mirror. You know how to help them dance—without kicking the crutches out from under them. When they're trying to turn dreams into reality or struggling to free themselves from the conundrum of escapism, you are indeed put in their path by the universe to help.

You evolved Virgos have the vision of a night hawk. Nothing escapes your keen perception. You cope very well with the double entendre, so one can't foil you with vagaries. You've got a perfect grasp of your own fall from grace. You can't be scared with that. You've been baptized in the name of higher powers, so you know you aren't going to catch leprosy from rubbing elbows with those unfortunates in the valley.

The happiest of you know that the rational mind may be the comedian of the piece, but the chaotic, emotional unconscious will always be the star. And that's where your relationships comes in.

Though you'll try to checkmate poetic fancy with logic, you need someone to slip you a mickey every now and then. You evolved Virgos can take it. You retreat into neither masochism nor frigidity. You can enjoy the music as well as the news. You deal best with all those gorgeous, hypnotic lost souls out there, the sinners that saints are always trying to save. Yours is the irony of the stoic and his Achilles heel, the nun with her one unshakable habit.

The happiest of you have learned that the deepest point you can reach in any major relationship is that point at which in one instant you have been abandoned by your fantasies and touched by a higher power.

The Miracle: Letting Go

How can you get back to that original point where you saw another person's shining potential, their blissful inner divine being? Once the light goes on and the champagne is worn off, if there's no illusion, can you maintain your interest?

In fact, you nervous, never-blink-for-a-minute-'cause-you-might-miss-a-trick Virgos do indeed hold on to your idealism about relationships. No matter how many whipped-cream pies you wipe off your face, each time you meet someone, you know "this is different," and a new sensation of holiness is created. The miracle exists also in keeping that mystical sense of union, not just in new relationships but with long-term associations.

How?

You have to try to remember what you first found beautiful, consciously trying to focus on the contributions a relationship has made to your life, consciously trying to keep from magnifying the undermining aspects of that bond. You need to remind yourself that it is your contact with people that frees you from your fretful, conundrum. So it is hardly productive to scream, *"J'accuse!"* to your deliverer. When frightened, hurt, or disillusioned, you Virgos shrink from contact and communication, lock yourselves in a tower or your bedroom to meditate on how horrible people are and how good you are. And it's when you are the most disillusioned that the miracle can happen.

You have to retire alone to collect yourselves (a lot of

you sleep alone quite often) and then slowly review the relationship and acknowledge your participation in the charade. You have to view your partner coldly, without rancor of judgment, and accept the fact that with wine often comes intoxication. You need to see a partner not as a seditious guerrilla, plotting your secret downfall, but as an old, old soul, that lost, lost sheep you first opened your heart to in the first place.

All it takes is one person to hold a little match to the giant glacier that is your emotional resistance and—*splash* —three towns are under water.

When you are touched by another human being, not only does your chastity belt fall off in one second, but your body falls away as well, and you become the spiritual being you really are. Nobody has more faith; nobody trusts more; nobody is less fearful of taking the plunge. Through contact your fear of contamination is dissolved. What you really want is a soul union anyway.

It is your sworn and solemn duty to worship your mates until they betray you, at which time you'll berate them for all their wickedness, but once you've connected with them on that mystical level, once you've seen the artistic, musical, or special gifts and potential shining at the depth of their soul, you'll never really lose sight of those special talents, no matter how mad at them you get. The deeper the experience, the madder you'll have to get at some point, because disenchantment comes to all—especially you Virgos. It must be said that some of you hold on to your bitterness until the very end, and it is buried with you. Once you get over the shock of your mate's sinfulness, your trust and love for them sneak back, albeit slightly tarnished by the force of reality. Once you have that mystical experience, though, you rarely return to normal.

Working the Miracle: Forgiveness

You Virgos enter people's lives to help them strengthen their sense of productivity. To keep you interested, though, they'll have to try to keep swerving you off your course. The best thing you'll do for your mates is help them make their fantasies come true, even if you are unable to participate fully in those fantasies. If one wants tangible results for efforts in any direction, one should seek out, hire, or marry a Virgo.

If one comes upon a Virgo, one should treasure the find. Even while supporting and respecting the Virgo's work and need for distance, the seduction should by all means be carried on. If one breaks the trust of a Virgo, a humble apology might help. That usually melts a Virgo. One shouldn't push it though. You Virgos have come to the point on your own when letting go is possible.

But can your mate help you let go? They can't simply say to someone who is a dithering nervous wreck, "Now, just forgive your enemies and all the figures on the Sistine Chapel will start dancing." Some of you Virgos find it hard to let go, because you have been cheated or lied to or disappointed by one parent or the other, as well as by a stream of people who followed. You unevolved Virgos never forgive anything, maybe just grant a general amnesty to all deserters every seven years or so.

But you evolved Virgos, disappointed every bit as often, are totally connected to the flow of the universe. You are motivated not out of a desire to say "I told you so," but out of your love for people and your wish to be clear and to shine a light through the fog. You organize your relationships not around the neurotic game of sin and pardon but around your power to provide clarity for those who seek it, observation without judgment for those who want it. You evolved Virgos have overcome your mad love of meddling.

It's hard for you Virgos to exist in an unclear situation. You have to define and redefine the relationship, measure your mates limits, contain and monitor them. Even as you're kissing them, you'll sometimes be actually thinking, "Hmm. So this is a kiss. Not bad. Not bad at all." You cannot easily just turn off your head. Your gift to a relationship is your magnificent power of perception, definition, and diagnosis. But you can't just shut up and enjoy the ride without giving a running commentary on the scenery. And to be in a relationship, that's just what you have to learn to do. Just to *be*. And that's where your mates can help you. With a wash of reassurance, they can restore perspective. Sometimes they have to drug you to get you, a little gerbil, off your wheel, because often you squeeze your eyes shut and tremble till the fun is over, so you can get back to a normal level of worry. The magic comes when your partner can ease you into letting go enough to perform some healing magic on yourself, so you can allow yourself the joy of sharing and permit yourself to partake of the ecstasy you have sought someone out to give you. That comes only with the restoration of trust.

People have to be patient with you Virgos, show you there's room in their heart even for people like yourselves who find it hard to forgive.

Your mates will buy you champagne or flowers when you're feeling cynical, shower you with kindness. You'll be furious, but you'll never be able to resist open-heartedness. It will help you grow. People shouldn't preach but practice love on you.

Your partners task is to show you that when there is forgiveness, there is a relationship. You are all consummately humane and are ever in the process of mastering the art of forgiving.

Gift Ideas for Virgos

● A kaleidoscope. So Virgo can learn to see a million different abstract images changing with every turn of the wrist. Every time Virgos are convinced that there is only one right answer, one right way, one right solution, you should be handed this device.

- A bottle of sea-sickness pills also makes a nice Virgo gift. This will remind you Virgo that you are not actually on dry land at all, but always being moved by the tides and currents of emotion.
- A paint-by-numbers set will show Virgo that a simple black-and-white picture can have more depth, subtlety, dimension, and beauty if it has color. It takes patience, aesthetic discipline and inspiration, and a love of the whole picture to achieve it.
- A bottle of red or white wine made from natural organic wood pressed grapes can show Virgo a balance is possible between being a goody-goody and having fun.

Reading Material for Advanced Virgos

Of Human Bondage, by Somerset Maugham

Guardian Angels: Movie Stars

 Movie stars watch over your relationships because they symbolize the classically glamorous and idealized figures that serve as deities for our culture. They are bigger than life, the Olympian-sized icons to be worshipped from afar—a favorite way for you Virgos to relate.

They are anything you want them to be. They are yours, there in the dark; they hypnotize you, take you out of yourself, take you away from dreary, everyday reality and make life bearable by providing fanciful diversion from your cares and woes.

They are false in the sense that they are not really there. They are unreal projections flashed in front of a screen, actors taking parts, fooling you for a brief magic moment into thinking they are actually a desert sheik or a bewitching siren.

The roles they play are convincing and their goal is to

make you believe they are who they say they are. They represent all the glitz and glamour that normal mortals rarely ever see. Their lives are wondrous, magical, full of fabulous voyages, luxurious pilgrimages to the East for enlightenment, champagne, and fancy cars. They symbolize the total freedom from the cares of the world that only fabulously successful artists can know.

You Virgos idealize other people's lives in this glamorous way. Movie stars are chosen as your guardian angels also to provide an ambiance of glamour, to add a mystique to life. They comprise your pantheon, archetypes to play off in the eternal dichotomy between art and life.

Even without your knowing it, movie stars make your life more liveable, by periodically taking you away, removing you from your own experience.

When the lights go on, movie-goers file out and return to reality, just as you Virgos cannot indefinitely use relationships to escape from the realities of work and service that are your lives.

We do not expect that movie stars will eventually step off the screen and kidnap us, save us from ourselves or our responsibilities, but the romantic illusions they create fill our dreams with secret possibilities.

You Virgos see people in that Hollywood haze. You need to learn that relationships provide a richness and add dimensions of beauty to your life, but that you must continue to carry on your work when the lights go on and the movie is over—hold no rancor toward the "actors" on the screen, have no bitterness to find out that the roles were not real, and the illusions they fostered were openly part of a movie.

The spiritual truth for you is the impermanence of all phenomena.

Celebrity Astro Game

You'd be surprised how many ways people reveal themselves in everything they say and do. To sharpen your sensitivity to other people and to learn more about the ways renowned Virgos handle their deepest relationship issues, look over the following list and pick out the people who interest you most.

Do a little sleuthing about their lives. Observe their actions; listen to what they say in public. The songs they sing, the roles they play, the particular contributions they make will enlighten you about the relationship patterns of this sign.

Joan Kennedy   Lily Tomlin
Sophia Loren   Jane Curtin
Queen Elizabeth I   Billy Preston
Ingrid Bergman   Barry White
Anne Meara   John Ritter
Anne Bancroft   Paul Williams
Lou Piniella   Raquel Welch
Bill Murray   Isabel Sanford
Itzak Perlman   Freda Payne
Michael Jackson

Chapter Seven

LIBRA

The Mirage: World Champion of Everything

You Libras, describing your mate to a friend during phase one of a relationship:

> "Rugged individualist. That's the word. I've never met anyone who was so daring and outspoken and brave and exciting. I feel like I'm with one of those pioneers, those wild people who conquered the West —do anything, go anywhere—you know the type. And that's what I need to get me going."

If someone's in the shower and singing "I gotta be me," a Libra will hear them clear across town. Independence makes you all prick up your ears and take up the scent. If one ever finds the most confident, self-assertive, independent heroic individualist in the whole world—one male and one female of such a species—one should freeze them both immediately and save them for any Libras one knows.

The Libra woman loves Ward Bond types. Remember him—the tough, tobacco-chewing wagonmaster from every western made in Hollywood? You don't always like to admit it, but you get tingly beside an ex-Marine with a deer carcass across his fender and a gun in his pocket. Libra men love aggressive women, and though you're all mad as hell at your moms for manipulating you, you're putty in the hands of a tough woman. Eternal bliss for a Libra man: to be banished to a desert island with Aretha Franklin. And you can bet Bruce Springsteen's wife knows who's really boss.

You Libras, men and women, spot your mates' self-assertiveness and zero in on it. You swoon and sigh quietly to behold how masterful, what truly independent spirits they are. They call things as they see them. They seize the reins of their life, fling themselves into the abyss of experience, eat major decisions for breakfast—they don't worry about their lives—they do it. It doesn't really occur to them to ask advice, except maybe after the fact. And they survive quite well on their own—beef jerky, TV dinners, and soup for-one.

When the government asks for volunteers to go to the moon, you will expect your partners to volunteer, because you always see them as fearless and ready to pick up and leave everything behind.

Though it's horribly difficult for you to accept, you want your mates to lead the dance. When they're angry, you love it when they explode right there on the spot, openly dealing with issues that you would nurse quietly into ulcers. When the iron gets hot, your loved ones don't go around taking surveys; they strike. They fire the first shot, undo the first button. And to you that's astounding, because to come out ask for what you really want, you usually have to wait for general amnesty day, and take valium to get up the courage.

You see everyone as positively Wagnerian. They are all Siegfried, Atlas, and Unsinkable Molly Brown, the first man on the moon, the first woman in Rotary Club, world champion of everything, captain of the Starship *Enterprise*. They're the key to your ignition system, the match you've been looking for to spark your fire. And . . . you're hoping that maybe a little of that strong cologne your partner is wearing called *identity* will rub off on you.

The Monster: Self-absorbed, Egomaniacal Outlaw

You Libras talking to the lawyer:

> "I hung on much longer than I should have. I couldn't face it. When you're with somebody, you overlook a lot. You have to. That's what makes a relationship work.
>
> "But eventually, you get to a point where you just can't kid yourself anymore. And you know that if you're ever going to have a shred of self-respect, you've got to look this thing in the face and make a break for it."

BUT . . . Nothing turns you upside down more than *not* being validated as a human being. You're crushed to see a partner's selfishness and narcissism. It takes you a long time to face it, because you look up to people so much, admire their spirit and courage. It hurts to confront the fact that what you thought was independence is really a lack of interest in anything but themselves. Their boldness was more a reflection of their rashness, perpetual anger, and thoughtlessness.

Your head was in the right place. You were giving your all. And while they might want company while shopping or having dinner, you see that you've had as much importance and meaning to them as their shadow. So when they just go ahead and make that major decision without consulting you, you do your best to undermine it.

And they can forget that Chinese restaurant they've had their heart set on; they'll never taste an egg roll. You won't come right out and refuse to go there, but just as their hand is on the doorknob of the restaurant you will feel "compelled" to suggest a darling little Italian place down the street.

If you think they've been selfish or insensitive or law-less (lawless meaning they didn't consult you before they took out the second mortgage on the house), you will retal-iate by acting out an even worse caricature of selfishness and insensitivity. So your mates shouldn't give you tit if they can't deal with some immediate tat.

What a pig of selfishness others can seem to you. You feel that they're just yanking you around, like a baby who's dragged around to bars and ignored by his parents. Your blood rises in your throats if a mate plays Big Brother and doesn't give you power to decide anything at all. You drool secretly with rage, swallow your tongue, and still manage to keep smiling. You boil when you behold a balloon of ego ever expanding and pushing you up against the wall.

Before you know it, people can get you turning into pretzels, running yourselves ragged to get your chores done, so you can be ready when they show up and need to be related to. Because you've played down your own needs in the beginning, it pains you to face the fact that those you love are not really listening to you at all and are not inter-ested in what you have to say.

Often there's a long gap between the moment you know it's all over and the moment when you actually call the lawyer. There must be horrendous pain for you when you take that cold, hard look at someone and see that you have tolerated ghastly behavior only because you've been afraid to be alone, fearing that if you made too much of a fuss, you'd be sent away.

Even if you admired it yesterday, when you Libras see the full depth of another person's self-involvement, you are stunned. Your greatest fear is that your sincerity will be abused and that in the final reel it will turn out that you are more involved with others than they are with you.

And after catering to them, chauffeuring them around, mirroring and fulfilling their every thought and desire, run-ning idiotic errands for them, boy do you ever feel like the back end of the proverbial stage horse.

You are then horrified to see that what you mistook for healthy self-assertion on their part was no more than the fact that they're actually a bundle of unbridled aggression, an egomaniac who has absolutely no regard for you or anybody else—an outlaw.

The Real Thing: Powerlessness

Your kidneys float to your eyeballs when you behold your partners' consummate absorption with themselves to the exclusion of you. You have often been abused in this way. You've been treated like a TV set by narcissistic parents, related to when no one else is there, then whisked out to play by yourselves when the adults had more important things to do.

Today as a result, if one is in a room with a Libra and the phone rings, one shouldn't stay on but should tell the caller to call back. You Libras cannot tolerate being ignored.

You don't want to be single. Libras with distorted views of the opposite sex and its power over you have adjusted to life alone, but you all see success as a function of your ability to cooperate and share. You Libra men are mad at your mothers for making you feel powerless. You Libra women get angry at men for being put down by them or for being forced to accept a second-class citizen's role in a man's world.

What lies behind your anger is your sense of powerlessness. To be overlooked, not consulted, passed over—to be moved about by an individual who has no real consciousness of what drives you to the violent acts of which you are capable—will force you to quit smiling, explode, and commit murder.

A partner can get away with a lot for a long time. You Libras are accustomed to smiling silently while someone's full weight rests on your toes. When the moment comes when someone gets your karate elbow in the ribs, it will be for some little bitty indiscretion that has been positively the last straw for you.

If you wanted to be single, you could simply dive into a pint of ice cream, accompanied by your *TV Guide*. And truly, the strain of being sensitive to others takes its toll on you and you do find relief just plopping down in front of the tube. But you're really not a loner.

The happiest of you Libras are satisfactorily working out your dependency issues by relating to people and do not see others as your ticket to power or identity. That would be the false trip, of course, because when we think that somebody else is going to bring us identity, we invariably end up resenting them for making us part of them. So what lies behind even this issue of powerlessness for you is your ambivalence between the aloneness of keeping your power and the danger of losing all your power in a relationship.

You love your partners for their headstrong manner. Then you set about to crawl inside them, often so they can help you fend off other powerful engulfing figures in your past. You try to merge with them, feel frustrated if they don't permit it, lose respect for them if they do. You sometimes erroneously think that a strong self-image is going to rub off on you. You resent your mate's dependence if they give themselves up to you, fight them if they try to make you the more dependent partner.

It is natural and healthy for you to be heavily invested in the success of a relationship, because you are naturally and healthily awake to the dynamics of a living relationship. While the demands of other people drive you nutty, you are a born master at guiding your ship through the mined waters of your opponents' territory. You are drawn to people who seem often to be asleep to relationships, and this often puts you in the position of working harder to make the union work.

It's ironic that your partners exist to show you that the sun does not rise and set around you—your mates have a whole set of motivations, desires, responses, activities, and needs that are simply none of your business. There's a whole history that doesn't include you, people your mates enjoy relating to without your presence—in short, whole areas of their life that are fulfilled without consulting you on every aspect of existence, from "What's my mother's phone number?" to what color chintz is good for the couch.

You can't bear this; a partner's singularity bugs you. And you often distort a mate's independence and interpret it as cruel and purposeful exclusion of you.

On the other hand, you enter people's lives to show them that if they were as damned self-sufficient as they protest to be, they would have already moved to a desert island and wouldn't have to have dinner or sleep with anybody. And if they do want to have dinner or sleep with somebody, then you cannot be treated just like an ironing board they can fold down when they need it and slam into the wall when their real date rings the bell. If they want a Libra in their life they have to share their power.

The Burning Question: How to Deal with Anger and *Not* Confuse It with Hate?

Your mates have to be able to show you they're mature enough to maintain their commitment to you and not abuse it. But they shouldn't be too nice to you, though. You can't stand it. Your passions are stirred by aggression even though you detest it. You've had your fill of it in childhood and think you'd like to eliminate it from the world.

Fat chance.

When a lamp gets broken over somebody's head, by all means there's sure to be a Libra in the crowd. Your passive way of expressing your aggressions will lead people sometimes to declare war and go after you with a hatchet—at which point you'll gasp with surprise, shock, and disappointment and withdraw until they've come to their senses and can talk things over calmly and rationally. You love peace but can't fulfill your function of restoring it until there is war. So while you try to calm your partners down, you lose a little respect for them if they lose their dynamism. You love them because they're irrational, impulsive, blind and rash. You'll spend a lot of time talking about them behind their back. But to their face, you'll mirror everything they do.

This may sound untrue when you first hear it, because so many of the Libras you know seem to be spontaneous, aggressive, and challenging individuals.

This is false.

You Libras often make a big show of how you told off the butcher or the lady at the bank, when in reality you never, or almost never, truly express your rage and anger to the person at whom you are really angriest, the person who holds the key to your security.

The most contented of you Libras have confidence that voicing your true feelings will not jeopardize a relationship but strengthen it, result in not alienation or rejection but in greater closeness. No matter what one thinks of Yoko Ono, did she in fact bring John Lennon to a greater senser of personal power than he had ever had before, even if maybe she did destroy the Beatles? With the help of his primal therapy, maybe it was Yoko who got him to be able to release all his anger and reach fulfillment in a relationship.

You have really had your anger buttons disarmed by one or both parents who allowed themselves to act out but made sure that you felt guilty as sin for expressing any rage at all. So you are now still trying to make nice-nice, while other people are permitted their selfish tantrums. When you act out, you are sent to your room or your shrink. Ironically, you're often so angry for having your anger controlled that you provoke others, then force them to control their anger.

A good part of your life is spent, then, handling aggression and trying to express these feelings appropriately. You hold it in and chat about Aunt Maud's X-rays and the cow across the road with anthrax, but you don't show what's going on underneath.

If we were to be little flies on the wall in the life of rock star Sting, would we see that beneath his piercing mysterious image, there's a man striving to express freely his aggression toward and love for women? Consider another

Libra—Mahatma Gandhi. Gandhi expressed his anger passively; he wouldn't eat. Was Gandhi's struggle really only about India, or did his mother fit somewhere in there, too? We can almost hear her talking to the Indian version of Dr. Spock: "I don't know what's the matter with this kid. He won't eat!"

You grown-up Libras know the difference between anger and hatred and, thus, do not simmer quietly away in a private vat of radioactive acid. You recognize that voicing honest comments or objections does not mean you are selfish or guilty of in some way wishing to kill a figure in your life who pretends to be weak and vulnerable but is actually monstrously manipulative.

You successful Libras are the greatest partners of all. You're provocative but not galling or argumentative just to show others you're there. You will help your mates gain insight by helping them, sometimes gently forcing them, to acknowledge sides of issues they had once closed the book on, and, thus, you help them fill out their perspective in practical ways, like psyching out the boss or dealing with the in-laws.

You mature Libras are not afraid of anger. You have learned how to meet intimidation if not head-on, then at least obliquely. You have often been intimidated by aggressive role models you both admire and detest. For a period of time your partners can get some real mileage out of your fear of their retaliation and a tenacious clinging to a relationship. You turn yourself into a pretzel to avoid conflicts, partly because you're afraid to be alone and because you have a real sense of responsibility to the aliveness of the relationship.

You Libras who achieve the greatest intimacy have conquered your fear of anger and have made for yourselves a distinction between it and hatred. You know that people get mad at one another not because they are bad or sick but because open conflict clears the air.

But it's hard for you. You'd rather just take off and not call people who've offended you than sit them down and tell them what's really wrong. You must face your fear of the loss of love. To avoid open war, you'll resort to trickery and deceit. To be successful, you must free yourselves from the spell cast by Mary Poppins on your whole sign and be able to dispel the saccharine cloud that prohibits clear, honest communication.

Ultimate Challenge: Their Identity vs. Your Identity

In the most successful relationship, there should be some flexibility in role-playing, but not as much as many pop psychology books would have us believe. In the best relationships, both partners have realms in which they are the masters. While they should always remain alert to each other's growth in those areas, and open to change, they have to have confidence enough in themselves to maintain the position of mastery and, by so doing, keep the foundation of the relationship intact.

Similarly, in areas where they are weaker, they have to be able and ready to accept another person's expertise and superiority.

You unevolved Libras always stick your fingers in the machinery of the relationship because of this. Because the position of submissive receptor pushes your "nuclear holocaust" button, you will try to muscle in on the other guy's territory and stick a twig right in the spokes of the wheel.

You singing-with-joy Libras have enough self-esteem to know where you are strong and can accept where someone else is strong. Gaining a rightful place for you does not mean making yourselves indispensable. That can only lead to rejection or failure. Accepting and encouraging another's superiority in a given area is not an admission of defeat or a humiliating recognition of infantile dependence. On the contrary, it is the key to Libran success in relationships.

There are indeed alternatives besides masochism or bloody divorce. In examining Libran action (or lack of it) in relationships and exposing the monster of self-absorption for what it really is, we have to explore an issue basic to all human beings, but especially deeply rooted in Libra consciousness: competitiveness.

The astrological symbol of Libra, ☍ , can be fancifully interpreted as two people lying down, one person lying on his or her back, the other above with his or her bottom in the air. While fanciful, it is not a frivolous interpretation of this symbol, because you Libras reflect the perfect union of the active and passive, strong and weak, the giver and the receiver, the one dishing it out and the other taking it. So your relationships, maybe more than all others, are organized around issues of male-and-female role-playing. On the surface, many of you present the perfect picture of white-gloved female and gruff, hairy male. But one must always remember that one never knows what's going on in a relationship unless one is in it. We should ask the Springsteens how they feel about this.

Whenever a Libra is involved, we are always dealing with the socialization of primitive aggressive instincts. You participate in other people's lives to teach the monkey in them to say *please*. Aggression is always a key issue. You want them to make the first move, but you are dedicated to countering it with a move that forces them to consider you in any decision they make.

"Li'l ole me?" you cry as the butter fails to melt in your mouth. "Competitive? That's ridiculous."

Ask Martina Navratilova about that after she's just trounced Chris Lloyd for the sixth time. You Libras are fiendishly competitive. And facing that about yourself gives you some insight, perspective and humor in the game you are always playing.

You are all trying to "find yourselves," and you take up one heroic role model after another, rejecting them all because they don't fit. You hate just being somebody's other half, and no matter how many times you end up walking behind them and carrying their train, you need to throw off your subservient role, get some distance from your self-imposed enslavement to them, and be your own person.

Sick to death of being overpowered by a partner's strong identity, you explode or withdraw, fighting madly against a dependence you nurtured from the first. Once you've assassinated someone, or at least gotten away from them for the weekend, you begin work on your own identity.

Lo and behold, when you go far enough and deeply enough within yourselves a voice inside says, "Get married, already. People are starting to talk."

And you awaken to the fact that, indeed your identity is found with their identity. Who you are is about how you relate to people and what people you're relating to. And you are challenged to confront your mate's identity, deal with it, be guided to a large extent by it, yet *not* be engulfed by it.

The Miracle: Self-esteem

When you Libras distort your understanding of what self-esteem is, you're at your most misguided and embarrassing point. You act out, selfishly thinking the monkey with the longest reach gets the banana. You model your behavior after some grotesque paragon of aggression, and totally confuse hostility with right action. You're mad at everybody, falsely thinking that if you get enough people thinking you're tough, then maybe you'll be tough, and tough people must think very highly of themselves.

Wrong.

Self-esteem comes in many different shapes, sizes, and colors. You Libras are in a funny spot, it's true. To think highly of oneself, one must be successful. Yet to be successful, one has to think highly enough about oneself to permit it to happen.

Success for you Libras means successful juggling what you want and what your partner wants. Once you Libras become aware of the juggling act you have to do, you're less inclined to push people away, less angry that you have to develop your diplomatic skills. Now the miracle can start to take place. The more successful you are in developing tactical skills and dealing with people, the more you get what you want. The more you have what you want, the more you think of yourself and *voilà*—self-esteem.

Of course, you have to get over your rage at yourself for your constant need of approval. Now often you will degrade yourself to get it before you take to the object of your approval with an electric knife. But as you grow, you mellow. You make great lawyers and generals, because you know exactly how to psyche out the enemy, know almost before the enemy does how, where, when he's going to strike. You highly developed Libras support others when their actions are right and true, oppose them when they're off the beam. Part of your miracle is to help your partners develop. This way you can foil their plans when they get too grandiose or brash, and encourage them in just the right place *at* the right time.

What you need from others is an encouragement to do *your* thing, whatever it is, and not fear punitive action on the part of a partner (formerly played by the parent in childhood).

When your relationships flower, both partners flourish, both think more highly of themselves and each other, and thrive independently as well as together.

Self-esteem comes from a feeling of accomplishment and fulfillment—not as judged by any outsider but as measured by you yourself. You need to feel loved and approved of, but you absolutely have to be proud of the actions that got you love and approval in the first place.

Part of your self-esteem comes from developing healthy long-term relationships. Those relationships will be organized around complex intellectual, sexual, emotional, spiritual, and professional needs of both parties, and the satisfactory meshing of those needs will invariably lead you to a feeling of greater self-worth.

Working the Miracle: Open Confrontation

One would think it would be easy just to speak up for what one wanted or be simply able to say quite casually, "Excuse me, sir, but would you mind not blowing that smoke in my face. I really can't stand it."

Easy for one as long as one isn't a Libra.

Every time you Libras are about to let it all hang out to that one person who's taken complete advantage of you (it's usually the person you're most emotionally/financially dependent on), a hand claps over your mouth and silences the scream.

In this case, silence is not golden. In fact, in no time it will turn the whole relationship a sickly shade of green. So if anything wholesome is to develop, there has to be open communication between the parties involved.

Open communication means open confrontation means fighting for the sake of the relationship. The alternative— *not* fighting, peace at any price—leads to war anyway. Everybody knows that. So to work the miracle of developing mutual self-respect, both parties have to be allowed to be. Both have to have a voice, have to be heard, and above all, they musn't be afraid to fight. Good, clean fighting stirs up the blood, creates excitement, stimulates the exchange of ideas, challenges thinking, forces a change of position, and clears the air.

Many Libras have to elbow their way through the foxholes of their own lives, scared to death of landing on a mine, resorting to sabotage and sneaky tactics. They tiptoe toward old age and death, not upsetting their mother's pacemaker, not daring to cross their fathers, holding their breath when the boss walks into the office, running stupid errands just because their brother is bigger than they are.

These Libras have all had a lobotomy, even without surgery. Their ability to challenge another human being has been removed, without their permission.

And to hear them tell it, everything is hunky-dory, fine, lovely. But these people are like a grenade with the pin already pulled. Bump into them wrong on a street corner and *blammo*!

Their lack of ability to confront comes out often in a stream of narcissistic sputtering, a monologue of trivia no human being could possibly ever be interested in. As a way of fending off this murderous rage they feel inside, and to make sure one doesn't get power over them, they don't let one get a word in edgewise. When one finally hangs up on them, they're insulted. Until the next time, when they can bludgeon one all over again with prattle.

Fortunately, there are evolved Libras.

You evolved Libras don't just pretend to listen; you do more than blab. You talk. You really talk to others. Even though you may stutter and get sweaty palms, you'll tell others nicely that they've just driven their truck over your feet and it didn't tickle.

You know about your tendency to offer to help others move out of their house, and then get angry about having offered. You show up four hours late and then feel so guilty you not only help them move but paint the new apartment. You evolved Libras *never promise more than you can deliver*.

You strive to say yes when it's possible and though you usually have to gulp down a couple of Hail Marys, you've learned to say no. You can stand up pretty well for yourself, not constantly picking at others for trivia but talking to a partner about what is really going on in your life and what's going on between the two of you. You are a giver to the nth degree but you also *get what you need*.

You're working on maintaining a dynamic equilibrium between survival and service. Though you can give your your mates a left hook when they need it, you don't need charm-school lessons—you know exactly how to move through society. People like and respect you.

Gift Ideas for Libras

- Two sets of boxing gloves—that would help you on your way. And large framed photographs of your mate are nice, too. This gesture lets you know they're still thinking of themselves and gets your blood stirred up.
- A rejection letter. By exploring the consequences of rejection all the way down to the bottom, you learn to deal with the raw feeling of failure and loneliness and climb back up to see that squaring off and facing the enemy is not to be avoided; on the contrary, it's the key to ultimate success.

Reading Material for Advanced Libras

War and Peace, by Leo Tolstoy.

Guardian Angels: Superman and Supergirl

Superman and Supergirl symbolize a thoroughly unique blend of unlimited personal power and a total dedication to helping others. They guard Libran relationships because through your relationship, you help develop your partners' leadership qualities and abilities to accomplish superhuman feats while you, too, experience the elation of moving mountains—for you, the ability to juggle yourselves and other people successfully.

Superman and Supergirl represent an idealized picture of the height of individualism, a quality you admire and need to help develop in your partners. The two superheroes are also a side of you seen only occasionally. Like Superman and Supergirl, whose truly powerful identities are kept hidden behind meek and mild-mannered masks, so you Libras pose for the world as shy, timid creatures—until an emergency arises, at which time your fearless natures emerge, as if with extraterrestrial strength you then lift automobiles, outrace trains, and buck all the forces of the universe if doing so will alleviate stress, pain, or trouble for a fellow human being.

Superman and Supergirl express also an equality in strength between the sexes. Both have timid shells; both are courageous when it comes to saving others from disaster. Their one common vulnerability—a piece of meteorite from their home planet—suggests the eternal struggle you Libras have not to fall prey to the same weaknesses that plagued you in childhood and not to let earlier patterns destroy your present strength.

Though they take an ordinary, even mediocre, place in society, Superman and Supergirl hide their overwhelming strength and wills of steel; the power lies dormant beneath, waiting until someone in need calls upon them. And then their powers are unleashed to right wrongs and restore justice.

The fact that Superman and Supergirl always retain their timid identities and never reveal who they really are describes the way in which you Libras must develop your true strength indirectly, never taking advantage of your superior position—that of rational understanding and tactical know-how—which only you know exists underneath.

The secret of their powers lies in their birthright, something handed down before the Superchildren were cast out of their dying home planet. This further suggests the inevitable course from which you can never long diverge: you cannot go home again. You cannot hope for the shelter or protection of a world that is no more. You find yourselves in a world full of hostile, underdeveloped beings who desperately need the help you can and are willing to give, but too readily would exploit your kindness for their own selfish purposes.

So Superman and Supergirl must remain in partial hiding while devoting themselves to the benefit of all other beings.

A Libra paradigm, to be sure.

Celebrity Astro Game

You'd be surprised how many ways people reveal themselves in everything they say and do. To sharpen your sensitivity to other people and to learn more about the ways renowned Libras handle their deepest relationship issues, look over the following list and pick out the people who interest you most.

Do a little sleuthing about their lives. Observe their actions; listen to what they say in public. The songs they sing, the roles they play, the particular contributions they make, will enlighten you about the relationship patterns of this sign.

Eleanor Roosevelt
Art Garfunkel
Dwight Eisenhower
John Lennon
Sting
Bruce Springsteen
Jim Henson
Michael Douglas
Mark Hamill
Edward Villella

Susan Sarandon
Chevy Chase
Lee Harvey Oswald
Ben Vereen
Marie Osmond
Dave DeBusschere
Suzanne Somers
Pam Dawber
Martina Navratilova
Ralph Lauren

Chapter Eight

SCORPIO

The Mirage: The Rarest Emerald in the World

You Scorpios, when you view someone through your telescope from across the street:

"I want that."

Right from the first instant you're excited by those who acknowledge your magnetism, validate your creative superiority and your powers as a healer. They may not even know it's happening, but you know. With you it's immediate, instantaneous, chemical. When you spot somebody who triggers off your chemicals, it's all over. You're in love, and all you have to do is face it. You don't have to hear violins, run a credit check, or find out their I.Q. All major decisions, both business and personal, are made downstairs, out of sight, by the real power behind the Scorpio organization—the Gut. Deep within you is a highly developed scanning device. It registers what people look, feel, sound, and smell like, it takes note of people's taste in clothes, everything about them, including how much they are responding to your electromagnetic signal.

153

The results are tabulated in about three or four seconds, at which time prospective partners are given a rating of *yes*, *no*, or *maybe*. Nos and maybes are tabled at once, but yeses are another story. Yeses are placed immediately on a pedestal under electronic surveillance. From the moment one becomes a Scorpio yes, one is treated like a precious jewel that is treasured for its rarity and matchless beauty. A new mate's worth becomes at once unmeasurable, because a priceless possession cannot be valued in earthly terms. How much is the Sistine Chapel worth, or King Tut's death mask?

Your utter workship of your love objects makes you irresistible as a suitor—in business or personal life. You Scorpios would all carry your mates around on a velvet pillow if they'd let you. You'd joyfully obsess over them, salivate at the sight of them, dab them off with a silken scarf and delight in showing them off to the entire world—at a safe distance of course.

You Scorpios see the objects of your desire as prizes to be won, something to slay dragons and risk death to compete for. You hold your partners in rare esteem. You look upon them as golden chalices that will be awarded to you if you prove yourself to be strong, beautiful, creative, sexy, and powerful enough to land them. They're the giant marlin over the mantle, the Ming dynasty vase in the front hall. They're an eight thousand acre ranch full of cattle and avocados; they're Shakespeare's first edition and Grandma's gold locket all rolled into one.

You see a relationship at first as a symbol of fertility, something rich and productive and life-affirming, and you believe that by connecting with another human being you can assert your own life-affirming qualities. You see a partnership as a stable foundation to build your house upon, a safe place to store everything you hold dear, materially and emotionally.

You know instantly that your love objects are trustworthy, and you view them as a rich symbols of those things that people come into the world in the hopes of someday possessing, something expansive and ultimately nourishing.

Against the smoldering Scorpio soul your mates appear sparkling and forever, solid and permanent. You view them with wonder and delight, the way alien beings who had traveled light-years through the blackness of space might be awed to behold the rich green bauble of the Earth.

The Monster: A Green-Eyed Fiend of Jealousy and Greed

You Scorpios, when you're chewing your leg off to get out of the trap:

> "I won't be owned by anything or anybody. Nobody owns me!"

BUT . . . when you Scorpios start to be owned by your own possessions, you feel a pair of strange hands around your throat, pressing tighter and tighter. For one thing, once you have attained the priceless jewel, some of you get terribly insecure. You're afraid somebody's going to take it away from you. You obsess, can't think straight, worry about being robbed, follow a mate around day and night with a camera to make sure there's not a hint of betrayal and to make sure he or she still belongs to you. And if you even catch a whiff of what you perceive to be disloyalty, you pursue the perpetrator with the wrath of a Holy Crusader and the diligence of a bloodhound, watching every movement of someone's eyes to see if they're looking at someone else. You begin to interpret the relationship as another person's hold on *you*, and you ascribe all sorts of plots and schemes to him or her. Eventually you consume the relationship with your own jealousy as if it were a leg of lamb, leaving only the bones.

And when you can't deal with your own possessiveness, greed, and jealousy, you put it all on the other person.

You're attracted to people for their earthy practical value system, because they're solid, but when you get paranoid you'll drain them, test them, make them give more and more of themselves. If they hold out, you're shocked and disillusioned at their stubbornness or what you perceive to be their greed.

Money becomes the tool of power and symbol of loyalty. You'll be horrified that they could actually reduce the lofty relationship to the level of dollars and cents. At first it excites you if your partners know about stocks or real estate, but if they start to apply any pressure at all or dare a squeeze play over money, your alarm sounds. You can't bear to be manipulated by practicality. Your religion is creativity and emotion, and even though your deepest yearnings cry out, "Possess me! Possess me!" you Scorpios won't be possessed by anyone or anything.

Why did Ike love Tina, Simon love Garfunkel, and Nichols love May? Maybe the relationships worked as long as creativity was the dominant theme. When banal issues of greed or fiscal control came into it, was degeneration inevitable?

You Scorpios detest the purity of your art to be compromised, and yet you are always battling the specter of prostitution. Though you are drawn to solid figures who are deeply rooted in the world and its material concerns, you are stunned to see that crucial decisions could ever be made solely on the basis of economic expedience. Though you may be seduced by the promise of the good life, you are horrified if your mates actually try to compromise your integrity with the bait of good Scotch or a feather bed. You are devastated to perceive, wrongly or rightly, a deep materialism in another person—it's a side of yourselves you'd rather not look at. Greed is a monster you'd rather belonged to other people—not you.

Possessiveness always enters the piece—it's the fly in the proverbial Scorpio ointment. Will it someday be a major hurdle in the relationships of both Sam Shepard and Prince Charles, if they discover private cookie jars in the kitchens of Jessica Lange and Lady Di? For you materialism is betrayal, and you'll do anything to overcome it.

Once betrayed, or even if you imagine betrayal, you declare a silent war that could last a thousand years. This is Scorpios' carryover from the time you were carnivorous arachnids—and you all once were—with one instinct only: survival.

The Real Thing: The Nature of Desire

The creative desire is insatiable, hungry, passionate, yearning for validation, constantly seeking expression. It is searching and sweeping for contact with life, reaching out for manifestation in the world. You Scorpios are grappling always with these primitive instincts. Beneath that confident smile, which could kill an army of Huns, you are loading weapons against the onslaught of existence itself. Life is an ordeal, punctuated with sheer delight.

You are the most complex creatures of all. Your restless minds scan the world for a suitable object for your ceaseless creative urges. You yearn for physical contact, and you are like a bodiless soul craving incarnation. You mature Scorpios have evolved beyond insatiable yearning. You have purpose and direction and are supremely focused. You exude confidence, and when you walk into a restaurant, you get served right away. You know what you want, how to go after it, and how to keep it once you have it.

You primitive Scorpios, on the other hand—who are sometimes called lower Scorpios—haven't even dreamed that there's a difference between wanting something and having something. You keep yourselves in a state of semi-frustration, ever on the prowl for some shred of gratification, one little lick of satisfaction. You know only the condition of desiring something, not having it. Your desires dominate everything you think, say, and do. If it weren't for the fact that you get rejected from time to time, you'd be total sex fiends, because you drift in a hot haze of perpetual lust.

You Scorpios get caught in the web of the monster

phase when the desire takes over completely. You either squeeze the life out of a relationship by embracing it too hard or by draining a partner's resources so low that he or she has to step back to avoid complete psychic, emotional, or financial exhaustion—at which time you get angry and feel rejected.

We all have desires, of course, but desires are strongest in members of the sign of Scorpio. We can describe it only in hyperbole, because it's the power that gives a peach tree peaches and fills the spaces between the stars. It's like a million tons of lava, boiling and seething within, lightning striking the Scorpio soul, three, four, seven hundred times a minute, and filling it with the light and power of creation.

So naturally you are not the feet-up-in-slippers type. You're hot and intense. You unevolved Scorpios flail with aggression and longing, crawling along in a vague search for satisfaction. Naturally, you can never be satisfied with what you have. You have to crush your possessions, feel choked by any real relationship, because it interferes with your eternal search for gratification.

But you evolved Scorpios have a handle on the desire nature, if not total control of it. You're the Roy Lichtensteins and Carl Sagans and Calvin Kleins. You know what that power is about and don't waste your lives on obsessive, prurient pursuits. Every Scorpio alive is reaching out for real, meaningful, earthly physical contact. You are the most expressive, protective, and affectionate critters around. While you all enjoy your scary reputation for being slathering carnivores, you're all looking for that simple earthy figure who can tame the beast, hold those desires in check, and develop a lasting bond.

The Burning Question: Does Money *Always* Have to Come into It?

You are the artists and healers of the world. You have secret gifts, powers that other people don't have. One

shouldn't believe a word of it when one hears people say
they don't like Scorpios. Everybody loves this sign to
death; make no mistake about it.

But not everybody can take the power. You Scorpios are
utterly powerful. You can see others nude even when
they're fully dressed, and that can be disconcerting. You'll
walk among lepers and dance through a mine field, because you don't really believe death would ever dare come
near you. And because you'll ride a bicycle, no hands,
along the rim of Hell, you can do things nobody else can
do. You are contemptuous of economic practicality and re-
pelled at the thought that what common people think of as
earthly realities could ever interfere with your passions,
instincts, and desires.

It's true, though, that you have a pretty cold streak.
When Aunt Maud takes a turn for the worse, it's often a
Scorpio who rushes, sobbing, to the bedside to ask her
what she plans to do with the figurines on top of the TV
set. You do have a practical side, which rushes to the surface when death is near or the wolf is huffing and puffing
at the door.

But in general, you tend to live at the edge, in fact take
a mate with you right to the edge. So at the last minute,
when the two of you are about to cross that bridge, he or
she had better have the money to pay the toll, because we
can bet you won't have the exact change. Sooner or later
the American Express bill comes in and somebody's got to
pay for everything the mad Scorpio genius charged up
while busy creating. No matter how you Scorpios try to
keep George Washington from sleeping in the marriage
bed, money always comes up. In fact, in every major relationship you have, it is the burning question. Does money
always have to come up?

You never form a business partnership or marry purely
for economic reasons, because then the dollar would compromise your passions, and you can't abide that. If, on the
other hand, you blind yourselves to fiscal truth, moving
only out of desire or creative urges, then you'll be brought
up short by a partner who, for some reason, is usually

destined to be the type who has a deeply practical streak.

You Scorpios will love your mates if they're solid, sol-vent, square, and even a little on the beefy side. They have to be interested in Wall Street and enjoy better hotels and restaurants, although you will fight their materialism tooth and nail.

The happiest of you Scorpios have a healthy sense of humor about the politics of sex and money. You know the one real thread that runs through every successful relation-ship involves the issue of whether it's the "man" or the "woman" who brings home the bacon. You Scorpios know how to make the world pay for your gifts, and in every successful relationship, there will be a mutually satisfying sharing of resources. Conflicts that exist between who is more personally magnetic or creative and who exerts finan-cial control will be a source of friction until both sides are willing to open up and negotiate openly, discussing various questions. Who is pulling the purse strings? Who is sup-plying the creative juice, and who is the economic support?

These questions cannot usually be answered simply, be-cause it is usually *both parties* who supply the creative and economic support. You Scorpios may not be materialistic, but the question of possessions must always be satisfacto-rily answered. It will eliminate the palimony-alimony squabbles and open the door for solid bonding.

Ultimate Challenge: Attachment vs. Nonattachment

Maybe you are all just misguided souls who failed to read the fine print before you came to Earth. Perhaps one day up in Heaven you looked down and saw people on Earth racing cars, painting great paintings, eating cotton candy, and ordering room service in fancy hotel rooms. When told that you would need a physical body if you wanted to carry on in such a way, you Scorpio-to-be souls probably didn't even flinch. You just hollered, "Go for it!" and nine months later you were born.

It never occurred to you, though, that the flesh had limitations, such as only one body at a time, high maintenance costs, eventual death, etc. And because you have come to Earth for the sheer excitement of the experience, you're really of two minds about settling down here, fettered by mortgages and modern conveniences. You love being here, but you always prove that nothing on Earth can hold you permanently. You'll smoke three packs a day for twenty years, then wake up one morning and *whammo!* you go cold turkey forever. Even if you guzzle champagne and bathe in whipped cream, you could always give it up whenever you wanted to.

The same goes for your security. If you were truly sold on it, you'd never immerse yourselves in the vats of boiling acid you're always diving into. When you do lose your sense of balance between your dangerous urge to prove your nonattachment and your obsessive need for security, you get into horrible scrapes.

You're attracted to people whose hold on the Earth is much simpler than yours, unfettered by philosophical dialectic. You Scorpios need your mates for their couches and immovable oak cabinets, even as you tell them they're too attached to material things. Actually, it's you who must find a balance between your ferocious need for security and your compulsion to prove you can walk away from anything or anyone.

You refuse to be owned by any of the commitments you make and yet you only want the permanent kind. To resolve this dilemma, you need to find some equilibrium between art and business, passion and practicality.

You Scorpios often come from a family where at least one parent (often the parent of the opposite sex) was emotionally possessive or financially controlling. It sometimes becomes your pattern to try to disassociate from these traits, externalize them, and then seek out relationships with people who exhibit those exact characteristics. Thus, in your relationships, issues of attachment always come up.

You demand that chemistry dictate the course of your relationship. But when the obsession grows, on either part, and threatens to engulf you, you break away, go cold turkey, trim the relationship out of your life like fat off a rib roast—all to prove your superiority over any addiction, appetite, or attachment.

In order to have what you want, you have to know what you want. You have to overcome your urge to throw it away just because you got it. You need to be able to cope with attachment, on your part or on the part of your partners. You are a seed looking for rich soil to grow in. You Scorpios need to appreciate the experience of being nourished by the soil and not fear strangulation by it. Meeting your challenge will lead you to accepting this kind of attainment. Wanting something will become having something, permitting yourself to *have*, rather than merely want.

The Miracle: Manifestation

The successful Scorpio relationship usually results in tangible issue—it is always a horn of plenty. The creative power, when securely planted in another human being, always comes to fruition.

For all your incessant brooding and tempestuous yearnings, you are happiest when settled down and, strangely enough, the most productive. You'll deny it, though. Many of you believe you have to live totally alone, surrounded by overflowing ash trays and empty coffee cups, if you're going to be creative, and that you should always have at least one room that no one would dare enter. But the miracle of you all is your power to nurture and grow and bring some fruitful issue into manifested being—through the power you bring to a relationship.

When a Scorpio is near, a garden grows. People make dough, property expands. In some way, standards of living rise and resources develop when touched by a Scorpio. But you will always make your partners spend some money on you to do it. For you to achieve this miracle of issue and manifestation, though, you have to share control, allow containment, substitute delayed for immediate gratification. You have to change your habit of desiring a thing to being able to have a thing.

You Scorpios are accustomed to pacing down miles of dark corridor in your mind, tearing your feet on thorns of desire as you scramble onward. To you in your primitive unevolved state, a relationship is an ice cream cone to be licked and eaten before it melts. You have to learn how to cherish what you have and not consume it. You need to handle your resources gently, deal with what you already have, in an effort to make it grow. You need to remember that a relationship is not a cattle drive. It is a delicate mating dance designed to bring two people together and hold them together long enough to produce some mutual tangible reward.

Accepting containment will permit you to reduce your threshold of need, erase your desperate quest to override deprivation. When you can allow yourselves to have something *and share the control*—the miracle occurs naturally.

You no longer have to go on madly searching for release, relief, reward. The carrot that has been dangling in front of your eyes just out of your reach is within your reach at last. To allow yourself to have something, you have to overcome your greed, because you disapprove of greed and will always punish yourselves for it by throwing away what you have. Once you can be contained by what you seek and no longer feel choked by it, seed and soil are one and the relationship is fertilized. Ask anyone connected with a Scorpio. Fertility always comes with the package. You simply need to learn how to value things and people without consuming them.

Working the Miracle: Cherishing Loyalty and Permanence

You enter people's lives to make them aware of their financial responsibilities and powers and to help make resources grow. Ironically, at the same time you're there to remind others not to be overattached to anything they possess. You'll scare people to death and take them on a fast ride past the cemetery at midnight or the poorhouse at noon, drag them away from their dear old Mother and give them thrills they never dared enjoy before.

If there's one thing your mates must help you do it's learn how to cherish the values of loyalty, trust, and permanence. Otherwise, there's no sense bringing you out into the light. If there isn't real transformation, people should just leave you alone in your cave.

They'll have to respect your privacy, because they'll never get you to tell them where you've been, and they shouldn't think they can stop that infernal sexualizing you do, because you'll probably never give it up. But the more they can help you see the value of permanence and loyalty, the higher the vines will keep growing. What develops this trust is an intricate dance of remoteness and intimacy, hiding self, sharing self, playing alternatives, and gradually letting options go.

You evolved Scorpios don't fear your dependency needs and don't have to exercise cheap sexual controls over people. You are not prima donnas who have to be pampered and protected. But you all need your privacy. Your mate shoud allow indiscretions and not magnify them. You seasoned Scorpios come to understand the importance of letting go of your obsessive desires in favor of a deeper exchange—taking something precious but giving something back equal in lasting value.

Scorpio's partners have to remain desirable, a little aloof, a touch unknown. This is difficult, because many of you Scorpios are bloodhounds. The minute you're with them, they have to hand over their bank books and diaries and submit to constant surveillance.

But if they possibly can, they shouldn't give everything away. Once you bankrupt them, you'll leave them, so they should hold back. It will pay off in the long run. In a personal situation, your mate should hold off the sex as long as possible. You Scorpios will pull all the stops and go into high seduction gear, but the more clearly they get the practical things squared away, the happier your life will be thirty years from now. Remember that you're both trying to bring something lasting and permanent into being. Scorpio relationships are deep. One can't think one is going to touch a Scorpio, be touched by a Scorpio, and then go la-di-da off into the sunset.

Your partners have to be spiritual about this relationship, because it can get messy—games of emotional/financial blackmail, overindulgence of appetites, and addictions, etc., so they've got to learn how to play the game of Br'er Fox and Br'er Rabbit, Tom and Jerry, any game where there is hunter and prey. At the same time they have to try to keep the relationship on a higher plane.

You Scorpios believe in sharing all your mates' possessions, and there will be trouble if you find out they've got a secret stash. But if they're smart, they shouldn't sign everything over to you right away.

The only way to materialization is slow growth and long-term nurturing. A Scorpio relationship is like a living plant, and you Scorpios have to learn about watering and caring for the life of something you yourselves have seeded.

When you have learned to value what you already have and can cherish the precious gem you first saw sparkling at the beginning of a relationship, the result for both of you is wealth.

Gift Ideas for Scorpios

- An inflatable globe of the Earth. Your partners can buy you this gift at a map and atlas store. This will symbolize not only how much they'd like to give you, but it will characterize the permanence of the relationship. Besides, it will be your breath that expands the Earth, and that will give you a sense of power. They should be sure to include in the gift box a large hatpin, which will let you keep the power to create and destroy your own world.
- Financial backing for some creative project. That's probably the best thing your mate could do, from a set of paints to a Broadway show—that's what most of you Scorpios would love the most.
- A plaster sculpture of a banana split, something delicious you can't eat up in one sitting. This will show you that the longer you keep something without devouring it, the longer you'll love it.

Reading Material for Advanced Scorpios

The Tibetan Book of the Dead
Sigmund Freud's complete works

Guardian Angels: Elsie the Cow and Elmer the Bull

Elsie and Elmer rule over Scorpio relationships because they symbolize, first of all, a vast commercial success. When they are productive and nurturing, Scorpio relationships bring a giant return on an investment, financial or emotional. They represent identifiable symbols of commercialism readily recognized by everyone in the culture. We could have used Betty Crocker or the Jolly Green Giant or any symbols from any other country or time. Although they stand for stability and permanence, brand names we can count on, in fact everything in our world is in constant flux. The masses seize fervently on symbols, embrace them, identify with them, come to rely on them and believe in them, and then—*poof!*—they pass away into nothingness. This is a truth of life that you and your partners need always to remember, because the tendency to become too caught up in things of this world is great.

But at the present time in our culture Elsie and Elmer suggest widespread acceptance on a commercial level— they are a pair involved in a profitable enterprise.

Foodstuffs, their major product line, symbolize the constantly replenishing wealth, contact with the Earth. Nowhere in this section have we focused on the sexual aspects of Scorpios and your relationships.

But aren't we always hearing about Scorpios and their famous sex lives?

In truth, the sexual aspect of your relationships is always understated, thanks to the cool heads of your partners. Elsie and Elmer are definitely united on a visceral, physical level. The products they represent signify the organic nature of the union they personify, a relationship that brings forth from it something nourishing, a cooperative effort that reflects their mutual power to bring home the bacon and cook it.

Elsie is usually pictured in an apron, and Elmer is often smoking a pipe, suggesting traditional role-playing. Sexual roles are crucial in your relationship—especially when it includes the question of who earns more money. A successful facet of your diamond-studded mating depends on the resolution of this question to the satisfaction of both parties. Invariably during your relationship, inheritance questions come up that challenge the economic and sexual balance, and a major adjustment is then required.

If we had to find one key word to describe what Elsie and Elmer stand for, in a material, emotional and spiritual sense, it would be *wealth*. They symbolize the richness of a well-endowed life, both in the daily interactions of people and in the swirling realms of passion.

Celebrity Astro Game

You'd be surprised how many ways people reveal themselves in everything they say and do. To sharpen your sensitivity to other people and to learn more about the ways renowned Scorpios handle their deepest relationship issues, look over the following list and pick out the people who interest you most.

Do a little sleuthing about their lives. Observe their actions; listen to what they say in public. The songs they sing, the roles they play, the particular contributions they make, will enlighten you about the relationship patterns of this sign.

The Shah of Iran	Carl Sagan
Billie Jean King	Jaclyn Smith
Dale Evans	Telma Hopkins
Roy Rogers	Richard Dreyfuss
Paul Simon	Stefanie Powers
Mike Nichols	Larry Holmes
Prince Charles	Tatum O'Neal
Linda Evans	Calvin Klein
King Hussein	Natalia Makarova

Chapter Nine

SAGITTARIUS

The Mirage: A True Renaissance Person

You Sagittarians, during those first, few fascinating moments:

> "My God, it's three A.M. already. Do you have any idea how long we've been on the phone?"

You Sagittarians like television anchorpeople, United Nations delegates, and gossip columnists—anybody who's got their finger on the pulse of the world. You like security, too, but you don't exactly like the idea of *being married*. It's confining. You tend to run around at parties and kiss the married ones, so if your mates are jealous type, they'll spend a lot of time harrumphing on the way home in the car.

It's a mental connection with you—that's the main thing. You can't be categorized very well otherwise. You like all types for all reasons. Some of you men are into well-endowed females, while others go for the flat-chested Waspy type. You Sagittarian women, too, like 'em all.

But there's one thing all you Sagittarians agree on: you have to be able to talk to your mate. He or she has to be able to speak to you, on your level. You don't want any

169

stupid dunces around you, so apart from the various physical fetishes you might have, a satisfying partner has to be able to speak to you intelligently on your favorite subjects, whether it's architecture, Nicaragua, Jack Nicholson, or how dare Aunt Tillie say what she did to Uncle Art.

So your mates have to be pretty facile to keep up with you. And no matter where their curves and muscles fall, their appeal will largely depend on how well they can bluff their way through a *deep* conversation. They probably don't have to be terribly intelligent, but they certainly have to *appear* to be intelligent. You Sagittarians are taken with a quick, nimble mind, so your chosen companions to be able to skim a book, then talk about it, quickly get the gist of a conversation and join right in as if they stepped out for just a moment.

You all need to be amused, so if your partners can tell a joke without ruining the punch line the way you do, they're in. It's probably their agility you idealize the most. Your relationship has to reflect their supreme flexibility. You adore it if they can do it on the run or on the phone; you love that writer of mystery stories who can become the hero, the beautiful young girl, the butler, and the old lady in the garret all at the same time. You like the impressionist who sounds just like Jack Benny *or* Lucy Ricardo.

A perfect blend of everything, that's all your mates have to be—the epitome of versatility and androgyny. You want them to be at least fifty people at once so they can keep up with your changes, stimulate your mind (God forbid you should get bored), so what sets you to chase after them, or to permit them to chase after you, is the fact that they have a hundred costumes in their trunk, they're ready to be something new every day, that they can return the serve of a tennis ball or badminton birdie without missing a stroke.

You want them to indulge your whimsy and act as your jolly accomplice in crime with a little good-natured scolding, cover for you when you've just told a big one and your nose is growing bigger by the second. They've got to be able to make the best of a night spent either on a luxurious sofa or in the back of the van. They've got to have more changes of clothes than Barbie or Ken, because with you the climate will always change.

An ideal mate must be the original Renaissance person, multifaceted and multitalented, just a bubble in a glass of champagne. You see a partner's charm as therapeutic as well as intoxicating—so to you he or she has to be as heady as an Alka Seltzer tossed into a bottle of Dom Perignon.

The Monster: Schizo!

You Sagittarians, when threatened by your mate's split-off side:

"I've got a nut on my hands!"

BUT... You are always expecting that cheerful Dr. Jekyll to be swallowed up by the inevitable Mr. Hyde. You expect your loved ones to run off with the next-door neighbor, because what lies underneath is your monster—your vision of them as tragically flawed and unreliable character who will go on for hours chatting gaily, then get a bug up their nose and slam the door in your face. They turn out to be two-faced, two-timing schizo who would tear the wings off a fly while recording the whole thing on a tape recorder. The monster for you is madness, and it doesn't matter if your mates are clinically nuts or not. To you they are.

What you Sagittarians first perceive to be a mate's darling Peter Pan personality you soon perceive as a thought-disordered fragmentation of selves. The skittishness, lack of consistency—the stream of capricious random actions devoid of discipline, devoid of loyalty. You are horrified when you contemplate what you see as a partner's faithless lack of commitment, dedication, or continued interest in anything or anyone.

Huge swings both excite and frighten you. With you it often becomes patient-shrink. You see people as crazy, and while you readily include yourselves in that category, you really see yourselves as wise, sane, and intelligent people whose lot it is in this life to have to deal with dim-witted inferiors. For some reason, Sagittarians have been put on the Earth to cope with dull, brain-damaged psychotic people who can't see past their noses.

Can it be true that all you Sagittarians had at least one parent who exhibited incomprehensible behavior, and are you all living a symbolic reaction against this parent's relating style?

For some reason, you are usually waiting for the madness to poke through. Although you do everything you can to keep busy so it doesn't happen to you directly, you do often seem, according to the way you tell it, to get hooked up to class-A, genuine, one-hundred-percent-certifiable nuts.

When you Sagittarians want to see the monster, you start looking for the holes in your partners' Swiss cheese. If on nine out of ten issues they're sane, then you'll suddenly see the tenth—the one issue where they're split off, cracked, that one place in their life where they lack insight and exhibit inconsistent, childish, or neurotic, even psychotic behavior. If you get stuck staring at that, you have to flee. Dealing with it means confronting your own fragmented self.

The Real Thing: Restlessness

It's your own ambivalence, of course, that draws you to people who turn you on, then turn on you. It's your own resistance to sitting in one place and finishing something that leads you toward restless or frivolous characters. One would think you'd get sick of yanking half-baked cakes out of the oven. And many of you do. Isn't Bette Midler, for example, now finally trying to put down some roots? But even when you people do decide to get serious, then you find someone else to act out your restlessness—and you marry people who can't sit down and finish their homework.

If we looked at Woody Allen's mother or Tina Turner's father perhaps we'd see why you Sagittarians do the things you do in adult life. When it comes to relationships, you have a very "ditzy" side. Part of the reason you say you need your space is that when you get close enough to see the whites of their eyes, you know you'll see the craziness behind. Woody Allen's characters have to be the shrink in their relationships. But the women in his real life might tell another tale—that maybe he drives them crazy, then offers them the ride back to sanity. Where does the restlessness come from? Whether or not you move from city to city, divorce, and remarry ten times, or just do your living rooms over every six months, you Sagittarians are restless people. You'll sign a lease for a year and move out in seven months, because when it's time to move on, it's time to move on. You start a million things, but to finish any one of them, ironically, you have to leave them all.

It's your own reluctance to be pigeonholed that draws you toward people with similar problems. It probably helps to know *why* we do some of the crazy things we do, but does knowing we are crazy and why we are crazy make us any less crazy? Maybe what attracts and repels you Sagittarians so much toward and from odd people is the fact that you spend a lot of energy proving to yourselves that you are sane. Intelligence and sanity are such enormous issues for you, one just knows you must have your doubts about both.

The nervous fidgeting that irks you so reminds you of either a parent you had or a side of yourself you'd rather not deal with. That's why you're such smiling deniers—you are simply refusing to crack. You believe that if one denies a problem long enough it eventually goes away. So when you hear a strange ping in your car's motor, you simply turn up the radio.

The source of restlessness? Your minds are thirsty and if your mates don't give you a drink, somebody else will. On the other hand, if they were to give you all the stimulation you want, then they'd have to be the three faces of Eve to the tenth power, at which time you'd think, now, what do I need *this* for? This creep's a nut.

You Sagittarians often lack discipline, so you search out people who won't confront you. You procrastinate like mad, so you seek out those who indulge you. You lack follow-through, so you look for partners who won't make a big issue out of tables that get stripped down and never get sanded and other unfinished projects.

You end up, then, drawing undisciplined, procrastinating, self-indulgent children to you, and that does not make you happy. The resolution begins when you awaken to your own pattern. What separates human beings from animals is the knowledge of what we are doing and why we are doing it. This is your task in life and the gift you bring to the mature relationship.

The Burning Question: How Can One Have a Relationship with Someone Who's Only Half There?

You want them there, but you don't. You Sagittarians require your mates to be on the road, out of the house, traveling for business, coming and going, moving about, and out of your hair for at least half the time. You might complain about it, but partner shouldn't give in and sit home holding the yarn for you, because if they don't leave, you will. The more they keep rolling, the happier you are.

The relationship has to be flexible enough to thrive on motion and commotion. It will *never* be like the movies, where people come down to a sterling-silver breakfast table looking like a million bucks and saying "Good morning, darling." Sagittarian mealtime is more like a lunch counter in Grand Central Station with people standing up and eating on the run.

But if somebody is gone half the time, what kind of consistency can ever be set up? How can there be any

long-term communication if there are more distractions
than there are connections? If someone is with you, male
or female, they had better understand that it's going to be
relationshipus interruptus, and, strangely enough, the sepa-
rations and the absences will probably be the source of
what keeps you together and gives you something to talk
about, and it will often be a little like telling your shrink
what happened between sessions.

You may want a partner to move on a moment's notice
but will fault one who is too capricious. You like impulsive
people who act quicker than a knee jerks at the touch of a
hammer. But lack of thought or insight that accompanies
any of their actions will bug you to death, and that same
burning question will come up again, this time regarding
not their geographical whereabouts but their mental facul-
ties—which as far as you're concerned will really need
some serious professional evaluation: How can you have a
relationship with somebody who's only half there?

If, as you reason, your partners have a mental blind spot
that they don't understand (you, of course, understand it
perfectly), then how can a sane relationship be conducted,
if in a given area they can't be talked to or reasoned with?
If they're closed off to communication in their crazy area
and that area happens to be crucial for the health of the
relationship, what are you to do?

In fact, the question could be turned around to ask it of
you, but you rarely think of that. Do you require their
periodic absence because in reality you cannot be there all
the time? And is the focus of their mental state a conve-
nient red herring to distract you from viewing that space
between your own ears, that little spot in the brain that
hasn't been filled in by some interesting fact, that tiny void
where madness glares through?

The split-off side of every person is real and must
always be communicated with—even on a part-time basis.
In Sagittarian relationships there are often some real issues
of morality (or amorality). The more rigid you are about
the codes you set up, the more likely it is that others will
break you and teach you a lesson. The successful Sagittar-

ian relationship, then, is built upon the integration of paradox into every moral, philosophical, or psychological system.

Ultimate Challenge: Their Behavior vs. Your Sanity

When viewed intelligently, even the craziest behavior can be understood as a reflection of someone else's view of reality. Behavior is absurdly relative, and customs that are accepted as normal and healthy by one group can be considered antisocial or pathological by another. In one culture alone, traditions change drastically over the years, and what is looked upon as sane behavior today would have sent our great-grandparents to bed with an infusion of eucalyptus tea.

With your great and expansive mental capacities you Sagittarians are often called upon to make huge jumps of morality and understanding, not by viewing or studying other cultures and other times but by the very relationship you choose to have.

Religious views, moral attitudes, social codes, political leanings, always pop up to challenge the Sagittarian relationship. What you believe to be right and true behavior may be completely antithetical to the code of your partners, who are, of course, chosen exactly for their differences of point of view.

The most fulfilled of you Sagittarians can embrace behavior they don't understand without signing a mate up against his or her will for shock treatments. You know what you're doing when you get mixed up with people in the first place—you need to keep things jumpy and a little unsteady. You smart Sagittarians know the difference between eccentricity and craziness, and you don't rule out a mate's behavior just because it isn't your own.

Consider a long-term couple like John Cassavetes and

Gena Rowlands; why did they last all those years? Maybe there are some sick needs lurking around down there we don't know about, but surely both people recognize, confront, and acknowledge where exactly they were both quite sane and both quite crazy. No blame, no patient-doctor bullshit, no priest-or-felon scene.

You Sagittarians are successful in real relationships when you come to accept that the behavior that you have in your ignorance judged as bad or crazy, you have in fact attracted to yourself to challenge yourselves and your own prejudices and bring you to a new level of awareness of your own behavior. The minute you interact closely with other people, you are often made to adjust your notions of right and wrong.

The most successful of you are not merely permissive or enabling but can live with other people and see them as different but not necessarily mad. It will always involve the resolution of opposing points of view, conflicting lifestyles, or contradictory moral systems. You wise Sagittarians know the trap of permissiveness. You don't just quietly help someone stuff their mother into the trunk of the car if they promise to let you get drunk afterwards. You know that if you act like Santa Claus all the time, they'll eventually kick you in the teeth for not making them grow up. You are in fact constantly challenging yourself to expand your understanding of human action and interaction and to communicate that knowledge to your partner so that you can both become more responsible and thinking beings.

The Miracle: Communication

You evolved Sagittarians do not split when things get rough. You talk, don't run from honest dialogue—in fact you help your mates conquer their own resistance to it. When one hears a Sagittarian couple bickering, arguing, interrupting each other, contradicting and correcting each other on the accurate details of a story, one shouldn't think for a moment that they're not having a grand old time.

Because you Sagittarians do tend to gloss over things before your enlightenment, sometimes your partner will feel frustrated when they must bring up difficult issues. When a relationship is festering away below the surface and unspoken rules get set up indicating that nothing real ever gets said, an eruption is inevitable and often takes place in a more public situation, where allies can be found and support gained for confrontational issues.

The happiest, luckiest, and most successful of you Sagittarians are in the process of mastering the art of communication in relationships. That means reaching out and speaking in somebody else's language. Coming to another level of comprehension. When we consider the research currently being conducted in the areas of getting monkeys to talk and of conversing with the dolphins, we must think of you Sagittarians and your partners.

Communications skills are the profound key to success for you. All you have to do is tap these talents and your relationships *work*. You are sometimes afraid that other people are too fragile and unstable to really talk and that is often your own fear projected into them. Besides, knowing how to confront and communicate with even the most unstable person is in fact the miracle of your versatility and flexibility.

You want a deep mind link and often pick people who communicate only superficially, without the consciousness of a deep mind connection. It is your task to provide that deep mind relationship without sending the other guy into orbit.

In English, then: you Sagittarians excel when you are helping a partner be conscious, by being more conscious yourselves. Greater consciousness provides confidence. When you are less threatened, you don't feel other people's craziness is a threat to you. You're not defensive about it and can thus express yourselves freely without putting others off. The secret to success in your relationships lies in the art of communication, in the art of speaking one's mind and being able to accept it when others do the same. Not just talking at each other and smiling politely, blocking out what someone else says, but listening, responding, building on a theme, going with it, fighting a point of view without branding it.

You need to be able to suspend judgment of your adversary's position and be ready with cogent arguments to defend your ethical, moral, or psychological stance. You need to develop the capacity to walk in the other fellow's shoes, see through a partner's eyes, to determine in what ways, incomprehensible though it might be, you are contributing to, even causing in a mate, behavior that you have been judging. You need to keep your consciousness elevated and be able to present information in a nonthreatening way and, through communication, to embrace the competitive volley that is the game of relationships.

Working the Miracle: Mental Flexibility

You Sagittarians enter people's lives to remind them that connected to that hand of theirs that is forever changing the channels there is, after all, a brain, and maybe it does matter whether they watch the public TV special on wild birds or just glue themselves in front of the *Woody Woodpecker Show*.

Of course, their job is to try to prove to you that there really isn't much difference between those two TV programs. However you choose to have your dialogue between cartoons and college, the miracle in this relationship is achieved through the resolution of mental and moral paradoxes—by coming to an agreement on the meaning of words. Words are the bond between you—the nuances, the tricky shadings of meaning, all those "gray" areas where truth is stretched until it screams in pain and laws are bent till they crack like a chicken's wishbone.

You Sagittarians elevate the consciousness of your mates sometimes by teaching them something, then testing them to see how well they've learned it so they have to take over *your* role, point out *your* behavior to *you*, help you wake up and grow. Idle chatter (you hate it) is not communication. Learning to communicate means being open to learning. This goes for you as well. You need to learn flexibility, to stretch your mind to encompass behavior you can't understand.

In this relationship there must be mental flexibility. Neither you nor a person you're involved with can stick rigidly to a set of ideas, principles, or goals without a willingness to shift position in the light of changing circumstances or reception of new data. One simply cannot go on in the same house if a six-lane highway is now passing right through one's living room.

Your relationship will provide new dimensions, new horizons, and horizons will expand for everyone involved. But if you are to have a successful relationship, you must not be feverish about your particular brand of orthodoxy. If your goal is wisdom—and you Sagittarians are always looking for that—then you will invariably come upon situations that challenge your current thinking. If you cling to a moral point of view, the minute you have a relationship, that point of view will come into serious jeopardy. And conversely, if you fail to develop a healthy ethical code, your relationships will fail, because the healthy code is what you're supposed to bring to a relationship.

Mental flexibility means being open to learning, observing behavior without slapping a quick label or diagnosis on it, recognizing that a relationship with someone who exhibits a particular kind of behavior is a particular kind of behavior in itself. The partner's actions mirror one's own inner life; everyone is there to teach everyone else a valuable lesson. If one is sane, the other crazy, in a repeated constantly repeated pattern from one relationship to the next, then is seeking crazy people its own form of craziness?

If it cannot be changed other than on the most superficial level of behavior modification, then can any relationship succeed? Is madness the common denominator—are we doomed to it?

Perhaps it is your task to rethink the whole subject of behavior. This, of course, may be the true path for all you Sagittarians—rethinking your behavior and that of the people you associate with.

There's no one more generous in the whole Zodiac to have a relationship with. You Sagittarians are absolutely astounding. Don't ever believe it when the doctors call you in and sadly tell you the news about yourselves. You all have unbreakable constitutions, and when the war is over, the Sagittarian flag is still flying. You Sagittarians bring freshness and motion to a relationship, goading your mates to new levels of experience. You'll have them trekking through the desert, going up and down the Grand Canyon on a mule, or rafting in white water.

You will definitely perform brain surgery on your partners one way or another, and their heads will never be the same post-Sagittarius. Their outlook on their own relationship to culture, morals, and religion will change when they fly with you. They're going to have to be willing to camp out and cook like an aborigine while they're between homes, but the experience will leave their mind expanded.

Just remember one thing. You Sagittarians want to do exactly what you want to do when you want to do it. If your mate goes along with you, they'll go exciting places, do unusual things, see the sights. But if they try to challenge you, they're crazy!

Gift Ideas for Sagittarians

- A toy phone, preferably red, to signify a hot line. Since the greatest and closest communications one will ever have with you will often occur over the phone, this toy will provide endless hours of amusement and enlightenment. If you and your mate are in a room together and you need to do some serious talking, they can just have you call up on the little red phone.

- A real WATS line—installed, of course. This will enable you to simply lift the receiver and begin speaking to them wherever they are. It will eliminate the need for any middle person, which will drastically reduce the dangers of triangulation and transmission of garbled messages for which many Sagittarians are famous.
- A box full of beautiful hand-carved black onyx question marks is not only a witty conversation piece but could have so many hidden meanings that you could spend months trying to figure it out.

Reading Material for Advanced Sagittarians

The Biological Basis of Schizophrenia, by Jon Karlsson, M.D.

Psychoanalytic Technique and Psychic Conflict, by Charles Brenner, M.D. (especially chapters on countertransference).

Guardian Angels: A Team of Ape Language Researchers

 A husband-and-wife team of ape language researchers watches over Sagittarian relationships, because they signify the great achievements men and women make when they devote themselves wholeheartedly to the task of communicating over insurmountable barriers.

They represent, too, the zeal and daring of people united on a quest for rare adventure, joined in a common cause that challenges intellectual prowess and develops a bond of shared mental interests.

People in the process of teaching apes to talk and learning the language used by apes to communicate among themselves are used as Sagittarian symbols because they denote the need to join minds with creatures that seem at first to be lower on the evolutionary scale. You Sagittarians also involve yourselves with individuals whose communication skills have been developed in a wholly different mode, as if on another wavelength. Both for the ape researchers and for you Sagittarians, the very effort it takes to jump the huge communication gap demands its own sharpened form of intelligence and highly developed skill. The joy and reward will be learning about these creatures, who have their own special modes of communication and codes of behavior.

This is the search for unique expression in relationships and a burning desire to make a mind link with another intelligent individual.

The researchers, like you Sagittarians, come to the relationship with a set of preconceived ideas, hypotheses, and notions. But they can be successful only when they surrender up their beliefs and prejudices and learn from beings who do not have a similar set of preliminary dispositions.

You Sagittarians have to learn to relate to people who interact with you but who do not in any way participate fully with your belief systems. The crucial ingredient in successful Sagittarian relationships is not at all the difference in level of intelligence but the disparity of social organization. As the apes and man live worlds apart, so you Sagittarians need to find people whose lifestyle may seem incomprehensible but actually serves to challenge your powers of understanding and expands your understanding.

Celebrity Astro Game

You'd be surprised how many ways people reveal themselves in everything they say and do. To sharpen your sensitivity to other people and to learn more about the ways renowned Sagittarians handle their deepest relationship issues, look over the following list and pick out the people who interest you most.

Do a little sleuthing about their lives. Observe their actions; listen to what they say in public. The songs they sing, the roles they play, the particular contributions they make will enlighten you about the relationship patterns of this sign.

Joe DiMaggio	Caroline Kennedy
Tina Turner	Chuck Mangione
Woody Allen	Abbie Hoffman
Andy Williams	Bette Midler
Jeff Bridges	Richard Pryor
Ted Knight	Dick Butkus
John Cassavetes	Donna Mills
Jane Fonda	Dionne Warwick
Don Johnson	Leslie Stahl
John F. Kennedy, Jr.	Phil Donahue

Chapter Ten

CAPRICORN

The Mirage: The Nursing Mother

One of the first ten questions you Capricorns will put to a prospective mate:

"Do you like to cook?"

It takes you Capricorns a long time to figure out the difference between what you *think* is going on between yourself and other people and what is really going on. Because in every Capricorn relationship, much more is happening than you'll ever see on the surface.

Just think of Capricorns like Diane Keaton or David Bowie—have they, too, had to make vast jumps from fantasy to reality in their relationships?

One rarely thinks that superstar Capricorns like Mary Tyler Moore would be looking for love or security or permanence like the rest of us. But maybe it's true. Capricorns, all of you, from Nostradamus to Richard Nixon, have an ideal you might not even be aware of—that perfect, gentle, nonthreatening somebody who can make you relax and take the starch out of your soul.

You're looking for the mommy's bosom you can bury your heads against, man or woman.

You Capricorns often feel you're being chased by a re-
lentless dog, and you're trying to get into the house before
the dog bites the seat of your pants. And the house you're
running toward is a relationship. When you look at your
partners, you see smoke rising from a flagstone chimney, a
house with geraniums, and wild pine trees sloping up a
steep hill. Below a rocky incline a brook babbles by with
clear water from a nearby mountain.

Inside, a woman in her ninth month is slicing tomatoes
and onions from the garden. A couple of kids are coloring
in a book. Grandpa sits by the woodstove, carving something for the little ones. With a rush of air the door opens
and handsome, muscular MR. enters with wood he's just
chopped.

You Capricorns see partnership as your deed to that
family scene. You project onto people all the fantasies you
have about doing what comes naturally, so you see them as
a mass of glands and feelers at the mercy of the Moon. You
like it if they eat spaghetti and scream, "Shaddap!" while
hanging the laundry in the living room.

By the time you are ready to meet someone you are so
fed up with having to conduct yourself according to Robert's Rules of Parliamentary Procedure that you welcome a
little good old-fashioned organic living.

You like them always to be a touch agoraphobic, just so
they'll always be there. (Remember the old woman in the
shoe: Her husband was probably a Capricorn.) And you
fully expect them to get you to either move out of the city
or at least stay in bed longer.

You surround them with the mystique of Mommy—you
see them as your nourishment, so it helps if they can cook.

You relate to nurturing so here we need to look at the
Capricorn mirage in terms of what breasts symbolize.

Breasts are the containers of mother's milk. Equipped
with a nipple, the breasts provide the source of nourishment for an individual while offering the opportunity for
the child to reestablish the intimate bond with its mother.

I'll admit it's difficult to imagine Reverend Sun Myung
Moon or Dolly Parton cooing at Mother's breast, but just

because it's hard to picture doesn't mean it might not be possible. Beneath the suave, I'm-totally-in-control-folks exterior of every Capricorn is a baby madly searching for nourishment.

You Capricorn women, too, are looking for Mommy's sweet nipple. It's harder for you, because you are searching for a man who doesn't mind playing wet nurse.

Before you're released from the hospital into the custody of your parents, you Capricorn babies are all stamped with a Good Housekeeping Seal of Good Behavior, and you grow up looking over your shoulder at an angel who's got a ledger and a pen filled with indelible ink.

So when you see your mates responding naturally and spontaneously like a crab to the tides of their own natures, you believe you can get in touch with your own natural instincts by merging with them.

You see them as your release valve. You hope that through them you'll be able to return to a primitive instinctual harmony with the universe you lost when your ancestors crawled out of the sea and got into real estate. Take a look at Janis Joplin or Elvis; and one thinks, Hey! Those guys all seem like they're pretty in touch with *their* natural instincts. And Ethel Merman didn't need primal therapy to scream. But it's still true, though many of you are publicly expressive, you Capricorns lay the mirage of Mommy onto every relationship, male and female.

The Monster: The Yowling Brat

BUT ... When they start needing and needing and needing and needing, you try to scrape them off as if they were leeches. If they cling and try to get too cozy, suddenly you think of a million things that have to be done, like cleaning out the garage or paying the phone bill. Blondie Bumstead has to be the ultimate Capricorn wife—the way she'll haul Dagwood out of the tub just when he's getting comfortable. It's the Capricorn way to restore order and purpose to those at leisure. The image of the mustachioed landlord ordering a pregnant woman into the blizzard is certainly a dark picture of this great sign.

You Capricorns like to go out to business in the morning and bolt the castle shut so when you come home at night your mates will be there, scrubbed, bright-eyed, doting, and uncorrupted by the world. You adore the tableau of family, but because it's as real to you as a Nativity crèche, the reality of family makes demands on you that you find emotionally draining. You expect a partner to be a pillow you can lay your head on, but neediness weighs you down. In your younger, more idealistic years, you think that having a baby means posing with the little thing on your lap before a red velvet curtain. Motherhood and Fatherhood are goals, the way some people want to go to Rome and see the Colosseum or own their own home. But in reality, the emotional bond for you Capricorns can be a difficult experience. Not that you're not sexy or don't make good parents. You are, and you do. You set goals and examples, and by the time one has grown up under a Capricorn regime, one is definitely an expert in some kind of marketing.

But the reality of intimacy sometimes creates a monster. You see your partners as clinging and needy and absurdly vulnerable to their own internal clocks. You want them to be wet and seductive, all right, but make sure they take that birth control device to bed. You hate bloopers.

First you see them as a porcupine of emotion who will help activate your shriveled glands, someone you can protect because they're *too sensitive to deal with the world*. But then—oh, God—a mouth that always wants to be fed. A yowling, screaming bundle of insecurity, a ball of clinging nervousness with no mind at all, just a lump of consciousness focused on food and responding to worry. A mass of ganglia responding to external stimuli the way an amoeba moves away from the point of a pencil on a slide. Always needing, needing, crying out, arms outstretched.

You Capricorns spend a lifetime trying to be economically free so you don't have to "depend" on anybody. Actually the dependence you are escaping is not economic at all but emotional. But you'll do everything you can to make your mate emotionally dependent on you, then recoil at the monster baby they've become.

You relate to them as a parent relates to a baby. And you have the same resistance to their emotional needs that you have to a child's need to be a child. Many of you Capricorns feel you turned thirty just before your eighth birthday. You don't feel you were allowed the full reign of childhood.

In the beginning of your relationship, you see your mates as expressive and emotionally loving, probably the result of what in your fantasies you regard as a good home. But after a while, too much tenderness makes you lean over the sink.

The Real Thing: Giving In to Nature

You Capricorns are drawn toward fertility. You are attracted to lush gardens and wild flowers. That's why your mates are in your life. You require a partner to be the TLC that makes those flowers grow.

But you are also threatened by the nature's wild tendency. You Capricorns are dedicated to society and sidewalks. You Capricorns are about as casual as a Swiss watch. You love weed killers and bug spray. Your purpose is to subjugate nature, suppress nature's tendency to proliferate wildly. You Capricorns are about as casual as a Swiss watch. You can't just lie back and be casual, rely on hunches, or make major decisions just because your nose itches or a crow flies south or something deep inside "tells" you a move is right or wrong.

Does Diane Sawyer use Capricorn strategy to figure out which offer from which network is right? Like all you Capricorns, does she need people in her life who move on a more feminine intuition? Intuition is the quality that all Capricorns admire, fear, loathe, and ultimately respect.

The socialized Capricorn man or woman responds in ways that are agreed upon as appropriate. You can burp aloud only in an Arab tent, where it is expected. You don't have many natural instincts. You can't usually just smell when a child has a fever or needs a little loving. You Capricorns need Dr. Spock to tell you it's all right.

Behind your passion for and repulsion to a mate's glandular way of responding to life is your own fascination for and terror of the consequences of living according to instinct. To you that is primitive, foreign, dangerous. You adore the idea of ethnicity and large families, passing the stuffing on holidays, but in reality, it's all too chaotic for you. You Capricorns are crying out, "Simplify! Simplify!" and the only way to do that is to be ruled by the head, not the heart.

But you love it in others. You business types revere the artists; you well-tailored upper classes are fascinated by the gum-chewing hoi-polloi who scratch their armpits and bellow with laughter in the laundromat. It's attractive to you, alien to be able to *be*, to exist, live by the wind and the sea and *not* by the click of the machine. How much work did Henry Miller accomplish when he fell upon Big Sur?

And that scares you—to think that if you actually give in to your love of gardening or golf, it will be "good-bye, life," and the next thing you know—foreclosure. You can cook, swim, make love, or rough it in the Amazon jungle —*if* an eventual *How to Cook, Swim, Make Love, or Rough It in the Jungle* book is to come out of it.

When you behold a child of nature, you're glued. You watch your mates like a leopard would marvel at Tarzan's baby—but to live like they do, completely—no thanks. Those little squirrels in the park that start running around gathering nuts for the blizzard, in the middle of July, are all Capricorns.

You Capricorns will be impressed with innocence, excited by ease. When confronted with a natural phenomenon, you are seized with a desire both to protect and crush it. Finding a balance restores you to a wholesome place in the relationship world.

The Burning Question: Is It All Right to Feel?

You Capricorns are actually gentle people, and it's not your fault that the Wicked Witch of the West was your grandmother. You missed out on a lot of that kootchy-kootchy-koo stuff that makes people naturally warm and responsive in later life. You're able to cope with enormous stress and handle any kind of situation that requires that a person *not* fall apart. You were all born in the dead of winter, so your entrance into this world was under adverse climatic conditions. And because your childhood ended shortly before it began, you are very ambivalent about indulging children or feelings in general.

You want to be babied, you want to baby your mates, but you cannot allow yourselves to be babied, and you always force other people to grow up. If they let you, you unevolved Capricorns will completely infantilize them. You'll take control and be very solicitous of their needs and slowly construct a playpen around their life. Then when they reach out, you'll slam them and tell them to shape up! You are needy but can't show it easily. You tend to see your relationship with them as strictly parent-child, with the roles changing according to your needs.

Male or female, you like to be the level-headed, serious-thinking daddy who brings home the bacon, tells others to calm down when they're hysterical, and "let's see how together we can work out the problem." It is rarely an act of conscious evil on your part that you can be both infantilizing and punitive. You long to be an infant, embraced in the safety and comfort of a loving mother's arms. But you also have disdain for that longing, and even if you turn your mate into the infant you want to be, you often feel a compulsion to crush that "child" and all its needs, just as the child within you was suppressed at an early age.

Your partners have to be a veritable cornucopia (you'll set them up with a grocery budget, of course), but you resent being there if your emotional needs are too pressing.

If one has any parent-child issues going on, you Capricorns are ultimate companions. You are all working to find an equilibrium between the fantasies of omnipotent parent and powerless child.

You Capricorns who had tyrannical parents tend to form relationships in which you get to play powerless infants and controlling adults. And you Capricorns who have developed beyond the primitive parent-child pattern often provide a strong role for a partner without crushing the relationship in the vise of an insecure baby's embrace or the grip of a rigid parent.

Though you fear it, you are calling on other people to evoke a feeling response in you. You may be ever grumbling to regain control of yourself and brush off the hay so that nobody will know you were up in the hayloft, but half your life and most of your joy comes from the feelings that relationships have helped you to awaken in yourself.

You Capricorns have to give yourselves permission to feel anything. You are always thinking so your partners shouldn't be insulted if, five minutes after an especially loving scene you roll over in bed, plant a kiss on their cheek, and say, "Richman had better sign those contracts he promised to deliver by Friday, or the deal's off."

Feelings, warmth, lovingness, closeness—ironically, these qualities come out in Capricorn relationships and they are precisely the qualities you bring out in your partner.

You've got that "untended since the age of five" air about you that makes your mates want to fix you a drink or run their fingers through your hair till you fall asleep. But they've got to be able to talk business at the same time.

Though you have to bite the bullet during moments of intimacy, your greatest relationships will open up your emotional center and help you answer that burning question: Is it okay to feel?

Ultimate Challenge: Office vs. Home

If you completely gave over to your fantasies, you'd *never* go to work. You'd live in your slippers and TV recliner and get fat watching reruns of *The Waltons*. You are always fighting agoraphobia and force yourself out of bed and out of the house each day to prove you can do it.

You Capricorns have such a deep love of home and family, one can't judge that by the fact that you are almost never there but by the size of the mortgage payments.

You Capricorns exist for the upkeep of the family. Your stand on abortion could be a tad fuzzy, though, because you are as much for pragmatics as traditional values. But when push comes to shove, you will vote the ticket for truth, justice, the American way, and tax breaks for summer homes and college tuitions. Though you spend ninety percent of your time and energy away from those cute little hungry faces, you'll be the first to say you're not out dancing in a nightclub somewhere but working late to scratch up the capital for the little guy's latest toy or the little lady's formal dress. In a way that is unassailably noble, you Capricorns are indeed working to preserve the family, and doing it at a perfect arm's length away.

You'll say business trips make you lonely, and you'll mean it. But when you're home on vacation, you are often reading, discussing, calling on the phone, or secretly hatching a business plan you can execute as soon as the holiday ends and you can pick up your life again. Your end of the deal is the business end. It's harder for a woman to get a man to go along with her need to be the breadwinner, so you Capricorn women like starving artists you can support.

Why do you do this?

You were programmed in the nursery; tape recordings were played in your tiny ears as you slept: *Make something of yourself. Pay your bills. Support the family. Don't depend on anybody. Support the family. Support the family.*

You can act only in the way you know how: responsibly

and coolly. As if you've got to do it all. Your soul may be as stiff as your upper lip, but you people are really warm in your own cool way. Your reticence and stuffiness notwithstanding, you guys are the sincerest and often the most passionate pals one can ever have.

You take on the serious role because that's how you are comfortable.

You are all rising to the challenge of family, as family symbolizes your heritage and your responsibility to your personal life. Every one of you wants one, but the demands of a personal life will always take you away from your true home—the office.

And it doesn't matter what the career is, whether it's politics, publishing, show business, or a dry cleaning store, you Capricorns take your jobs seriously. You give your time and dedication to it freely with diligence and love. Your mate shouldn't get in the way of it. One shouldn't think Faye Dunaway will stay in bed with you if she has a five A.M. call on the set of her new movie.

You are often being confronted by your loved ones to share more of your time and give more of yourself. But it's hard for you. You feel you're betraying yourself if you have more than one piece of toast—let alone relax into a plate of pasta. You work to be successful, to achieve worldly mention, and win awards.

You all want to be part of a home filled with loving beings who live well, eat well, and enjoy their lives. You are striving to balance a clawing ambition for material success against an equal need for security on an emotional level. Your goal is not to sleep your way to the top but to create and maintain ties of tenderness and loyalty as the years go on. One shouldn't believe it if you flounce in the door like Loretta Young. You're tough old birds, and you all went to J. R. Ewing University.

But neither should one buy the act of a Capricorn who pretends to be Ebenezer Scrooge before the fateful Christmas Eve. On the other side of the heartless mogul, there's a little boy or girl curled up with cookie in hand or thumb in mouth, just waiting for Mommy to come home.

On your own you stay at work as late as possible, but in a relationship, the home is important. You need your mates to put down roots. Oh, you can carry the mortgage and haggle with banks and locksmiths, but your relationship has to be the medium in which your culture truly grows.

For some reason, left to your own devices, you Capricorns will sup on a bit of cold mutton and left-over porridge. And it's up to your partners to provide the pancakes and butter sauce. Though you'll try to keep them from eating anything that tastes good, you love it when they heap ice cream under your nose.

You Capricorns are trying to balance your personal and professional life—as we all are. You usually see your relationship as providing the home base. On your own, you'd eat somewhere near the office or just order Chinese. But it's your union with a mate that creates in you the need to have a "real" home.

The Miracle: Intimacy

It's a mistake for others to think that nothing goes on inside you Capricorns but a lot of figuring of the prime rate. You may be stiff in public, but behind closed doors, you can outcozy a puppy. You are capable of deep and lasting intimacy. You do ice up sometimes when your mates get hottest, and if they're sick, they've got to get well in a day or two, because when your supply of sympathy runs low, it's rarely refillable. And yes, you want only tenderness from other people.

But nobody provides security like you Capricorns, even if it's hard for you to just put your tootsies up on the couch and enjoy it. Real contact for you brings out all the emotion that lies buried at the bottom of your being. You Capricorns know you have struck oil when through a relationship you wake up the child within you. After you have passed through the horror of facing your neediness, you embrace your mates totally, deeply, and forever.

You mature Capricorns neither hide your need nor detest

it in others. You deal equally well with both worldly problems and your own emotional needs. One should never try to blackmail a Capricorn emotionally though. You're trying to overcome your fear of intimacy, so for you it can be one step forward, two steps back. And when you contract and withdraw, it's like opening a clam shell to win you back. You are all walking slowly away from a childhood that deprecated tenderness, and you're not really in familiar territory in the emotional area. It takes you time to unwind and open up, but when you do, you'll take care of a mate until the last cow comes home.

You unevolved Capricorns are rebelling against your upbringing and are emotionally obsessive, believing that if you can be accepted by the individual with the wildest emotions, it will rub off on you by osmosis. This results in chaotic relationships, destructive life behavior, such as overdrawn credit and physical excesses, all leading to eventual rejection of the relationships.

You experienced Capricorns are cautious and sincere, and aren't scared of being boring any longer. You are not closed off to dependence and have a balanced view of the head and the heart. You are someone people count on, caring, sensible, intuitive, and though characteristically Un-Capricorn, *very* psychically tuned.

If you are not wholly empathic, then at least you are supremely aware and sensitive, always able to present diplomatic and viable alternatives to help your partners out of any jam they're in. You act like the village elders when you give advice, so your mates have to grit their teeth a little. You men twirl your mustache in a knowing fashion and while you women do much to retain your feminine complexion and demeanor, you are not the buttons-and-bows type—and some of you even have a mustache.

You emulate the tenderness you see in others and strive to imitate the intimacy other people have a natural gift for. It's hard for you, though, to just relax and be a kid.

You are by nature parental—you support your partners' worldly ventures, applaud their successes and feel utterly protective of them if others dare to blemish their name with criticism. But you're the first to narrow your brows when they fart at the dinner table, so they should strive for decorum always. Although you cannot resist punitive comments and digs, you are their staunchest allies as time goes by.

You evolved Capricorns recognize the child within you and have no fear of it, and thus have no particular compulsion about naturalness or the emotional needs of others.

You know who you are, embrace your potential, develop your capabilities, and accept your limitations. You neither envy nor detest your mates for the families they grew up in and the needs they have today because of it. You can participate and enjoy their naturalness or fiery expressiveness without having to merge with it or stamp it out like a fire on your wall-to-wall carpeting. You are hip to the parentchild game and do not pretend you are not playing it. *All you Capricorns play it.*

The happiest of you are wise to the dynamic and know when to lose the wrestling match with your "child." You are superfine-tuned to who's in need and who's in control, who's the baby and who's the grownup. You savvy Capricorns know that financial control puts you far in the lead but that it can never take the place of your need for security and enduring love. And in that sense, *your mates* are always in control of you.

You can at least partially let go of your head, so to achieve your miracle, you need to understand intellectually the function, purpose, and benefit of emotional fulfillment. That way you will not be threatened by it. You have to approach it the way a busy executive would come to see that meditation and exercise could be good for his business.

Once you have understood fully the need for an emotional life, you can master it. When you've seen for yourselves the function personal intimacy serves, how it rounds out your life, how you deserve it, and why it's no sin to have it or practice it, your obsessiveness abates. And then you move toward permanent personal attachments, albeit slowly, with certainty and trust.

Working the Miracle: Bonding

Every relationship has a starting point, a moment when it begins. For all signs of the Zodiac, that first encounter, the planting of the seed, creates a potential on which the reality of the entire relationship will eventually be based.

But of all the signs, this seeding process is most crucial for you Capricorns. Your method of emotional bonding will reflect so many of your deepest patterns that it merits special attention. If you are attracted to feeling types but mistrust your own instincts, then the beginnings of your relationships will be a measure of how much you are in or out of touch with your emotional natures.

A Capricorn who is cut off from his or her feelings will be unattractive and drab, and easy prey for any fast-talking smoothie who's been around the park in a carriage. As sharp as you Capricorns are in the interest-and-loan department, you can be naive when it comes to love, and your business acumen fails when feelings come into play. You know this, of course. That's why you're forever stamping out feeling as if it were a brush fire. You Capricorns who fear engulfment by your own need for emotional sustenance, of course, get engulfed by it. You are vulnerable to sexual opportunists. Thus, you get involved in situations where initial bonding is *not* developed appropriately. Insecurities create chaotic situations, and in an effort to deal only half-heartedly with your personal vices, you're attracted to unavailable or dangerous people who end up confirming your fears and driving you further into your shell.

With maturity, though, you usually get a better perspective on your weaknesses and strengths. As you mature and get a handle on your acting out, you tend less to overcompensate for your feelings of inferiority. At that point you women can enjoy being with a man who has a decent job, and you men can allow a woman to be more than a child. You grown-up Capricorns have gotten over your passions and resentments for your mothers and tend to form very different relationships from your unevolved cousins (and your earlier selves). And in the first encounters with a new person, there is less frenzy, hysteria, and obsessiveness, and a greater sense of building something real with a life of its own that will grow and develop healthily.

Your partners will have to expect periods of contractions and withdrawal—budget cutbacks and bear markets. Or maybe you will cry out against cholesterol and calories.

This could be a clue that there's too much warmth and closeness for your comfort. You might feel that a mate's growing dependence on you is cloying, and this is your way of backing off a little.

You Capricorns enter people's lives to get them to open up more, to help *you* open up more, deepen the bond. But you will from time to time cough up the banana like a little baby, and that should tell a mate to wise up, slow down, and back off.

You choose specific people because they have an expansive emotional nature. They choose you because you can usually keep your head even after a whole bottle of wine.

If you want to work your miracle, you have to learn to relax that muscle that involuntarily contracts, that automatic *no* response that keeps you isolated from deep contact.

Since most of you Capricorns are smart, it usually dawns on you that maybe the reason you were a dud in high school was your *own* fear of letting your hair down and having fun—because that *judge* was always standing nearby. Yeah, sure, your mothers restricted your life, but beyond that, there comes a point in every Capricorn life when he or she realizes that (a) success is great, and while thanks to your parents you can't live without it, it certainly ain't everything and (b) success is unachievable when people suppress their personal needs for too long.

It is then that you step bravely into the arena of emotional response. There you are, a great ocean liner in a stormy sea with no radar, but this is where your true strength comes out. As grave and stodgy as you are, you know how to take that plunge into a relationship.

The power and guidance you supply connects your mates permanently to the real world, and they find themselves striving upward, motivated toward achievement, with goals within their grasp they once thought impossible.

Meanwhile, you too, are blossoming like a winter flower, protecting your mate, and, with growing confidence in them, opening up emotionally.

In that mutual safety in the privacy behind the closed doors of the relationship, something wondrous is conceived—the seeds of your future are being planted—a bond that no man or woman can ever put asunder.

Gift Ideas for Capricorns

- The deed to the house. If someone deeds the title of their house over to you in your name, it will give you an idea of their trust in you. And it will give you also a sense of responsibility toward them that you usually need before you can open up emotionally. Giving you security and control will increase your confidence.

- A large pizza with everything on it. This will act as a mandala to remind you of the stomach and all the parts of the body not ruled by the rational mind. It will suggest eating and all the other processes of nature you sometimes like to take a pill to forget. Most of all it will act as a picture of all the gifts of nature, including mushrooms, green peppers, sausage, and even anchovies.

- A comforter your mates knitted themselves. A doll, or a teddy bear. These gifts will evoke happy childhood memories you might not even have, but it will give you something to cuddle with.

- A dangerous gift is a baby bottle. You have so much infantile material buried beneath the surface that if you take one sip from the baby bottle, somebody had better be on hand to call the therapist.

Reading Material for Advanced Capricorns

The Secret Life of the Unborn Child, by Thomas Verny
How to Achieve Compassion and Kindness (available at Buddhist temples)

Guardian Angels: The Couple from *American Gothic*

The *American Gothic* couple guards Capricorn relationships because they stand for long-term commitment. They are not wildly expressive or jubilant, but they do represent firmness and solidity. These two obviously have no social pretentiousness at all.

You Capricorns often need to have your overambition corrected by a relationship with one who helps your career, supports you in your climb, but who reminds you of who you *really* are as a human being. The "American Gothics" are just plain folks from down home. Plain as you please. They took some time out to have their pi'chure took so's they can send 'em on to the kids in the city, but soon's this silly session's over, they've got work to do. There's hay needs stackin', and that pie in the oven' just about to burn.

This couple symbolizes the clear distribution of duties and shared responsibilities of a long-term relationship. We must not look at them and try to determine which of them is the Capricorn, because regardless of who plays which role, the successful Capricorn relationship is the result of hard work and cooperation—both people pulling their weight. This relationship is their enterprise, their business, their farm. Regardless of sex, they pitch in for each other at four A.M. with the milkin', and Mom's been up there patchin' the roof during a thunderstorm more than once. Why, Dad even fed all eight kids from a baby bottle himself for nearly two months when Hannah the goat up and died.

This relationship is their pride and joy. The farm symbolizes the total involvement with which you Capricorns approach your commitments. The American Gothics are not young people—they are chosen because they represent the longevity of every Capricorn relationship. You Capricorns are not the wild honeymooners of the Zodiac. In your relationship, your love for each other grows as the pine trees down at the end of the driveway grow. Can't even see the house from the main road now, but when those trees were planted (a week after the wedding) your knees were higher than they were.

Your guardian angels present an iconography for the strength of your bond. Everything about you suggests endurance through weather, over generations, fruitfulness, tradition, and a deepening of roots as time goes on. You are the symbol of men's and women's social consciousness perfectly integrated with the vastness of nature.

Celebrity Astro Game

You'd be surprised how many ways people reveal themselves in everything they say and do. To sharpen your sensitivity to other people and to learn more about the ways renowned Capricorns handle their deepest relationship issues, look over the following list and pick out the people who interest you most.

Do a little sleuthing about their lives. Observe their actions; listen to what they say in public. The songs they sing, the roles they play, the particular contributions they make, will enlighten you about the relationship patterns of this sign.

Diane Keaton	Carlton Fisk
Jose Ferrer	Jon Voight
Elvis Presley	Donna Summer
Richard Nixon	Ben Kingsley

Martin Luther King, Jr.
Cary Grant
Howard Hughes
Ava Gardner
Humphrey Bogart
Larry Csonka
Hanna Schygulla
Barbara Mandrell

Victoria Principal
Alvin Ailey
Mercury Morris
E. L. Doctorow
David Bowie
Rod Stewart
Muhammad Ali
Dolly Parton

Chapter Eleven

AQUARIUS

The Mirage: The Star!

You Aquarians when you're telling a friend about your partners:

"This is a class act I'm talking about. A class act."

If a prospective mate has a hyphen in his or her last name or a title before it, that's a good start. You Aquarians like class. Pizazz, though, people have to have pizazz if they want to shake you up. They must have that *je ne sais quoi*, that don't-you-recognize-me-I'm-a-star quality that turns heads when they walk down the street and makes the whole world wonder who they are when they come in the room. They don't have to go to Harvard or have a Ph.D., but they must have that special elan, that separates the big people from the little people.

The one with the cigarette holder, poised before the airplane while a photographer snaps their pic—that's the one you Aquarians want. And if they can get up in front of a crowd and captivate them, you are theirs.

You go after them if you think they have class. Of course, you don't always know class when you see it, and you sometimes confuse gold bracelets with taste, but if they're gay and debonair, full of flash and flair, witty and urbane, even if they just spent their junior year abroad, you will follow them around. You'll see them as a dashing cavalier or worldly courtesan, and the more ports of call flash on their jacket lapels, the better.

No matter what they're really like you Aquarians see other people as the romantic lead. You men don't have a lot of confidence usually, and when you try too hard to be romantic, you come off like Alice Cooper doing Rhett Butler. You often stumble over your feet on your way to the bedroom a la Jack Lemmon. With a few exceptions, of course, you Aquarian women do a better imitation of Carmen Miranda than Catherine Deneuve.

So it has to be your partners who dip you on the dance floor. They have to jet around like a big producer. If they're down and out, with their head in cement, they should keep away from you. You expect your partners to perform the entire opera smashingly this evening, no matter what their X-ray report said this afternoon. Though they might feel that they're about to fall off the world, you will see them as unassailably stable—with a few snits and affectations, maybe, but basically a light of unmatchable constancy, brilliance, and warmth. That's what really ropes them in. If they can get you a little closer to show biz, you'll get closer to them.

What gets you totally is their remarkable self-possession and strength. You Aquarians are like boats that have pulled away from their mooring, balloons that have escaped from a little child's hand. What you are looking for is somebody who can pull you back in when you've gone too far out. You're skittish, though, and because of what happened to Icarus, you're scared of melting your wings if you fly too close to the sun.

But you can't resist tanning yourselves in the light of a strong, self-expressive and confident ego. You gain strength from being pulled into its sway; it restores your equilibrium when you've wobbled too far out of orbit. An individual's focused constancy and commanding presence, together with a few well-placed fashion trends that aren't yet fads, will yank you in for a closer look.

The Monster: MussoliniNapoleon

You Aquarians, when you're confronting your mate's ego:

> "Quit acting like a child. It's not going to get you anywhere."

BUT... When they start controlling you, do you guys run! You Aquarians will flee from a mate's ego when it's too inflated. You will not accept being tyrannized and manipulated by tantrums and outbursts that put you at a disadvantage, because you crumble when you see people upset and acting out. So where you once admired bold self-expressiveness, you rebel if you think others are resorting to overdramatized tactics to inhibit or control you.

You may have secretly coveted your some people's cute little devices for getting what they want at the beginning of the relationship, but you really don't approve of the artistic temperament.

And they shouldn't try to turn your mustang into a gelding. If you think they're trying to change you, forget it. You'll bolt through the window, crashing through glass like a Hollywood stuntman in an effort to get away.

Because you are hypersensitive to control, you can blow out of proportion any of a number of what normal people might think are reasonable requests. When they want something from you are not prepared to give, you'll do everything you can to foil their plans, gum up their works, spill your drink on their party clothes. Tyranny frightens you to death, and you perceive it in all kinds of places.

What you once perceived as sophistication and *savoir faire*, you suddenly see as their sickening need for constant admiration, mirroring, and approval. Their flair changes to their vanity, and all at once you see them not as a great-looking package, but as a pastiche of hair dyes and face lifts and insecure bids for compliments.

When you see how they play the crowd to build up an ego that they say is fragile but in reality could surpass the Egyptian pyramids in durability and size, you flee. You think you want a star, but you do *not* adapt well to the role of make-up person who has to dab somebody's face with powder every five seconds, spritz them with hair spray, and whisper "You're terrific, J.C. Just terrific." And you throw up when you hear them say for the nine hundredth time, "You really think so?"

When you get close enough to see your mates preening in that mirror, you may retch, but until you do, you'll never be able to feel how hot they really are, and that's what you Aquarians like—a hot, hot person. The bigger their ego the more alluring they are. Once they've made you fall in love with them, then they start trying to change you, eradicate your precious eccentricities, bring you in line, scrub you behind the ears so you can meet their parents.

Your relationships have to have a slightly offbeat, off-color quality to them and yet you want your partners to try to make you go straight. Even though you're positively fanatical about not getting married, you want someone who will demand that you settle down. But wise partners know they're better off keeping you as the weirdo diversion in their life.

Jack Lemmon and Paul Newman have both been married for a couple of thousand years. But at some point did they have to pass through the test of fire and face the fact that they needed in their lives a strong woman to help keep them centered? Without that force, you Aquarians sometimes pull a John Belushi.

You all make a big deal out of your independence, but you are always looking for someone who supposedly could help you adapt to life on the planet Earth, catch you, and hold you. It's quite a feat, because even though you flirt with strong individuals, when you feel you can't just

wander, when you believe they are threatening to disinte-
grate your precious freedom, you fly. You Aquarian males
have a tough time accepting a relationship if you think it
means castration. And you idealistic Aquarian princesses
will not be happy to find out your father has sold you into
slavery!

The Real Thing: Direction

But not all you Aquarians are so paranoid! Once you get
wind of the fact that relationships don't destroy your talents
at all but develop them, then comes the dawn. Then when
the conductor raises the baton, the first violinist (an Aquarian) is not loudly upwrapping a peanut better and jelly
sandwich but is right there, bow raised and ready to make
beautiful music.

You Aquarians are all looking for strong mothers and
fathers you can give the finger to occasionally. You're odd,
versatile, sexy, in an alien-being-from-the-planet-Uranus
sort of way, and you bring a spark of electricity to a
partner's life that will add spontaneity to any situation he or
she are in. You can change a person's whole life in five
seconds flat by walking in or out. The guy who passes soap
bubbles through an electric current in a laboratory and
turns them into tadpoles is probably an Aquarian. That's
how clever you people are.

Though you're enormously powerful, your energy needs
a field of direction. You're a symphony of possibility in
dire need of an experienced conductor. But you are afraid
your genius will be lost if you obey the maestro's wand. So
while you'll be drawn to your mates for their power to
make you dance, you sometimes resist the legitimacy they
offer. What you cannot resist is their power and potency.
Take Zsa Zsa, for example. She may need a man to keep
her grounded, but when the honeymoon's over does she
start to pull a lot of crazy, infantile stunts? Aquarians often
do that. You want to be part of a great company, but you
will insist on altering the master plan, probably because to

follow anyone's lead reminds you of an autocratic parent you found insufferable. Did Mia Farrow love Frank Sinatra because he was tough and controlling?

Many of you Aquarians are coming from a scene where one parent was trying to run a tight ship, while the other was periodically rocking the boat. You want to be good and behave, and you honestly try not to lead with the left foot at the parade, but from earliest childhood you have been made mindful of the harmful effects of mind control on freedom of speech and thought, so you are trying not to repeat the process.

You don't like to make correlations between your personal relationships and your parents though. You will say that Freud was probably a nice man, but definitely a nut. You prefer to think your behavior is motivated by impulse alone and if one looks much further back than five minutes, one is wasting one's time.

You Aquarians see yourselves as wobbling on stilts, and while you like to focus on some symbol or person to keep you steady, you're really more dedicated to your wobble than to steadiness, so one shouldn't fall into the trap of steadying you too much.

Marriage often makes you do a 180-degree turn, and you find yourself pushing baby carriages, playing canasta, and changing political parties. We can ask ourselves what happened to Ronald Reagan when he married Nancy.

You Aquarians will often knuckle under and for years do exactly what your mates tell you, but then just when they've got all the best china teacups, perfectly balanced on the tray and they're walking into the dining room, guess who bangs through the same door in the opposite direction.

What lies behind your mixed feelings for strong-dominating figures is your attraction/repulsion for direction.

You want to be the controlling one. Sure it's usually for the betterment of mankind and the love of humanity, but you Aquarians want your mates to help you kill off the boss so they can start doing things *your* way.

You know you need a boss, but you hang on so desperately to your love of your so-called freedom, and you're so afraid to sell out, and—God forbid—be normal that you keep throwing off the yoke you put on yourselves.

You're so convinced that your fabulous genius don't-bother-me-with-details-can't-you-see-I'm-composing mentality will be compromised if you go along with the world—i.e. your *mates*, i.e. your mother and father—that you identify them with some mind-controlling despot you must whisper about beneath the stairs with the servants and eventually overthrow.

The Burning Question: Love or Friendship?

You're dying to play in the big leagues love-wise, but you can't always hit the ball quite right. You're so damned scared of getting burned. So you often look for safety in numbers. What your mates think is going to be a little tea for two will turn out to be a picnic for thirty in the park. Many of you Aquarians make great partners, but your incessant triangulating makes it hard sometimes for an intimate love match to work (although the fact that you keep bringing in ringers probably saves the marriage). You can't resist putting yourself at the apex of several triangles at once and being a friend to all.

You don't usually want to hurt anybody, and you are idealistic about how people should all live in harmony and peace and this is the dawning of the Age of Aquarius and everything. But. . you just can't help bringing a "friend" home for dinner, or a stepdaughter from a previous relationship. Or maybe you get your zipper caught on the merry-go-round of someone else's marriage.

Some way, somehow, an Aquarian will always have a gang in the lifeboat, so there will always have to be enough rations for an unexpected guest.

This is the only way you keep survival distance from a partner and keep yourselves from being dragged in and burned to death by what you are afraid might be your mate's flaming ego. So no matter how mad you are about someone, you'll drop little crumbs now and then to let them know about the competition.

You're never comfortable if it's only love. Although it may be your burning desire to be passionately, dramatically, shoot-your-lover's-lover in love, you still play it best when it's more of a friendship. That's when the relationship is true. You have to fall head over heels in love with them, but they can't breathe a word of it to you.

Your mates have to be your ardent lover when you're there for it, but when you're into being their "friend," they have to trust that your passion will return. And when it does, for Pete's sake they shouldn't be at the door with a rolling pin and a polygraph machine. You'll never belong to them, but they must always pretend to be jealous. They just shouldn't call in the loans or escalate the game. You want them to be all over you, but you must pretend to be somewhat uninterested in them while they're the madly adoring over-expressive, overreactive, over-theatrical, melodramatic sweetheart.

But if they act as cool as you do, they'll blow it. Too passionate, and you back off. You don't really respect naivete, so they shouldn't be afraid to whip out the mirrors and gold chains. The trick is to get them to think your whole world rises and sets around them, and then you will unexpectedly prove to them that it indeed does not. Though you desperately wish to have the adventures of characters in romance novels, you actually disapprove of the childish way that people act when they're in love. So often when you're most in love, you pose as a friend. That's how you're most comfortable—just friends—no strings, no attachments, nothing in writing, just hang loose, talk-to-you-soon type thing. It's up to your partner, though, to apply the heat, supply the games and Hollywood glitz, and make you admit you're in love with them.

When you're pretending to be *just friends*, your mates do best to let you be but shouldn't buy your act for a minute. They should respect your distance, because it's positively against your religion to show jealousy. The miracle of you futuristic phonies is that you're every bit as crazy on the subject of love as the rest of us prehistoric children that you are always trying to cope with. Robert Wagner's unending passion for Natalie Wood, Durante's eternal torch for Calabash—big relationships enter your life to show you that while we have to love all human beings, we can't really be in love with more than one at a time.

Falling in love alters the state of all beings. When one is in love, bluebirds tweet around one's head. One's heart hurts deliciously. One's *freedom* seems like just a bunch of cardboard letters spelling out the word, and one feels like Henry Higgins after Eliza Doolittle has ruined his life.

And it happens to every Aquarian alive at some time or other. The vacations you cherished alone become endlessly boring, an evening spent with friends without the mate is torture. The Aquarian miracle is that you have no immunity to this malady. As happy as you think you are as a free agent, you all need one person to be pulling away from and to be drawn to, one who knows you, calls you on your games, pulls you into line when you get too sassy, and can make you do what no one else can—behave.

Nothing frightens you more than giving yourselves emotionally or financially to an unworthy candidate. You act casual and loose, as if you were brought up in Hawaii, because you don't want to commit yourselves wrongly and get stuck with a mean bitch or evil bastard, even though bitches and bastards know how to turn you on.

Beneath your loose-fitting shells, you're a cautious lot, and your question of "Love or Friendship?" is at least in part your way of keeping safe. But to thrive, your relationships always need both.

Ultimate Challenge: Distance vs. Closeness

You jump out of airplanes and bed with equal speed. You'll tell a mate what a highly evolved being you are, whose mission it is to deal lovingly with all people, everywhere. Your path is the highway of humanity, and your door is open to all but because you try so hard to be distant, when you do fall for someone, brother, do you fall.

But you don't play the game of love easily or well. You show your affection by dipping pigtails in an inkwell or hitting someone over the head with a pizza. Sometimes what sounds like a shouted put-down across a dinner table is your version of foreplay. Because you're about as emotional as an astronaut, those who love you must be willing to say hello or good-bye at a moment's notice.

You Aquarians are wrestling with issues of distance and closeness, and there's simply no formula to follow to eliminate this conflict completely. You enter people's lives to force them to hang a little looser, throw an extra plate on the table at the last minute, or take one off.

You definitely want it both ways. You want to know which side of the bed to sleep on, so one shouldn't pull any tricks on you. You are already coping with so much internal unpredictability that you must be able to count on your partners for reliability.

But as far as you are concerned, no matter how tiring your life may be on the third moon of Uranus, you can never give it up. Your purpose is to show others that there are random encounters that will electrify them and change their life. When they're sure they got it all figured out, you come along driving a truck through a red light. In order for them to plug into you, they've got to be able to embrace unexpected change without initiating it.

So when they think they're in for the night with a good book and a piece of chocolate cake, they'll find themselves dashing around at quarter of eight, looking for their black shoes, because you've called to invite them out. And then, too, there will be nights when they're in their formal gear, sitting by the door, when the eleven o'clock news comes on, waiting for you to show up.

They can be sure of one thing. On the planet you come from, marriages take place one minute after two people meet. After that the couple see each other once every seven years. Between times, they communicate by answering machines. During the Aquarian mating season, you are passionate and intense, but five minutes later, you can't remember ever having had sex.

You will give someone a taste of your hottest moments in an airport motel a few minutes before takeoff. Then they'll call you up on the phone the next day and you'll promptly put them on hold for several seconds, minutes, or days.

You are battling to integrate a progressive, open-minded nature with a strong reactionary streak. You want to be far-thinking and futuristic, free from the filthy primitive traits of jealousy and possessiveness. And if you're going to practice what you pray for, you need distance. You've got to be able to go off to New Orleans, or your mate has to be able to go to Central America and nobody has a heart attack or gets hysterical with hives. A relationship that takes the wild bird in human beings and serves it up with cranberries is no relationship for you.

You need your space.

But only partially.

You also need to develop another side—a side that's maybe not so A.D. 3001 and progressive but one that's much more here, in the present, and answering the really frail human need of love, of having someone, that very special person that people who need people still seem to need on a cold night in February.

And that type of connection is not achieved by Telex or electronic mail. To titillate that side of your nature, you Aquarians need your mates there, just an embrace away. To make it with you, they have to be able to be close when you're apart, and be able to cope with some cool distance when you're together.

The Miracle: Loving

Aquarians have to learn to play the lover's game—complete with jealousy, competitiveness, the whole bit. You don't do it well as a rule, but when you deny it, you get lost and fall to the mercy of the sophisticated game players you invariably draw. Your miracle is achieved when you allow yourselves to get close enough to be warmed by being in love without getting fried in the process.

If you're going to be the cool cat who never shows the slightest ruffle over separation, then how can you ever show what you're really feeling? How can you ever *know* what you're really feeling? If everything inside you is created for the express purpose of being able to say good-bye without crying, if you always have to be a perfect brick about everything, what device is needed to break through to achieve the miracle of feeling, warmth, lovingness, and self-expression?

It's hard for you to differentiate between sincere expression and theatrical dramatization, and sometimes while guarding against the cheap imitation, the baby goes out with the bath water. The safe route for you Aquarians is to treat all feeling with the same slightly contemptuous, disdainful sneer. That way everybody's at a safe distance. Nobody takes anything too seriously. Nobody gets hurt.

You pretend so well not to be overemotional, overinvolved. You know that the only people who really get to express themselve in life are those who can throw themselves into the furnace, get melted down, reshaped into something burnished, polished, bright.

A lot of you are frustrated actors, musicians, or artists. Maybe it's because it was too impractical, but you've shrunk away from the creative life. You're not the star but the star's hairdresser. You're not the musician but the musician's teacher. You've perhaps looked upon the volatile artistic temperament as childish, self-indulgent. Maybe you've disapproved of the attention-getting devices of extroverted showpeople, judging them to be superficial and too involved with their own egos. But if you can't deal with the artistic ego, you can't be an artist.

Many of you Aquarians shun love for the same reason —it's too volatile, too emotional, too childish, too unpredictable. But of course you can't stand being on the outside looking in, so self-denial doesn't work. If you deny the ego in yourselves, you'll have to cope with it in a mate, step-children, or anyone whose need for attention mirrors the repression of yours.

You need your moment in the sun, though, your shin-ing, glorious instant. And you can have it as soon as you abandon your I-don't-give-a-damn-I-don't-have-to-suck-up-to-anybody defenses. And then, of course, your shield will be down. You'll be vulnerable. You'll open yourselves up to be hurt, laughed at, smashed, rejected, but oh, the glory of connecting honestly and truly, admitting and ac-knowledging your love of warmth. It's the ground hog squinting in joy at the sunlight, the surfer's great wave, the diva's high C, that pinnacle moment in the teenager's life when she gets to kiss Don Johnson.

When you admit the need for the great experience, your heart center opens like a garden of lotuses in full bloom. Your precious freedom is not lost, then, at all, but found.

You need to accept the performer within, and if you can't cut it as a creator, then you should team up with a self-expressive, outgoing artist and curb the temptation to inhibit him or her. You have to go a little lighter on the Ha! Ha! Love is for saps! routine and quit treating life as if it were a soap opera you are watching while you eat a cheese sandwich. You need to admit that in the bedroom depart-ment you have a lot to learn.

You are led straight to your miracle when you can turn to someone, acknowledge another person for the talents he or she may have, and accept some guidance and direction from people without making fun of it. For all your absurd and transparent defenses, you really can't help falling in love, and once you can face it, you are the closest friend/lover one could ever have. While you'll always need an hour or a night or two alone, the more you show how much you need people, the more your heart will open up. So to start living, all you have to do is be slain by Cupid's arrow and quit pretending it hasn't happened.

Working the Miracle: Coping with Limerence

Limerence: "the state of being in love." Cope with it, Aquarians.

All that Aquarian talk about distance, freedom, and friendship flies out the window when you fall off the Empire State Building in love. You'll carry on like a buddy and a pal but you can't prevent your own miracle from happening. You always overcome your fear of getting roasted alive in the fires of Venus's cute little furnace.

And in your own shy and goofy way, you, too, get to glow. Suddenly the clumsy ostrich becomes a noble crane. You may step on your glasses during the clinch, but somehow it doesn't matter. You've got the lead in life's high school play at last. And you're no longer just the smart kid or the athlete or a gangly brat from the wrong side of the tracks. Loving makes you adult, fills you out, adds a swashbuckling flair to your once awkward advances.

And you're all capable of it. Every one of you worships the Broadway producer, the tap-dancing fool, the rock musician. You aspire to the heights of entertainment but often feel too inhibited, bound by society, or caught in a web of family undoing, to try. But loving elevates you, frees you from your inhibitions, rekindles your sense of urgency to capture life's drama, swinging like Tarzan across the stage just once, and for you, loving is that leap.

It's hard to be in love, because when we are, passion takes precedence over practicality. We become chemically altered; we're not ourselves. We sit by a phone, play stupid games, drive by the person's house ten times until we "accidentally" meet. We pretend not to care, and then stay up all night counting ceiling tiles or smoking.

When we're in love, we're under the other person's spell. We are very, very sick, and the only thing in the world that can heal us is the special someone's simple presence. When we're with the person, we experience a wellness such as we have never known. All your hopes and wishes seem to be in your grasp. Your motivation is up 358 degrees, and we even find ourselves planning for the future.

In the east, the sun is rising, and it's going to be a beautiful day. If it rains, then that's great; the farmers need the rain.

—TWA may buy your company today or, who knows, your show may definitely get produced. All things are possible. All things come to people who taste that feeling of love.

You Aquarians reach out for relationships for precisely these reasons. Oh, you'd be hard put to admit such chemical carryings on. But relationships have been put in your path to perform heart surgery on you. So those involved with you should pull out all the stops. The more wildly they display their talents, the more you will develop. And in return you fly in at the eleventh hour like the cavalry to save your mates from ruin, revitalize their passions, awaken their creativity, and add a new style and sparkle to them. A new hairdo with a total rinse, perhaps, a high-voltage charge that will change them forever, bring them out of their hiding place, crack open their shell, and expose them to the world.

Gift Ideas for Aquarians

- A toy bow and arrow. One can find them in any toy or novelty store. On the arrow, your mates can carve your name. This will let you know that to have a real relationship, business or personal, you have to be gotten.
- An anklet serves the same purpose. The fad is long past, but for a man or a woman it marks not only an amusing out-of-date gift you Aquarians love, but it evokes an era of slavery, brands you with your mate's stamp, and lets you know there's no escape. Of course, the anklet has *their* name on it.
- A solid gold wedding ring is perfect for you. Although you will insist that this archaic piece of ritual jewelry is definitely not for you, it really is.

- An imitation gold-plated wedding band mounted on a stand. It makes an odd conversation piece and will keep you puzzled enough to maintain interest in their bizarre sense of humor.

Reading Material for Advanced Aquarians

The Madness of a Seduced Woman, by Susan Schaeffer
Of Love and Limerence, by Dorothy Tennov

Guardian Angels: The King and Queen of Hearts

 The King and Queen of Hearts symbolize supremacy in romance, the successful playing to and off each other of two adults in love. They symbolize top cards playing together, for high stakes.

They represent the power of being at the top, holding a responsible position and yet not forgetting the need to play. They keep their key spots in society and always remember that life is just a game.

The King and Queen of Hearts suggest also a romantic and chivalrous image, drawn from a time when people acted nobly, full of pomp and glory, when knights competed for their ladies. You Aquarians always aspire to a nobility and dignity that only personal relationships can give you.

But it is always a game, and though the stakes are high, both partners have power. Both are high cards, trump cards, next to each other in strength.

One should not be misled by the fact that the King is a higher card and that because he can take a trick where the Queen is played, she does not have similar power. You Aquarians are keenly aware of male-female competition, and you're not naive enough to think that males don't try to rule over females.

The successful Aquarian relationships are those where the partners rule together, *equally* fifty-fifty, straight down the line. There are always games of control and rebellion in an Aquarian regime. They keep such a relationship alive and dynamic.

But you set up a set of checks and balances so that when your partner takes the trick, exercises control, puts you in a lower position, then it's fair to strike back, pull back, knock down the house of cards, until equality is restored. The King and Queen of Hearts are two trump cards. They are the epitome of social exuberance. They play life not only to win but for the joy of the sport. They symbolize an opening of the heart center, generosity, zest for living that only comes from loving. They personify play.

Celebrity Astro Game

You'd be surprised how many ways people reveal themselves in everything they say and do. To sharpen your sensitivity to other people and to learn more about the ways renowned Aquarians handle their deepest relationship issues, look over the following list and pick out the people who interest you most.

Do a little sleuthing about their lives. Observe their actions; listen to what they say in public. The songs they sing, the roles they play, the particular contributions they make, will enlighten you about the relationship patterns of this sign.

Paul Newman	Alan Alda
Farrah Fawcett	Gene Hackman
Zsa Zsa Gabor	Vanessa Redgrave
Ronald Reagan	Tom Brokaw
Robert Wagner	Natalie Cole
Jack Benny	Gary Coleman

Sonny Bono
Morgan Fairchild
Christian Dior
Linda Blair
Tom Selleck
Angela Davis
Mikhail Baryshnikov

Robert Klein
Mark Spitz
LeVar Burton
Oliver Reed
Burt Reynolds
Chita Rivera
John McEnroe

Chapter Twelve

PISCES

Mirage: Lighthouse in the Fog!

The Piscean motto in relationships:

"Perfection in others!"

You Pisceans love commoners—shoemakers, farmers, seamstresses, and blue-collar workers. You adore labor, you are always looking for the sternest nun in the convent, the toughest cop on the parole board—somebody who's heard it all a dozen times and judges on performance, not excuses.

In the beginning of a relationship, you will salute your captors, immediately acknowledge their superiority and authority, stand at attention—if they say what they mean, mean what they say, and follow through on it. Marine Corps drill sergeants set your heart aflutter, and if your mates let you know that the last thing they believed in was Santa Claus, and that was thirty years ago, they've got you.

Elizabeth Taylor is the ultimate Pisces. Two thousand years from now, her picture will probably be on the Zodiac instead of the traditional fishes. She's been everywhere, done everything, gone to Hell and come back in a fur coat, looking great. She's been sick and gotten well, made it in the world, had lovers, had kids—you name it.

Way back when she met Mike Todd, she was just a gorgeous kid, moved about by directors, publicists, and studio bosses. "Smile! Act sad! Cry! Be sexy! Tell 'em you're just friends. Lean toward the light!"

And here comes Mike Todd. Granted, she had already been married to Nicky Hilton and Michael Wilding, so she wasn't exactly wearing white. But did the hard-driving disciplined call-it-like-you-see-it no-nonsense way Todd had of dealing with the world hit her very hard, as only a Pisces can get hit hard? And did Richard Burton get her in the same way?

You Pisceans are devastated by someone who can restore clarity to the murky realms in which you live. You're overjoyed when you meet a tough little person who knows how to eliminate the squid ink from the sea in which you reside.

When you don't feel like working, of course, you Pisceans simply do not hear the alarm clock. And you all need your share of mental health or bathrobe days. But you love it when you come upon someone who can consistently spring out of bed and be showered in time to wake even the rooster. The word here is *consistency*, because no matter how diligent you try to be, you Pisceans need time off to contemplate your navels. So you have to have a person in your life to empty ashtrays and change the cat litter. That's where your partners come in.

You are dazzled by their industry, awed by their ability to work even when they don't feel like it, and stay awake at their desk without the help of No-Doz. What turns you on is your mates can not only start a project, but finish it.

What you love most is their clarity of vision. They're not distracted every five seconds by something that passes the periphery of their eye. They can shut out so beautifully all the million and one sights and sounds that make your Piscean mind wobble and wander. Their mind boggles your heart, and you love how in one simple sentence they can cut through five hundred pounds of baloney. Their perceptions chop through like a meat cleaver, and you scream with pain and delight. They're so refreshing to you. You have often surrounded yourselves with other indulgent people who not only allow but nurture unproductive fantasies and encourage you to rationalize failure by deriding society.

But the people you snag are different. They're members of society. They're productive. They believe in progress; they even vote. They have a connection to this world that is wholesome and refreshing. There's nothing vague about them. Their body is here; their mind is here. Everything about them is here. You believe they have a clean way of reducing all abstraction to its lowest terms, and you love that. You respond passionately to their power to transcend the malarkey, tear away the dangling participles and double entendres, and get right to the heart, meat, and truth of every sentence. When they nail you to the wall by the seat of your pants, shine the light on you, and make you confess, you pant with ecstasy, because if there's anything a Pisces likes more than sin, it's confession.

Above all, their purity gets you. That they could be so much a part of this world and yet uncorrupted by it. Not only can they function without the help of booze or diet pills, but they are the uncorruptible virgin, faithful, honest, loyal, and true. And they have been brought to you by the universe to help you clean up your act, purify your system, streamline your life, turn your dreams into reality, help you pick your cotton, provide a remedy for what ails you—in short, they're a drop of earthly medicine.

The Monster: Parole Officer!

You Pisces, when charged with capitol crimes by your mate.

"Okay, I'm guilty, now may I please leave."

But ...

When that wonderful helper turns into a Spanish Inquisitor, you dive out the nearest window. What a pill your mates turn out to be. After a while, you find them acting the way Ethel Mertz would act if Fred ever really tried to get romantic. When you find out the depth of their cynicism, you recoil. How much they have to deny their natural self, suppress their emotions, in order to function. They could actually go into an orgy with their math homework under their arm and get it done. At first, such one-pointedness of mind is captivating to you, but soon after, you shrink from the coldness. In fact, that infernal dedication to work often becomes a thorn in your side. It excites you to imagine these highly motivated, busy little bees actually going to save you from your love of procrastination, but when you find out they got their training in the Marines, you go AWOL. Their industry comes between you and your desires. We can contemplate a possible moment when Pat Nixon realized that Richard was going to remain stiff in all the wrong places. When you Pisceans get the feeling that these people are trying to stuff you into a bottle and label it, your tides recede and you see them as petty, confining, and small.

It's natural for them to want to hang on to you, though because you're all so damned irresistible. You Pisceans can make an ugly old maid feel beautiful, so naturally they'll want to just throw a double bed in the dungeon and feed the key to the crocodiles.

But that's when the trouble starts. Once somebody tries to train you, it's all over. And yet didn't you want them to clean up your act? Did Oscar really want Felix to help him put his room in order? When you feel the hook pierce the roof of your mouth, your mates definitely take on a different aspect in your fishy eye. You see them as tragically narrow and repressed, while all about them the real drama of nature is buzzing and humming and tweeting, while they nervously press their knees together and pray for courage to resist.

If they give into your seduction completely, though, you lose respect for them. The closer you get to someone's sharp focus and narrow concentration, the more you admire them. But in the end, you have to admit their lifestyle is not for you. And when you get the sense that they think they know what's better for you than you do, and they're under the absurd impression that they really have you figured out, that's when you feel sorriest for their puny one-dimensional perspective.

You see them as uptight, fidgety, and frigid, lacking in true insight, unforgiving, and ridiculously moralistic. In fact, they may sincerely believe they're keeping up their half of the relationship by being the efficient one who handles things, but after a while you see them as the drudge, a rigidly programmed little drone computer that responds automatically like those toy birds that dunk their beaks in water then pee it out the other end. You begin to see their approach to efficiency as defensive and surprisingly inefficient. What seemed to you like refreshing practicality turns out to be simply another way of avoiding life. You see that they hide in work and that their analytic little brain is busy creating its invincible wall of insulation against feeling. While at one time this may have been attractive, you soon view it as ridiculous.

Though you don't accomplish much while soaking in a bubble bath, you feel it is criminal, the way your partners can take the blossoming lotus that is the universe and just throw it in the freezer with the ice cubes and chopped spinach.

In her meanest, most deflating moments, Alice Kramden, of *The Honeymooners*, symbolizes the worst side of relationships for Pisces. Bitter and cynical, Alice took her frustrations out on Ralph by never allowing him his dreams. She'd been burned. She had shared those dreams once, but fifteen years later, seated in her barren kitchen, she felt she'd been had. So there she stood with a hatpin, whenever Ralph showed signs of hope.

Where once you Pisceans revered clarity and earthly aplomb, you begin to see both those qualities as harsh reminders of what can happen to people who believe more in birth control than they do in birth.

So if your mates are no more than petty, judgmental little bureaucrats with pea-sized minds, afraid to roll up their pants and wade across the stream of life, they can forget you. You are a liver. When you see that they've elected themselves the posse that's going to head you off at the pass and keep you from going where you want to go, you'll disappear before sunup.

Because if there's one thing that scares an eight-foot tuna, it's the possibility of getting divided up neatly into fifty-two cans.

The Real Thing: Being Nailed Down

One shouldn't think you can't be materialistic or ambitious. It's just a lot nicer if somebody else can do the boring work. And one should never try to cram you into the cage of reality.

Was your imagination encouraged by one parent, crushed by another? Are you trying to prove that you don't have to be bourgeois to be happy?

What frightens you Pisceans is the danger of becoming one thing at the expense of something else. It's your blessing and your curse, of course. What lies behind your rejection of the material universe is not irresponsibility but a resistance to being categorized. You don't want to be known as just a butcher or baker. You Pisceans look upon your mates as monsters if they make you account for every move and thought for the past thirty days and project your activities, thoughts, and menus for the next thirty.

You need clearly defined limits and deadlines. But your cosmic purpose is to infiltrate and undermine every system. That's why you make your teachers fall in love with you—just to erode all the rules and regulations. You cannot be confined to one simple identity. Life on Earth is clumsy and trivial.

You are ambivalent not only about achievement and wealth in this life but existence itself. You do believe that you did not choose to be alive but that one day you were out for a walk in Heaven and fell through the clouds. So you don't actually enjoy being followed around with a clipboard and a tape recorder. You're not really a shirker, but the more your partners press and quote the vows you once made, the more you'll prove that vows were made to be broken.

Though you are stimulated by the thought of a ruler across your knuckles, you recoil from discipline without compassion. One shouldn't quote canon to a Pisces. Though you respect dogma and yearn for the achievement of seeing something through, you know you can never be attached to success.

This makes you sigh a lot. You will drive your mates completely crazy if they pin you down and ask you what you really want. You'll start fidgeting with the tablecloth and looking off to the right. You know you cannot be motivated by the trappings of culture. What happens to you has to come to you naturally, on the inside, like relief from gastric indigestion.

Your sometimes propensity for substance abuse is not so much your escape from a person as it is your escape from life on Earth itself. If somebody corners you, you'll flee into yourselves. If they wave the contract in your face you'll smile and tell them to sue you. One shouldn't ever doodle around with you or try guile. You've got enough guile for you and two thousand mates.

Yes, you'd like to turn your gas into a solid, but you're really no good for anything if once in a while you can't just dissolve, liquefy, vaporize, and simply vanish.

But people refuse to let you change your state. They try to hold you. Of course, you've sought them out because you want the most concrete, most specific relationship possible; you look for the most exacting person, with a thermometer in one pocket and a calculator in another. You force him or her, ever so subtly, to cruise around after you in their squad car and pick up the clothes you've dropped somewhere between your birth and the bedroom, but then you can't abide the constant surveillance, the reporting, the judgment.

You love being nailed down. If one gives a Pisces a specific task, one sees a true artist at work. No detail too small, no job too big.

The problem is the *consistency* involved with the completion of the task or the endless repetitions necessary to perfect a craft. It's picayune, stunting, paralyzing; you can't hack it.

You seek out relationships to help you get your shit together, only to realize that you have to do things your own way in your own time, and if it takes 3.2×10^{23} lifetimes, so be it.

You live always in the gulf between high-powered efficiency and sloth, and that's where your relationships are spawned.

The Burning Question: Why Work at Anything?

When one thinks of how maddening it could well have been to be Hamlet's girlfriend, it's not surprising that Ophelia killed herself! You Pisceans drive everyone crazy with your endless musing about the absurdity of existence. Yet when you hook into something or someone, you're a total zealot. You are totally dedicated to anything that strikes your religious fancy. In fact, you make great slaves, because you give yourselves totally and completely and unconditionally, more fully than Jerry Lewis gives himself to the telethon.

But it's best not to remind you of your commitments or make you at all self-conscious of what you are doing. It's much better to pretend to ignore a lot with you. Your loved ones have to know when to act unconscious. If they rub your nose in your actions, you'll automatically make mistakes. You cannot be bought or bribed for very long. In your heart you know nothing lasts forever, so you are not moved if somebody flashes last year's Valentine before you while reading, between sobs, what you wrote to them then.

You see yourselves as cosmic dough looking for shape. But just as you're about to be popped into the oven, you'll jump off the cookie sheet. You are always asking, questioning, doubting, considering life in California while building a house in Duluth. You want reality. You crave a practical outlet. But your mates should not be led into believing it's forever. You come into their lives when it's time for them to expand their spiritual awareness. Unfortunately, sometimes it doesn't happen until after someone has bopped you over the head with a frying pan and tossed you into the street. Even if you try to make them think they're going to clear up your life for you, they shouldn't bite that bait. The happiest Piscean is a little sad.

The question every Pisces relationship must answer eventually is Why work at anything?

You Pisceans see clearly through the tricks of civilization's slavemasters. You see the hordes of mindless masses chained to a system that certainly won't last much longer. The masters create products for the slaves to buy, then give them jobs in the factories that produce the products, in order for them to earn money to buy those products so they have to keep working—and so on. No way will you Pisceans just knuckle under and start marching in the zombie parade. And yet your dream is to fill some useful purpose in this useless world.

Not all you Pisceans are depressed, however. You simply cannot raise the enthusiasm for the fleeting interests and whims that catch the fancy of most people, and certainly refuse to be fooled by what society tells you to be excited about. You know better.

Many of you have jobs and wear neck ties and bras and do everything you are required to do. You want to do right, and you absolutely hate to make a mistake. So sometimes you'd rather do nothing than fail.

And yet in every relationship, work issues arise . . . the value of work, who works harder, what work is, and especially what the hell is the point of making anything work —even a relationship.

You often keep your work life separate from what you consider to be your *real* life, separate because you see yourselves as true spiritual artists, and sometimes you confuse any form of commercialism with a criminal human rendering of divine inspiration. So you are torn between the purely artistic life and a utilitarian's view of the world —your mate, of course, being engaged by you to represent the dour, dowdy, uninspired utilitarian's end of the dialogue.

A Piscean relationship that works, then, works because of common attitudes about work and an agreed-upon system of division of labor.

Ultimate Challenge: Reality vs. Romance

If your partners didn't need a little jazzing up, they wouldn't have attracted you in the first place. You're there to add a touch of human compassion to the scene. You come into a mate's romantic life to add glamour and intoxication. And he or she got to be able to float belly-up on a sea of uncertainty.

You Pisceans are big by nature. You have glamorous and grandiose views of your potential, even though you are shy, self-demeaning, and timid. You need your mates to bring you down, but you are going to fight it all the way. Does reality kill romance? Ask Carly Simon. Is her relationship with James Taylor a good example of where intoxication and glamour can lead?

People often get drunk on you when they have to learn *how* to be intoxicated, and you move toward them when it's time to go straight.

You Pisceans love to give things up for Lent, because yours is a long battle between indulgence and discipline. And when you cook for your mates, they'll often find cigarette ashes in the brown rice. Emotionally, it's a similar story. You can't quite decide which life-style is better— Louis XIV or a twelfth-century monk. You want your partner to put you on a diet of steamed vegetables and hard labor, but you will have to sneak off to the john for a puff of escape.

You highly evolved Pisceans have a healthy respect for the physical world as we know it, can move about freely here, interact with humans, *not* have the phone company threatening to terminate every other month and enjoy the fruits of earthly life without either fasting six out of seven days or ending up in a detox center.

The happiest of you Pisceans file taxes, pay the IRS some years, sometimes not. The challenge you must rise to is, of course, *mundane reality.* Not reality in the we-are-all-one-in-the-universe sense but reality as defined by the term get-up-at-six-and-drive-a-taxi.

You undisciplined Pisceans live in a world of extremes. You stuff yourselves, you starve yourselves. You indulge yourselves in slothful self-pity, then force yourselves over hot coals of self-abnegation. You wander aimlessly into the dream state of what would, could, and should be, then end up scrubbing floors. You go from glamorous fantasy to harsh reality, from dreaming about being a movie star or living barefoot in the Canary Islands to the wearying work-aday routines of real life. You need a balance between your dream life and your real one.

Once you've developed that balance on your own, you don't need your mate to pour a pitcher of cold water on your dreams. Because if you get them to act out the role of policeman, you'll ultimately have to reject them. You'll tend to see them as the smart one, you as the pretty one, so the contest for supremacy will often be between beauty and brains. But it will always be murky, so don't look for clarity. You are a master of the subtle reference, indirect suggestion. You gentle creatures will love *somebody* forever if they blurt out the truth as they see it. But you will ultimately teach them that truth is multifaceted and any attempt to draw a bottom line about the truth is not only vulgar but stupid. They shouldn't push it, either, because if they totally smash your view of life, you'll bring them down.

Through relationships you are trying to add a little levelheadedness to your deep inner drive—which is to put a sombrero over your eyes, sit under a banana tree, and meditate until things get better. You're sharp, though, and most of you are so conscious of your own tendency to cop out and escape that you'll purposely put yourselves in highly structured, highly disciplined situations, challenging yourselves—if your *mates* don't— to stick with a job just to prove you can do it.

Deep in your heart you are striving to hold on to the belief that life is a mystery, revealing itself slowly. It can never be known totally and certainly must be accepted as the mystery unravels. But you are always madly attracted to nuts and bolts people who want to know who, what, where, when, how, and how much. You Pisceans are drawn to the pragmatists of the world, to those who want to do it all, but with the light on and only for five minutes —no tricks, no shadows.

You Pisceans search for that delicate equilibrium between your gentle, personal existence and the harsh exigencies of the outer world. You don't mind feeling along blindly, being moved by the currents of fate. There's a spiritual correctness to the knowability of life, so what seems like a pointless, aimless drift to some is to you the way nature intended things to be. But you need also to be in the world, maintain a healthy body and function in a society that for all its modern appliances seems ridiculously cumbersome and outdated to you. Your success in relationships comes when you find the compromise between aimless drift and mundane purpose.

You believe in the inevitability of the unforeseen contingency. Nobody can predict how they will feel at some future time. And yet you crave dedication, completion, commitment. Only through cooperation with a world full of practical people can you achieve this balance.

The Miracle: Unfaltering Dedication

Despite your million and one fears of failure, you Pisceans
are the zealots of the world. You lose heart every hour on
the half hour, question your own worth on the hour while
an undercurrent runs through the whole thing—isn't life
ridiculous?

Funny, though, nobody loves life the way you Pisceans
do. You're touched by life's incessant tragedy in a way that
makes you a natural in any human endeavor that requires
feeling and empathy, from music to acting to fund-raising
for the sick and dying. You're amused by life's stupidity,
and so you can participate in absolutely anything, totally
and fully, by rolling your eyes heavenward and crossing
your fingers.

In the dark moments, it's hard for you to stay on track,
though, because when you see a partner's ardor for a task
that seems trivial and niggling, you tend to drop out, and
there's nothing anyone can do about it. That sometimes
means that a mate will be picking five bushels to your one.
In those moments of doubt, you will stray, wander, falter,
and deviate, and you need to strive at those times to stick
with somebody whose unflagging efforts could be a lesson
well learned.

You Pisceans bring to every relationship a scope your
mates would never have without you, and you teach a
partner how to throw away the book and rely on the inner
guides of inspiration and intuition. What you get from a
relationship is an inspiration of another kind.

Once you see the value of working and living health-
fully in the human world, you can fling yourselves into any
task and see it to completion. Once you have assimilated
(not with your mind, in which you wisely have absolutely
no faith) the use, value, and function of moving whole-
somely about in the world, you are a total giver. You as-
sume a vigorous blend of spiritual mission and tireless
practical labor that leads always to a plentiful harvest.

But you need to be able to allow your partner to help you bring your dreams into reality. You Pisceans get bored. Reality as we mortals know it is awkward for you. Once you get the gist of the blueprints, the real house doesn't have to be built. So you need people to help you see the value not only in dreaming of an orchard but in actually harvesting the fruit. (You will definitely want help with that job.) You need people to edit your lofty verse, trim away grandiosity, and occasionally haul you into a cold shower of truth.

You need to look upon attention to physical detail not as an abhorrent conundrum of fretfulness and worry but as a way of mastering a craft and perfecting a skill. You admire consistent, persistent drive, but without relationships, your own zeal flags. You are endlessly rethinking your position, reevaluating your job or position in the world, clarifying your actions and justifying your system, all while truly believing that none of it matters anyway, all while checking the stock quotations in the paper.

At very worst your relationships mimic a tired and weary dialogue between cynic and religious mystic, rebellious addict and disapproving therapist, sinner and saint.

To achieve your miracle of unflagging dedication you need to develop a consistent approach to everyday living. You need to master simple skills, perfect simple crafts, and maintain yourselves on an even level of functioning. This you learn from your relationships with creatures you once thought trivial and small. Once you are awakened, it is through your exposure to simple, hardworking folk that you then lead yourselves toward the excellence to which you aspire. You need a very real, very simple teacher to help you fuse into your baroque scheme a humble simplicity that leads to mastery.

Working the Miracle: Transformation by Example

One shouldn't make the mistake of thinking it's you who are the lazy, self-indulgent one. In a crisis, you could out-work 150 Virgos on diet pills. If someone is involved with you, their burning issue is just as much romance vs. reality as yours is.

One should not be led into the illusion that you people are consumptive weaklings who just love the feeling of sand being kicked in your face. Though you do get excited from the sight of a person in a uniform, you have definite limits to how much abuse you will take. Contrary to popular astrological mythology, you are *not* pitiable vegetables who can't get from the bed to the bedpan without help.

You've got plenty of good reasons why effort is useless, and you've got more compassion for yourselves than you'll ever really have for your partner. One shouldn't start whining to you about one's problems. Your Piscean motto is "Perfection in others." And you will not tolerate for a second escapist self-indulgence in any of your lovers, co-workers, or therapists. You can and will motivate your mate to achievement better than you could ever motivate yourselves.

You have unfaltering dedication despite all your horsing around. When the chips are down, your fears and prejudices vanish, and you always rally at the eleventh hour. In fact, that's the only time you hear the clock.

You do not wish to fail and are not necessarily socio-pathic. You're full of paranoia about government plots to poison the drinking water with mind-control drugs and full of disdain for the artists who sell out to the networks. Some of you Pisceans sit at the bar at three A.M. and tell people you invented the microwave back in the fifties but didn't get it patented because you knew it was harmful to humans. It insults your aesthetic even to consider existing in a culture that could even conceive of leisure suits or instant pudding.

Even if you have to come back from a state of advanced toxemia, though, you people are the purists and workers of this world. You've been everywhere, done everything, seen and sniffed it all, so nothing one can ever wave in front of your nose tempts you for long. You've followed every carrot there is. And for all your professed idealism, you know you have a streak of cynicism that would move even Alice Kramden to tears. You can and do keep jobs for years. Your practicality in regard to relationships is truly astonishing. It's amazing how long you'll keep a mate on if he or she help with the housework. One shouldn't be dismayed by your dramatic withdrawals. If one waits long enough, there will always be a humble return, because of all the signs, you Pisceans are the most dedicated partners *to people whose motives are pure*. You'll test a mate out, but if his or her heart is simple and true, you'll eventually prove to such a person that there is indeed a forever.

One should never think one can get a Pisces to do anything. You will all make it look as if you are capitulating, when in fact you got someone else to get you to do what you wanted to do in the first place, so that way it will be their responsibility if you either marry or divorce.

You'll jump at the chance to let them convert you, but such a conversion rarely lasts, so the miracle of dedication can only be accomplished not by proselytizing, badgering, or manipulating but by letting you come to the truth—whatever the truth for you is—on your own. You Pisceans do things you believe in completely beautifully and well and totally. Not just *believe* but *believe in*.

You will believe anything you're told. If someone says something with total conviction, you have no reason to doubt it, so you'll usually go along with it because the person was articulate and convincing.

But for you to believe *in* someone it has to be by example over the long haul. You'll test them, refute them, undermine, betray, and desert them a thousand times until you see the beauty and strength of their own dedication. And then, when you've seen the depth of the person's commitment to their life and work, when you contemplate their sincerity and effectiveness, then you take up their banner and fly it forever.

First they have to stick to their guns in spite of every destructive test you put them through. You'll play the heavy, the sinner, the impossible, irrational, unreasonable one, as a way of putting them through a ghastly spiritual exercise.

But then, it's over, and you follow them more loyally and zealously than they could have ever wished for. They shouldn't try to trick you into it. When you have experienced the purity of their heart, you return, more loyal and faithful than ever. And at that point the grapes will fill the vines.

Gift Ideas for Pisces

- An apple, real or wax. This symbolizes Pisceans need to shine up to the teacher, be a good student and learn lessons, do homework, and behave for the teacher. It symbolizes also the fruits of a harvest.

- A nice orchard or vineyard in northern California or southern France. You could work the farm when you feel like it, just drink the wine when you don't. You Pisceans are peasants at heart, happiest when working, but you have a confused notion of yourself as part of the leisured class, so owning a farm could give you your much-needed air of being the landed gentry while providing you with your much-needed ambience of back-breaking work.

- A gingerbread cookie mold makes a nice Piscean gift— preferably in the shape of a person. This will let you know that your mate knows you are one person and one person only and that they intend to make sure you stay in that mold till you're fully baked.

Reading Material for Advanced Pisceans

The Grapes of Wrath, by John Steinbeck
How Green Was My Valley, by Richard Llewellyn
Crime and Punishment, by Feodor Dostoevsky

Guardian Angels: A Pair of Street Musicians

 A pair of street musicans watch over your relationships because they symbolize the carefree joy of artists flinging themselves onto the mercy of fate, borne along by the exultation and dedication to their art. They do not perform in a vacuum or confine their music to the ears of an esoteric few. This is selfless community service in its purest form—a rolled-up-sleeves attempt to bring joy into the world of the working masses.

There they stand in the heat of summer, the cold of winter, singing and playing, untouched by the elements of weather or the ignoring attitudes of the passersby.

You Pisceans are ever looking for a person to help take your talents, make you practical, turn you outward, translate your inner songs into useful language. These guardian angels are not just paragons of selflessness, utterly depersonalized or removed from society. The street musicians want recognition, and they are out there, doing it, facing possible failure, defeat, and rejection, never knowing where their next meal will be coming from.

But it always comes. The music, coming from deep within the heart, always reaches the ears it's supposed to reach, and suddenly the upturned hat that sits on the sidewalk is filled with silver coins and green bills. The street musicians preach nothing. Their song speaks for them. Their very existence combats the dereliction and hopelessness that apathy always engenders. Despite your apocalyptic dialectic and firm stand against society's fleeting and foolish values, you Pisceans cannot silence your own exultant song.

Together this pair of wandering troubadours personify the work ethic and personal productivity. Though they are misfits and stand at the edge of society, they make a unique contribution.

Celebrity Astro Game

You'd be surprised how many ways people reveal themselves in everything they say and do. To sharpen your sensitivity to other people and to learn more about the ways renowned Pisceans handle their deepest relationship issues, look over the following list and pick out the people who interest you most.

Do a little sleuthing about their lives. Observe their actions; listen to what they say in public. The songs they sing, the roles they play, the particular contributions they make, will enlighten you about the relationship patterns of this sign.

Liz Taylor
Joanne Woodward
Pat Nixon
Ted Kennedy
Desi Arnaz
James Taylor
Mikhail Gorbachev
Julius Erving
George Harrison
Ron Howard

Laraine Newman
Tom Wolfe
Jim Rice
Liza Minnelli
Wally Schirra
Andrew Young
Deborah Raffin
Judd Hirsch
Patrick Duffy
Rudolf Nureyev
Daryl Strawberry

Part Two

THEORIES AND PRACTICES

Chapter Thirteen

THE ASTROLOGY BEHIND IT ALL

Now the fun starts.

By this time you've read through your own sign and the signs of those people you're most interested in. You've had many insights into your behavior and theirs, and it's been right on the money.

But not quite.

In some places you may have seen traits of other people in the chapter that was supposed to belong to you and then were able to find yourself described under signs you thought you had nothing to do with. Yet we *have* covered a lot of ground so far, and if you close the book right now, you will still have already uncovered solid material you could use and work on in your relationships for the next thirty years.

Up to this point we've been dealing with your Sun Sign only, the Sign of the Zodiac appearing to house the sun during the month in which you were born. We could scrutinize all the other bodies of the solar system as deeply—

Mercury, Venus, Mars, Jupiter, Saturn, Uranus, Neptune, and Pluto. We could then study the Moon's position as well. At that point we could examine the contacts the planets have to one another. Then we would have a much deeper understanding of your relationship patterns.

So you can see that this book is certainly not the last word on astrology and relationships. Volumes have already been written by serious students of astrology on the comparison of the horoscopes of two individuals, astrological compatibility, sign-to-sign combinations, and many other related subjects.

Without getting too technical, we should make some statements here about why an astrological view of a person can allow so many observations about how that person will behave in relationships. And then we can fine-tune the material you already have. We'll

A. dig a little deeper into every sign and see how the month, date, and year of your birth alter the general influences we've already described.
B. find the Rising Sign and cut to the very core of relationship patterns.
C. do a little predicting for the final fifteen years of the twentieth century so you can test the material you've been reading against the events in your own life.
D. include a technical chart for the real astrology fiends in the audience.

Why does it work? If you believe that we're here on Earth to eat a lot of sugar and drive fast cars, then certainly you can't take astrology seriously. When you start thinking about who or why your astrological chart could possibly describe so accurately your traits and patterns in relationships, you're faced with some pretty confusing philosophical issues.

If you're "you" because of your astrological chart, then where exactly does childhood fit in? Why do you have that particular horoscope, and why did you end up in that particular family?

Astrological lore tells us that human beings, as well as all other creatures on the Earth, are following a path of evolutionary transformation. This is hard to believe when one wanders through a busy shopping mall on Saturday morning, but we are all indeed moving toward greater consciousness and awareness all the time. Every reality we know to be real is, in fact, unreal—just a mask that humanity wears as it travels down this path of consciousness. Why we're traveling or where we're going, nobody knows. We're all at different places along this road, and astrology measures where one is. Your horoscope, a map of the positions of the planets and stars when you were born, describes your personal path.

But why enter the world when you did, and why pick the parents you picked? Go to India and ask a holy man. Maybe he can tell you how or why souls get to choose their respective parents before they enter the world. It's really quite a colorful alternative to Freudian theory, I assure you.

No matter what religion you were raised in or what belief system you currently hold, you confront the ultimate *why?* and eventually reach the most frustrating *because*. This is something all people must find for themselves.

The mechanics of astrology, on the other hand, are another story. The various mirages, monsters, and miracles I've conjured up are based on my observations of people over the last twenty or so years. Unless you just got off a UFO, you probably know what your Birth Sign, or Sun Sign, is—the Sign of the Zodiac the Sun appeared to be passing through during the month you were born. Because the sun is so much larger than the other bodies of the solar system, it is the one giant factor we use in determining your patterns.

But it is just one factor. From it we've already been able to see a lot. The kinds of people you draw to you will always reflect the inner requirements we've outlined in the previous chapters. But all the planets of the solar system interact with the sun as they move about the sun. In addition, the Earth rotates about its own axis, and this twenty-four-hour motion forms further celestial relationships with the rest of the cosmos. When you were born and where on Earth you were born determine these factors—and we can summarize them into one and call it your *Rising Sign*.

If you're an astrology fiend, these concepts and terms are familiar to you. But if you're a novice, you're probably only going to be interested in how all these astrology terms and theories and beliefs get translated into practical terms for your relationships.

To help you, we've prepared a chart to deepen your knowledge of yourself in relationships and increase your skill in the delightful and hair-raising game of human interaction. Some sections you read may contradict others you have already read, and the art of synthesis and interpretation is not one you can master by sitting down and reading one book. What you're reading here is one one-thousandth of what can be said about astrology and relationships—Venus and Mars together, for example, the Nodes of the Moon, etc. So let's look a little deeper.

Digging Deeper

QUESTION: When is a Taurus a Cancer?
ANSWER: When Saturn is in Scorpio.

The above question and answer is a complicated astrological way of saying that when major planets transit, that is, pass through signs opposite your Sun or Rising Sign, they will produce certain significant effects in your behavior toward relationships. The transits of a major planet through various signs of the Zodiac will reflect the needs you'll have and the demands you'll make on other people.

When Saturn passes in opposition to your Sign, for example, you will act like a Cancer because Saturn has special effects on Cancerian relationships. In the above example, since Scorpio is opposite Taurus in the Zodiac, when Saturn is in Scorpio, Tauruses will exhibit Cancerian characteristics. When Jupiter is opposite to your Sun or Rising Sign you will seem in many ways like a Gemini in your attitudes toward partners because Jupiter has special effects on Geminis. Uranus will give you a Leo flavor, Neptune will add a touch of Virgo, and Pluto will make you act like a Taurus, all for the same reasons as described above.

To give you added insight into those changing influences, we've chosen five planets to examine, to show you how they provide you with mirages, monsters, challenges, and miracles—other than those that you have already discovered assigned to your Sign (and the Signs of the people you're having relationships with).

When the Earth is in line between Jupiter and the sun, for example, it will give a Gemini twist to your relationships, no matter what sign you are. If Saturn lay on one side of the Earth and the sun on the other when you were born, you'll have a touch of the sign Cancer in your relationships and should read the section on Cancer as well. Uranus in a similar position will add Leo qualities to you, Neptune will make you see people the way a Virgo does, and Pluto, when it and the sun are in opposition, will add a Taurus dimension to all the major relationships you form, and you should read Taurus as well.

All the positions of these five planets for the twentieth century are accounted for, so all you have to do is find the period during which you were born and read the appropriate sections. Look through the charts carefully. Some of the dates seem to jump around and you might find your date in more than one category.

The more signs you are asked to read about, the more complicated your relationship life will probably be. That stands to reason, of course. The greater number of mirages, monsters, and miracles you're dealing with, the more complex will be the individuals you need to draw unto yourself.

Also, if you're born exactly right on the beginning or ending dates of any given period, by all means go to an astrologer and get it figured out exactly. If planetary positions changed radically around the time you were born, you'll require even greater challenges and changes in your relationships, and you shouldn't fiddle around in areas you don't know about. Rather than fidget with guesswork, you would do well to put yourself in the hands of a competent professional.

Remember:

The more sections you are asked to read, the more you will act like different signs in your relationships. This means your needs in people will be more complex. This reflects ambivalence and indicates that you are drawing people who are either only partially available or sending you mixed messages.

These people are those you have chosen to draw to yourself in order to experience growth and learning through dealing successfully with their complexity.

Here are the charts:

If you want to dig deeper into	*for the following time periods*	read section titled
ARIES	Transit: Jupiter in Libra	GEMINI

oct 11, 1909–nov 11, 1910
sep 25, 1921–oct 25, 1922
sep 10, 1933–oct 10, 1934
aug 25, 1945–sep 24, 1946
dec 13, 1956–feb 18, 1957
aug 7, 1957–jan 12, 1958
mar 20, 1958–sep 6, 1958
nov 15, 1968–mar 29, 1969
jul 15, 1969–dec 15, 1969
apr 30, 1970–aug 14, 1970
oct 27, 1980–nov 26, 1981
oct 10, 1992–nov 9, 1993

Transit: Saturn in Libra	CANCER

oct 7, 1921–dec 19, 1923
apr 6, 1924–sep 12, 1924
nov 20, 1950–mar 6, 1951
aug 13, 1951–oct 21, 1953
sep 21, 1980–nov 28, 1982
may 6, 1983–aug 23, 1983

Transit: Uranus in Libra	LEO

sep 28, 1968–may 19, 1969
jun 24, 1969–nov 20, 1974
may 1, 1975–sep 7, 1975

Transit: Neptune in Libra	VIRGO

oct 3, 1942–apr 16, 1943
aug 2, 1943–dec 23, 1955
mar 12, 1956–oct 18, 1956
jun 15, 1957–aug 5, 1957

If you want to dig deeper into	*for the following time periods*	*read section titled*
	Transit: Pluto in Libra	**TAURUS**
	oct 5, 1971–apr 16, 1972 jul 30, 1972–nov 4, 1983 may 18, 1984–aug 27, 1984	
TAURUS	Transit: Jupiter in Scorpio	**GEMINI**
	nov 11, 1910–dec 9, 1911 oct 26, 1922–nov 23, 1923 oct 11, 1934–nov 8, 1935 sep 25, 1946–oct 24, 1947 jan 13, 1958–mar 19, 1958 sep 7, 1958–feb 9, 1959 apr 24, 1959–oct 4, 1959 dec 16, 1969–apr 29, 1970 aug 15, 1970–jan 13, 1971 jun 5, 1971–sep 10, 1971 nov 27, 1981–dec 25, 1982 nov 10, 1993–dec 8, 1994	
	Transit: Saturn in Scorpio	**CANCER**
	dec 20, 1923–apr 5, 1924 sep 13, 1924–dec 1, 1926 oct 22, 1953–jan 11, 1956 may 14, 1956–oct 9, 1956 nov 29, 1982–may 5, 1983 aug 24, 1983–nov 16, 1985	
	Transit: Uranus in Scorpio	**LEO**
	nov 21, 1974–apr 30, 1975 sep 8, 1975–feb 16, 1981 mar 20, 1981–nov 15, 1981	
	Transit: Neptune in Scorpio	**VIRGO**
	dec 24, 1955–mar 11, 1956	

If you want to dig deeper into	for the following time periods	read section titled
	Transit: Neptune in Scorpio	VIRGO
	oct 19, 1956–jun 14, 1957 aug 6, 1957–jan 3, 1970 may 3, 1970–nov 5, 1970	
	Transit: Pluto in Scorpio	Read Taurus twice!
	nov 5, 1983–may 17, 1984 aug 28, 1984–jan 15, 1995 apr 21, 1955–nov 9, 1995	
GEMINI	Transit: Saturn in Sagittarius	CANCER
	dec 2, 1926–mar 14, 1929 may 5, 1929–nov 29, 1929 jan 12, 1956–may 13, 1956 oct 10, 1956–jan 4, 1959 nov 17, 1985–feb 12, 1988 jun 10, 1988–nov 11, 1988	
	Transit: Uranus in Sagittarius	LEO
	jan 1, 1900–dec 19, 1904 feb 17, 1981–mar 19, 1981 nov 16, 1981–feb 14, 1988 may 27, 1988–dec 1, 1988	
	Transit: Neptune in Sagittarius	VIRGO
	jan 4, 1970–may 2, 1970 nov 6, 1970–jan 18, 1984 jun 23, 1984–nov 20, 1984	
	Transit: Pluto in Scorpio	TAURUS
	jan 16, 1995–apr 20, 1995 nov 10, 1995–dec 31, 1999	

If you want to dig deeper into	*for the following time periods*	*read section titled*
	Transit: Jupiter in Sagittarius	Read Gemini twice!
	dec 10, 1911–jan 1, 1913	
	nov 24, 1923–dec 17, 1924	
	nov 9, 1935–dec 1, 1936	
	oct 24, 1947–nov 14, 1948	
	feb 10, 1959–apr 23, 1959	
	oct 5, 1959–feb 29, 1960	
	june 10, 1960–oct 25, 1960	
	jan 14, 1971–june 4, 1971	
	sept 11, 1971–feb 5, 1972	
	july 24, 1972–sept 24, 1972	
	dec 26, 1982–jan 18, 1984	
	dec 9, 1994–jan 2, 1996	
CANCER	Transit: Jupiter in Capricorn	GEMINI
	jan 19, 1901–feb 5, 1902	
	jan 2, 1913–jan 20, 1914	
	dec 18, 1924–jan 5, 1926	
	dec 2, 1936–dec 19, 1937	
	nov 15, 1948–apr 11, 1949	
	jun 27, 1949–nov 29, 1949	
	mar 1, 1960–jun 9, 1960	
	oct 26, 1960–mar 14, 1961	
	aug 12, 1961–nov 3, 1961	
	feb 6, 1972–jul 23, 1972	
	sep 25, 1972–feb 22, 1973	
	jan 19, 1984–feb 5, 1985	
	jan 3, 1996–jan 20, 1997	
	Transit: Uranus in Capricorn	LEO
	dec 20, 1904–jan 29, 1912	
	sep 4, 1912–nov 11, 1912	
	feb 15, 1988–may 26, 1988	
	dec 2, 1988–mar 31, 1995	
	jun 9, 1995–jan 11, 1996	

If you want to dig deeper into	for the following time periods	read section titled
	Transit: Neptune in Capricorn	VIRGO
	jan 19, 1984–jun 22, 1984 nov 21, 1984–jan 28, 1998 aug 23, 1998–nov 26, 1998	
	Transit: Saturn in Capricorn	Read Cancer twice!
	mar 15, 1929–may 5, 1929 nov 30, 1929–feb 23, 1932 aug 13, 1932–nov 19, 1932 jan 5, 1959–jan 2, 1962 feb 13, 1988–june 9, 1988 nov 12, 1988–feb 5, 1991	
LEO	Transit: Jupiter in Aquarius	GEMINI
	feb 6, 1902–feb 19, 1903 jan 21, 1914–feb 3, 1915 jan 6, 1926–jan 17, 1927 dec 20, 1937–may 13, 1938 jul 30, 1938–dec 28, 1938 apr 12, 1949–jun 26, 1949 nov 30, 1949–apr 14, 1950 sep 15, 1950–nov 30, 1950 mar 15, 1961–aug 11, 1961 nov 4, 1961–mar 24, 1962 feb 23, 1973–mar 7, 1974 feb 6, 1985–feb 19, 1986 jan 21, 1997–feb 3, 1998	
	Transit: Saturn in Aquarius	CANCER
	jan 19, 1903–apr 12, 1905 aug 17, 1905–jan 7, 1906 feb 24, 1932–aug 12, 1932 nov 20, 1932–feb 13, 1935 jan 3, 1962–mar 23, 1964	

If you want to dig deeper into	*for the following time periods*	*read section titled*
	Transit: Saturn in Aquarius	CANCER
	sep 16, 1964–dec 15, 1964 feb 6, 1991–may 21, 1993 jun 30, 1993–jan 27, 1994	
	Transit: Uranus in Aquarius	Read Leo twice!
	jan 30, 1912–sep 3, 1912 nov 12, 1912–mar 31, 1919 aug 16, 1919–jan 21, 1920 apr 1, 1995–jun 8, 1995 jan 12, 1996–dec 31, 1999	
	Transit: Neptune in Aquarius	VIRGO
	jan 29, 1998–aug 22, 1998 nov 27, 1998–dec 31, 1999	
VIRGO	Transit: Jupiter in Pisces	GEMINI
	feb 20, 1903–feb 29, 1904 feb 4, 1915–feb 11, 1916 jan 18, 1927–jun 5, 1927 sep 11, 1927–jan 22, 1928 may 14, 1938–jul 29, 1938 dec 29, 1938–may 10, 1939 oct 30, 1939–dec 19, 1939 apr 15, 1950–sep 14, 1950 dec 1, 1950–apr 20, 1951 mar 25, 1962–apr 3, 1963 mar 8, 1974–mar 17, 1975 feb 20, 1986–mar 1, 1987 feb 4, 1998–feb 13, 1999	
	Transit: Saturn in Pisces	CANCER
	apr 13, 1905–aug 16, 1905 jan 8, 1906–mar 18, 1908 feb 14, 1935–apr 24, 1937	

If you want to dig deeper into	for the following time periods	read section titled
	Transit: Saturn in Pisces	CANCER
	oct 18, 1937–jan 13, 1938	
	mar 24, 1964–sep 15, 1964	
	dec 16, 1964–mar 2, 1967	
	may 21, 1993–jun 29, 1993	
	jan 28, 1994–apr 6, 1996	
	Transit: Uranus in Pisces	LEO
	apr 1, 1919–aug 15, 1919	
	jan 22, 1920–mar 30, 1927	
	nov 4, 1927–jan 12, 1928	
LIBRA	Transit: Jupiter in Aries	GEMINI
	mar 1, 1904–aug 7, 1904	
	aug 31, 1904–mar 7, 1905	
	feb 12, 1916–jun 25, 1916	
	oct 26, 1916–feb 11, 1917	
	jun 6, 1927–sep 10, 1927	
	jan 23, 1928–jun 3, 1928	
	may 11, 1939–oct 29, 1939	
	dec 20, 1939–may 15, 1940	
	apr 21, 1951–apr 27, 1952	
	apr 4, 1963–apr 11, 1964	
	mar 18, 1975–mar 25, 1976	
	mar 2, 1987–mar 7, 1988	
	feb 13, 1999–jun 27, 1999	
	oct 23, 1999–feb 13, 2000	
	Transit: Saturn in Aries	CANCER
	mar 19, 1908–may 16, 1910	
	dec 14, 1910–jan 19, 1911	
	apr 25, 1937–oct 17, 1937	
	jan 14, 1938–jul 5, 1939	
	sep 22, 1939–mar 19, 1940	
	mar 3, 1967–apr 28, 1969	
	apr 7, 1996–jun 8, 1998	

If you want to dig deeper into	*for the following time periods*	*read section titled*
	Transit: Saturn in Aries	CANCER
	oct 25, 1998 – feb 28, 1999	
	Transit: Uranus in Aries	LEO
	mar 31, 1927 – nov 3, 1927 jan 13, 1928 – jun 5, 1934 oct 10, 1934 – mar 27, 1935	
SCORPIO	Transit: Jupiter in Taurus	GEMINI
	aug 8, 1904 – aug 30, 1904 mar 7, 1905 – jul 20, 1905 dec 4, 1905 – mar 8, 1906 jun 26, 1916 – oct 25, 1916 feb 12, 1917 – jun 28, 1917 jun 4, 1928 – jun 11, 1929 may 16, 1940 – may 25, 1941 apr 28, 1952 – may 8, 1953 apr 12, 1964 – apr 21, 1965 mar 26, 1976 – aug 22, 1976 oct 16, 1976 – apr 2, 1977 mar 8, 1988 – jul 21, 1988 nov 30, 1988 – mar 10, 1989 jun 28, 1999 – oct 22, 1999 feb 14, 2000 – jun 29, 2000	
	Transit: Saturn in Taurus	CANCER
	may 17, 1910 – dec 13, 1910 jan 20, 1911 – jul 6, 1912 nov 30, 1912 – mar 25, 1913 jul 6, 1939 – sep 21, 1939 mar 20, 1940 – may 7, 1942 apr 29, 1969 – jun 17, 1971 jan 10, 1972 – feb 20, 1972 jun 9, 1998 – oct 24, 1998 mar 1, 1999 – aug 9, 2000 oct 16, 2000 – dec 31, 2000	

If you want to dig deeper into	for the following time periods	read section titled
	Transit: Uranus in Taurus	LEO

jun 6, 1934—oct 9, 1934
mar 28, 1935—aug 6, 1941
oct 5, 1941—may 14, 1942

SAGITTARIUS	Transit: Jupiter in Gemini	GEMINI

jul 21, 1905—dec 3, 1905
mar 9, 1906—jul 29, 1906
jun 29, 1917—jul 12, 1918
jun 12, 1929—jun 25, 1930
may 26, 1941—jun 9, 1942
may 9, 1953—may 23, 1954
apr 22, 1965—sep 20, 1965
nov 17, 1965—may 4, 1966
aug 23, 1976—oct 15, 1976
apr 3, 1977—aug 19, 1977
dec 30, 1977—apr 11, 1978
jul 22, 1988—nov 29, 1988
mar 11, 1989—jul 29, 1989
jun 30, 2000—dec 31, 2000

	Transit: Saturn in Gemini	CANCER

jul 7, 1912—nov 29, 1912
mar 26, 1913—aug 23, 1914
dec 7, 1914—may 10, 1915
may 8, 1942—jun 19, 1944
feb 21, 1972—jul 31, 1973
jan 7, 1974—apr 17, 1974
aug 10, 2000—dec 31, 2000

	Transit: Uranus in Gemini	LEO

aug 7, 1941—oct 4, 1941
may 15, 1942—aug 29, 1948
nov 12, 1948—jun 9, 1949

If you want to dig deeper into	*for the following time periods*	*read section titled*
	Transit: Neptune in Gemini	VIRGO
	dec 25, 1901–may 20, 1902	
	Transit: Pluto in Gemini	TAURUS
	jan 1, 1900–sep 9, 1912 oct 20, 1912–jul 8, 1913 dec 28, 1913–may 25, 1914	
CAPRICORN	Transit: Jupiter in Cancer	GEMINI
	jul 30, 1906–aug 17, 1907 jul 13, 1918–aug 1, 1919 jun 26, 1930–jul 16, 1931 jun 10, 1942–jun 29, 1943 may 24, 1954–jun 12, 1955 sep 21, 1965–nov 16, 1965 may 5, 1966–sep 26, 1966 jan 16, 1967–may 22, 1967 aug 20, 1977–dec 29, 1977 apr 12, 1978–sep 4, 1978 feb 28, 1979–apr 19, 1979 jul 30, 1989–aug 17, 1990	
	Transit: Saturn in Cancer	CANCER (this is complex; profes-sional astrologer should be consulted)
	aug 24, 1914–dec 6, 1914 may 11, 1915–oct 16, 1916 dec 7, 1916–jun 23, 1917 jun 20, 1944–aug 1, 1946 aug 1, 1973–jan 6, 1974 apr 18, 1974–sep 16, 1975 jan 14, 1976–jun 4, 1976	
	Transit: Uranus in Cancer	LEO
	aug 30, 1948–nov 11, 1948	

If you want to dig deeper into	for the following time periods	read section titled
	Transit: Uranus in Cancer	LEO
	jun 10, 1949–aug 23, 1955 jan 28, 1956–jun 9, 1956	
	Transit: Neptune in Cancer	VIRGO
	jul 19, 1901–dec 24, 1901 may 21, 1902–sep 22, 1914 dec 14, 1914–jul 18, 1915 mar 19, 1916–may 1, 1916	
	Transit: Pluto in Cancer	TAURUS
	sep 10, 1912–oct 19, 1912 jul 9, 1913–dec 27, 1913 may 26, 1914–oct 6, 1937 nov 25, 1937–aug 2, 1938 feb 7, 1939–jun 13, 1939	
AQUARIUS	Transit: Jupiter in Leo	GEMINI
	aug 18, 1907–sep 11, 1908 aug 22, 1919–aug 26, 1920 jul 17, 1931–aug 10, 1932 jun 30, 1943–jul 25, 1944 jun 13, 1955–nov 16, 1955 jan 18, 1956–jul 6, 1956 sep 27, 1966–jan 15, 1967 may 23, 1967–oct 18, 1967 feb 27, 1968–jun 14, 1968 sep 5, 1978–feb 27, 1979 apr 20, 1979–sep 28, 1979 aug 18, 1990–sep 11, 1991	
	Transit: Saturn in Leo	CANCER
	oct 17, 1916–dec 6, 1916 jun 24, 1917–aug 11, 1919 aug 2, 1946–sep 18, 1948	

If you want to dig deeper into	for the following time periods	read section titled
	Transit: Saturn in Leo	CANCER
	apr 3, 1949–may 28, 1949 sep 17, 1975–jan 13, 1976 jun 5, 1976–nov 16, 1977 jan 5, 1978–jul 25, 1978	
	Transit: Uranus in Leo	LEO (this is complex; professional astrologer should be consulted)
	aug 24, 1955–jan 27, 1956 jun 10, 1956–oct 31, 1961 jan 10, 1962–aug 9, 1962	
	Transit: Neptune in Leo	VIRGO
	sep 23, 1914–dec 13, 1914 jul 19, 1915–mar 18, 1916 may 2, 1916–sep 20, 1928 feb 19, 1929–jul 23, 1929	
	Transit: Pluto in Leo	TAURUS
	oct 7, 1937–nov 24, 1937 aug 3, 1938–feb 6, 1939 jun 14, 1939–oct 19, 1956 jan 15, 1957–aug 18, 1957 apr 11, 1958–jun 9, 1958	
PISCES	Transit: Jupiter in Virgo	GEMINI
	sep 12, 1908–oct 10, 1909 aug 27, 1920–sep 24, 1921 aug 11, 1932–sep 9, 1933 jul 26, 1944–aug 24, 1945 nov 17, 1955–jan 17, 1956 jul 7, 1956–dec 12, 1956	

If you want to dig deeper into	*for the following time periods*	*read section titled*
PISCES	Transit: Jupiter in Virgo	GEMINI
	feb 19, 1957–aug 6, 1957	
	oct 19, 1967–feb 26, 1968	
	jun 15, 1968–nov 14, 1968	
	mar 30, 1969–jul 14, 1969	
	sep 29, 1979–oct 26, 1980	
	sep 12, 1991–oct 9, 1992	
	Transit: Saturn in Virgo	CANCER
	aug 12, 1919–oct 6, 1921	
	sep 19, 1948–apr 2, 1949	
	may 29, 1949–nov 19, 1950	
	mar 7, 1951–aug 12, 1951	
	nov 17, 1977–jan 4, 1978	
	jul 26, 1978–sep 20, 1980	
	Transit: Uranus in Virgo	LEO
	nov 1, 1961–jan 9, 1962	
	aug 10, 1962–sep 27, 1968	
	may 20, 1969–jun 23, 1969	
	Transit: Neptune in Virgo	VIRGO (this is complex; professional astrologer should be consulted)
	sep 21, 1928–feb 18, 1929	
	jul 24, 1929–oct 2, 1942	
	apr 17, 1943–aug 1, 1943	
	Transit: Pluto in Virgo	TAURUS
	oct 20, 1956–jan 14, 1957	
	aug 19, 1957–apr 10, 1958	
	jun 10, 1958–oct 4, 1971	
	apr 17, 1972–jul 29, 1972	

Cutting Right to the Core

If you want to gaze right at the heart of your deepest relationship issues, you really have to explore a little goodie called the Seventh House, which is probably the key to it all. The Seventh House describes your whole outlook on the world, how you see members of the opposite sex whatever your sexual preference, and what you expect people to do when you're in a relationship with them.

What you have to provide for this part is your time of birth. It's probably on your birth certificate or etched onto the silver cup you've got stashed away, or maybe Aunt Jeanette remembers what time your mother went into labor. If it's not listed anywhere and you can't find anyone who remembers, you may have to skip this section. But remember if you closed the book right now, you'd have a lot to work on.

If you do know your time of birth, get your horoscope calculated by an astrologer or astrological computing service so you can find out the exact placement of all your planets. In the meantime, however, we're going to take a shortcut. Instead of working out messy calculations and dealing with complex astrological terms such as ascendant and descendant, mid-heaven and sidereal time, we're going to find your Rising Sign in a quick way. Your Rising Sign is the Sign of the Zodiac that appeared to be rising on the eastern horizon at the time of your birth. We've sneakily incorporated information about the Seventh House and Rising Sign in all the material in part one of this book. Once you have your Rising Sign, you can return to part one, read the appropriate section, and you'll cut right to the core of your relationship patterns.

Here's a short cut to *approximate* your Rising Sign:

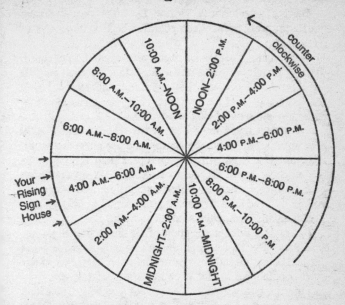

Just in case you don't know what sign you are, find your birthday on the following list. The word beside it is your Sun Sign. If you were born exactly on the day the signs change, you should consult an astrologer or computer astrology service to find out precisely what sign your Sun occupies. They sometimes vary slightly from year to year:

ARIES: mar 20–apr 20
TAURUS: apr 21–may 20
GEMINI: may 21–jun 21
CANCER: jun 22–jul 22
LEO: jul 23–aug 23
VIRGO: aug 24–sep 22
LIBRA: sep 23–oct 23
SCORPIO: oct 24–nov 22
SAGITTARIUS: nov 23–dec 22
CAPRICORN: dec 22–jan 19
AQUARIUS: jan 20–feb 18
PISCES: feb 19–mar 19

On the wheel above, locate the time period during which you were born. Write your Sun Sign in that sector of the wheel.

Now, using the list of signs above, find your Sign. Starting there and going down the list, write each successive Sign into the wheel, moving counterclockwise. If you reach the bottom of the list, keep going by starting back up at the top and moving down.

When you reach the sector of the wheel marked "4:00 A.M.-6:00 A.M.," write the appropriate Sign into that sector and stop. That Sign will be your approximate Rising Sign.

One little hitch: Because of the horrendous confusion with time zones and daylight-savings time and war time, you really need an experienced professional to help you. ·

But again, for now let's take a shortcut.

Below is a brief description of all the Rising Sign personalities. The Rising Sign doesn't usually describe one's deepest being but rather suggests the outer shell, the image other people have of one, even in a superficial way.

Find the one you've calculated for yourself. Then look at the ones before and after. If one of those descriptions fits you, chances are it's yours and your calculations were a little off because of the time zone mess. When you're reasonably sure of your Rising Sign, go back to part one of this book and read the section pertaining to that Sign as if it were yours. It will give you the core of it all, when it comes to relationships.

Thumbnail Descriptions of Rising Signs

Aries Rising

I may be about to have a heart attack from fright, but I always march into that burning building as if it's going to be a piece of cake. I want everything yesterday and pretend to believe in myself, not in fate.

Taurus Rising

Even if I'm down to my last thousand, I can make you think I'm as sound as a dollar should be. Even when I do cry poverty, I can make you think I'm rich. I talk about how much things cost all the time. I have a lot of plants and natural wood in my house.

Gemini Rising

In the last five years I have lived in at least three places. And if I haven't moved, I've thought about it plenty. In my day I have smoked probably about a million cigarettes, but I'm now turning over a new leaf.

Cancer Rising

I look about six-and-a-half months pregnant all the time, and my arms are a little too skinny for my body. I'm pretty moody and have plenty of sympathy for myself, especially when I see a lot of my mother in me.

Leo Rising

I have the pride of a Southerner and an ego that bruises more easily than a Dixie peach. I have sometimes lied about having affairs. They're not lies, exactly. And to tell the truth, weren't exactly affairs either.

Virgo Rising

I'm soooo good, and I make sure you know about it. It's a bit hard for me to admit when I'm wrong, and when I tell my stories, I'm usually the long-suffering victim of other people's sloppiness. It's only through divine Providence that I'm not still a virgin.

Libra Rising

I usually get you to think you chose the restaurant. I'm very gentle and sweet and kind, and sometimes when you talk to me my eyes glaze over and I smile lovingly at you while I pretend to be interested. I'm so damned accommodating, sometimes I actually make myself sick.

Scorpio Rising

My eyes are so piercing and my stare so intense that sometimes people don't sit next to me on the bus. People think I'm a lot sexier than I am, and that makes me happy. I don't tell anybody anything I wouldn't want everybody to know, so obvious I don't tell anybody anything.

Sagittarius Rising

Don't ever tell me a secret. I'm well-meaning, but I always blab. I'm the best-natured person you will ever meet. Even if it's maggots in a pail on the inside, the world sees only the smile. I'm a Christian Scientist at heart, I guess.

Capricorn Rising

I'm great at thinking why things won't work. I'm always trying to make something of myself, and no matter what I'm doing I am a sucker for those late-night TV ads where they tell you, "You can earn more money." I'm so uptight, it's ridiculous.

Aquarius Rising

I've always been interested in underground anti-social activities. In all my class pictures, for some reason I always stick out like the one from the planet Uranus.

Pisces Rising

I never really know what the hell I'm doing. And every time I try to get a grasp on myself and define who I am, it's like trying to grab the soap bubbles in the bathtub. But I have a lot of faith that things will work out just the way they're supposed to.

A Little Bit of Prediction

The planets are not standing still, of course. They've been whirling around up there since long before color TV was invented, and unless the Bomb or aerosol cans mess the whole works up entirely, they'll continue for a long time to come.

Since they do move around, though, influences change and attitudes shift, and you'll find that something or someone you're mad about for one, two, or five years all of a sudden doesn't interest you anymore. Or situations you never believed could happen do happen, and you're doing things you never thought possible. Let's look at some trends operating between 1985 and 2000.

In the following chart, when you come upon more than one influence operating during a given time period, don't go mad or give up. The paradoxes and conflicts reflect the ambivalence you will be having about your relationships, business and personal, during that period. Such ambivalence will be reflected in the availability/unavailability of the people you'll be involved with, some Catch-22's and mixed messages, all indicating your need during that time frame to experience growth through coping with complex individuals.

For example, in the following chart, see what will be going on in the lives of Leos in January 1998. In addition to acting like their usual warm and wonderful selves, they will be acting in their relationships like Geminis and Virgos—all at the same time.

Look at the following charts and test the predictions against the real people you are relating to during the time periods indicated.

For Sun Signs and Rising Signs	*during the period*	*In Part One read section(s) on*
ARIES	oct 10, 1992–nov 9, 1993	GEMINI
TAURUS	nov 10, 1993–dec 8, 1994	GEMINI
GEMINI	nov 17, 1985–feb 12, 1988 jun 10, 1988–nov 11, 1988	CANCER
	feb 17, 1981–dec 1, 1988	LEO
	jan 16, 1995–dec 31, 1999	TAURUS
CANCER	jan 19, 1984–nov 26, 1998	VIRGO
	feb 15, 1988–jan 11, 1996	LEO
	jan 3, 1996–jan 20, 1997	GEMINI
LEO	feb 6, 1985–feb 19, 1986 jan 21, 1997–feb 3, 1998	GEMINI
	feb 6, 1991–jan 27, 1994	CANCER
	apr 1, 1995–dec 31, 1999	Read Leo twice!
	jan 29, 1998–dec 31, 1999	VIRGO
VIRGO	feb 20, 1986–mar 1, 1987 feb 4, 1998–feb 13, 1999	GEMINI
	may 21, 1993–apr 6, 1996	CANCER
LIBRA	mar 2, 1987–mar 7, 1988 feb 13, 1999–feb 13, 2000	GEMINI
	apr 7, 1996–feb 28, 1999	CANCER

For Sun Signs and Rising Signs	during the period	In Part One read section(s) on
SCORPIO	mar 8, 1988–mar 10, 1989 jun 28, 1999–jun 29, 2000	GEMINI
	jun 9, 1998–dec 31, 2000	CANCER
SAGIT-TARIUS	jul 22, 1988–jul 29, 1989 jun 30, 2000–dec 31, 2000	GEMINI (this is complex; profes-sional astrologer should be consulted)
CAPRICORN	jul 30, 1989–aug 17, 1990	GEMINI
AQUARIUS	aug 18, 1990–sep 11, 1991	GEMINI
PISCES	sep 12, 1991–oct 9, 1992	GEMINI

For Astrology Fiends Only

Those readers of this book who are not versed in the language and symbols of astrology should skip this section and go right on to chapter Fourteen.

But for the real buffs, astrologers, and astrology fiends out there, the following chart is my attempt to encapsulate some of the more complex planetary configurations and fit them into the scheme of mirages, monsters, guardian angels, and miracle that we've worked out for the twelve Signs.

It's not totally complete, of course, but as astrologers you know well how much shading these astrological pictures always have. You'll be able to see from the following chart that when it comes down to synthesizing all the mirages, monsters, and angels, the horoscope is more of an abstract expressionist painting than a Jackson Pollack.

Use this chart, test it out, add to it, and cross out things you think don't work as well. Let time measure its accuracy by watching, hearing, and observing yourself and everybody around you: It will help you immeasurably in your transformation from ideal relationships to real ones.

If your Sun or Rising Sign is . . . —	*and/or you're involved with someone who is . . .*	*—and/or you have any of the following positions natally*	*Go back to Part One and read the section on*
ARIES	*LIBRA*	*☉ in 1. ♀ in 7, 10 or ♎. Aspects from ♀. ♀ in ♎ or 7. ☉ ☍ ruler of 1. Ruler of 7 in 7, 10 or ♎. Aspects from ♎, 7, ruler of 7.*	*ARIES*
TAURUS	*SCORPIO*	*☉ in 2. ♇ ☍ ☉. ♇ in 7, 10 or ♎. Aspects from ♇. ♀ in ♏ or 8. Ruler of 7 in ♏ or 8. Ruler of 8 in 7, 10 or ♎. Aspects from ♏, 8, ruler of 8.*	*TAURUS*
GEMINI	*SAGITTARIUS*	*☉ in 3. ♃ ☍ ☉. ♃ in 7, 10 or ♎. Aspects from ♃. ♀ in ♐ or 9. Ruler of 7 in ♐ or 9. Ruler of 9 in 7, 10 or ♎. Aspects from ♐, 9, ruler of 9.*	*GEMINI*
CANCER	*CAPRICORN*	*☉ in 4. ♄ ☍ ☉. ♄ in 7, 10 or ♎. Aspects from ♄. ♀ in ♑ or 10. Ruler of 7 in ♑ or 10. Ruler of 10 in 7, 10 or ♎. Aspects from ♑, 10, ruler of 10.*	*CANCER*
LEO	*AQUARIUS*	*☉ in 5. ♅ ☍ ☉. ♅ in 7, 10 or ♎. Aspects from ♅. ♀ in ♒ or 11. Ruler of 7 in ♒ or 11. Ruler of 11 in 7, 10 or ♎. Aspects from ♒, 11, ruler of 11.*	*LEO*
VIRGO	*PISCES*	*☉ in 6. ♆ ☍ ☉. ♆ in 7, 10 or 1. Aspects from ♆. 9 in ♓ or 12. Ruler of 7 in ♓ or 12. Ruler of 12 in 7, 10 or ♎. Aspects from ♓, 12, ruler of 12.*	*VIRGO*

If your Sun or Rising Sign is...	and/or you're involved with someone who is...	—and/or you have any of the following positions in your astrological chart	Go back to Part One and read the section on
LIBRA	ARIES	☉ in 7, ♐ 8 ☉. ♐ in 7, 10 or ♎. Aspects from ♐, 1, ♀ in ♈ or 1. Ruler of 7 in ♈ or 1. Ruler of 1 in 7, 10 or ♎. Aspects from ♈, 1, ruler of 1.	LIBRA
SCORPIO	TAURUS	☉ in 8. ♀ in ♉ or 2. Ruler of 7 in ♉ or 2. Ruler of 2 in 7, 10 or ♎. Aspects from ♀, 2, ruler of 2. ♐ in ♏ or 8.	SCORPIO
SAGITTARIUS	GEMINI	☉ in 9. ☿ in 7, 10 or ♎. Aspects from ♐. ☿ in ♊ or 3. Ruler of 7 in ♊ or 3. Ruler of 3 in 7, 10 or ♎. Aspects from ♊, 3, ruler of 3.	SAGITTARIUS
CAPRICORN	CANCER	☉ in 10. ☽ 8 ☉. ☽ in 7, 10 or ♎. Aspects from ☽. ♀ in ♋ or 4. Ruler of 7 in ♋ or 4. Ruler of 4 in 7, 10 or ♎. Aspects from ♋, 4, ruler of 4.	CAPRICORN
AQUARIUS	LEO	☉ in 11. ♀ in ♌ or 5. Ruler of 7 in ♌ or 5. Ruler of 5 in 7, 10 or ♎. Aspects from ♌, 5, ruler of 5.	AQUARIUS
PISCES	VIRGO	☉ in 12. ☿ in 7, 10 or ♎. Ruler of 7 in ♍ or 6. ruler of 6 in 7, 10 or ♎. Aspects from ♍, 6, ruler of 6.	PISCES

Chapter Fourteen

BLAME YOUR MOTHER

If you think your parents were totally wonderful, heavenly, perfect, divine beings, please skip this chapter. But if you've got any reservations at all about their sainthood, then here's a fascinating little experiment that will provide endless hours of thought and contemplation. You can't be literal, though. You've got to be open-minded in your interpretations, because we're going to be drawing archetypes and symbols that could actually work out in a million and one different ways.

Since we know that your parents' relationships to each other had a five hundred-megaton effect on you, then if we look at their relationship astrologically and see their celestial connection, we might be able to predict the astrological type of man or woman you'd be drawn to.

We say *type*, not the sign exactly, but the type described by one of the twelve signs. It's simply done. Look at the following list of zodiacal signs:

Aries	Libra
Taurus	Scorpio
Gemini	Sagittarius
Cancer	Capricorn
Leo	Aquarius
Virgo	Pisces

Find the Birth Sign of the parent who is the same sex as you. Going down the list and using that parent's sign as number 1, count until you find the Birth Sign of the parent of the opposite sex. Naturally, if you reach the bottom of the list before you get there, start over at the top and keep going. When you reach the Birth Sign of the parent of the opposite sex, stop.

Now find your own Sign on the list. Go down the list again and, using your own as number 1, count exactly the same number of signs.

When you've counted exactly stop and notice what Sign you've landed on.

Using the following table, go back and read the appropriate section. It will give you deeper insight into your relationship patterns.

If you've landed on	*Go back and read**
Aries	Libra
Taurus	Scorpio
Gemini	Sagittarius
Cancer	Capricorn
Leo	Aquarius
Virgo	Pisces
Libra	Aries
Scorpio	Taurus
Sagittarius	Gemini
Capricorn	Cancer
Aquarius	Leo
Pisces	Virgo

*You'll have to pretend you're a member of that sign for this part.

Once you've done so, you'll see more clearly how deeply your parents affect your relationships. Of course, when the sun is shining, a breeze is blowing into your face, and you're moving ahead in your own life, it's easy to be gracious about them. Come on, you think. Okay, so they didn't have the Dalai Lama's consciousness, but they did the best they could. You think of all the special gifts you have and you figure generously, Well, all this good stuff didn't come only from therapy.

On a bad day, though, when you're stuck in the cement mixer you call your life, you think of your parents and you're hit with tsunami-size waves of pain, confusion, anger, and guilt.

It hurts for you to think of their suffering and how, albeit unwittingly, they inflicted it on you. And it's all such a pea soup fog, besides. None of it is clear—who did what to whom and what you can do about it at this point. The rage that boils up in you when you think of how they lied to you, for whatever reasons, manipulated you, punished and brutalized you, distorted your view of reality to fit their own prejudices and fears, twisted you out of your natural shape into a grotesque Frankensteinian reflection of themselves. Though they might have said they were giving you the advantages they never had, they blatantly turned away from some glaring need you had that they refused to acknowledge.

And then, of course, when your murderous rage toward them steams to the surface and you're actually ready to level those charges against them, the guilt strikes. To have bad feelings toward your parents is wrong! Un-Christian, un-American, positively un-Cosmic! So then you slink down into yourself, pick a fight with your wife, say something absolutely terrible to your husband, screw up badly on the job.

No matter where you fall in the astrological scheme of things, you had parents, and if you had parents you've got troubles. And it doesn't do a bit of good to deny it all and say of your father, "He's too old and sick. He couldn't take hearing any of it now. I couldn't bring anything up to him.

It would be cruel. I couldn't tell him about all those things he did—it would kill him," or of your mother, "What's the use? She wouldn't hear me. If I reminded her of how she beat me up, she'd just smile and say, 'That's nice, dear.' She wouldn't hear a thing I said. She simply doesn't want to hear it."

You could pretend your parents were totally wonderful, but that's probably the worst thing to do in order to have a good, healthy relationship. If you refuse to acknowledge any of the undercurrents, you end up with just as negative an attitude deep down as if you thought only the worst of everybody. Aries, Virgo, Scorpio, Sagittarius: until you have a grip on the real story behind the first hot triangle in your life—your mother, your father, and you—you're nowhere on the road from ideal relationships to real ones. Behind, underneath, surrounding, and intertwined with your astrological sign, is your earliest relationship to Momma and Poppa.

In fact, this is the real source of the mirage-monster syndrome. When we are little, our parents are our gods. We worship them. Whatever they want for us must be right. These gods have given us life—hey, no small feat! So they must know a thing or two. And if they gave us life, they could probably take it away, so we'd better be good and please them. Besides, they're so beautiful. Look at a photograph of your parents taken when you were a child or just before you were born. You'll be struck with how gorgeous she was, what a hunk he was.

To us when we are little kids, our parents are the source and origin of love and beauty on Earth. So think of your own. If they treated you kindly, were warm and generous and consistently there to provide support in your shaky moments and constructive criticism when you were off the beam, then you're likely to be that way today. If, however they beat you up or mistreated each other, never giving you a break, if they competed with each other for your love or competed directly with you, put you down, always keeping you in a pre-earthquake state of uncertainty, then you are going to have a lot of trouble today sorting out the confusion over what love is and how to develop creative expression.

Many parents foster the image of themselves as gods. When they dress up as Santa Claus or play the tooth fairy, they get back a sense of their own divinity, their own magic power, which they probably feel has been lost by becoming an adult. Other parents use discipline of their children to alleviate their own suffering from the sense of inner powerlessness. Lavish rewards for good behavior, awesome wrath for bad, all make little children believe that their parents are God.

But when we step out into the world and see that *reality* has about fourteen zillion more facets than we ever dreamed, we often feel disillusioned by our childhoods. Whether you were happy or miserable under your parents' regime, you accepted it as reality—that's the way things *were*. And when you're out in the world and you see how easily and smoothly some people move about and advance in those areas you find most difficult, you think back to your parents' teachings and your very soul flinches.

These "gods" turn out to be desperate, crippled neurotics handing down their prejudices and distortions to you. You see their control and manipulation only too clearly, and you understand at last the Greek tragedy that was their existence. And you are angry to think that along with your brown eyes and curly hair, they passed the whole thing onto you. The further back you look, in fact, the more clearly you see the family curse, snaking its way forward, from Grandma's time right on down to the present, hissing at you right in the face.

You get angriest at your own blindness. What you thought was a sensitive parent was a weak parent; what you thought was good-naturedness was indolence. Eccentricity was infantile rebelliousness, and so on. The qualities you once revered now turn out to be your dilapidated model for a bogus reality, *molded* out of a couple's adaptive behavior to their own chaotic childhoods.

You are angry and disappointed, and here's where we get into trouble.

A wise person once jokingly said, "You can never forgive your parents until you've killed your own children." And there is some truth in that sweet little saying. Nothing gives you insight like your own life. And when you see what your children become because of your efforts and because of your problems, all you can do is hope they have kids someday. Because it's difficult otherwise to come to any deep understanding of how, in trying to do our best, we actually kill off part of our children. We do it by our own unconscious jealousy that their lives might actually be easier than ours, by ignoring some crucial aspect of their development that needs tending, or by crushing a part of them that is too difficult for us to face.

You can be sure of one thing: whatever you do today will be reported by your children to their psychiatrist in the year 2020 or 2100.

If you don't have children, then the buck stops here, and you have only your relationship to your parents to rely on to get you on the road. Children or not, a confrontation with the parents is the crossroads between ideal and real relationships for all the Signs of the Zodiac. To go from monster to miracle, you need to be able to ask questions, challenge positions, pursue the paradoxes and mixed messages your parents sent you. If you're adopted, then your adoptive parents serve the same function. Even if both your parents died early on, somebody had to raise you, and that somebody is the one you need to communicate with.

Some parents are defensive and controlling. They believe they did their best, made sacrifices, gave their children chances to grow and develop in ways they didn't, and they're not eager to hear the negatives. Very early on, many parents crush their children's will, never permitting the child to be bad or have unhappy feelings. When the kid is grown up, the parent still insists on maintaining this suppressive role.

Then, too, many children don't like to hear *back* any negative feelings their parents might have toward them either. They think theirs is the only case being brought to court. They can't conceive that their parents might have some good reasons to be resentful, enraged, and sick to death of *their* antics, either.

The unfortunate solution often reached: withdrawal of communication. Quick-frozen in the monster stage, the child (by now walking around in an adult body) exists in a depressed state, visiting singles bars and discos, always looking for that "right" person.

In an absolutely infantile effort to return to that glorious first idealizing state before the parents become monsters, some of us go after one unreal situation after another, never actually able to step outside ourselves to attain the miracle promised by our Sign, because we are looking for the mirage of the perfect parent.

Every time a potential partner exhibits a trait that reminds you of a certain monster in your past, does the relationship have to face the threat of disintegration?

Communication is the path from monster straight through to the miracle, no matter what sign you are. You must pass *through* the monster stage (there's no way around it) to be able to view partners and parents as human beings, not gods or devils—human beings with supremely loving natures. The guardian angels for your sign have been devised as a caricature of your parents, and coming to terms with them will bring you to a mature acceptance of your real self and of the positions of other real people in relation to you.

A lot, therefore, depends on our relationship to our parents. How we related to them, how they related to us, how they related (or didn't) to each other, everything we saw in those first days, weeks, months, and years, are all powerful determinants in our attitudes toward the opposite sex and our own sex.

Once real communication with parents is established, the monster shrinks immediately. If real contact is maintained with family members (you don't have to love them to death), the monster eventually blows up and withers away. Then your issues, questions, and challenges can be vigorously pursued with other people and you won't constantly get caught confusing a partner's conduct with your personal monster.

As you master your issues, answer your questions, and meet your personal challenges, the miracle occurs automatically. To help you establish and maintain a real communication with your parent or parents, here are a couple of suggestions.

Put in your mind the determination that every conversation you have with these people from now on will be a meaningful one. This does not mean a knock-down, drag-out fight every time someone opens their mouth. You don't, blurt out accusations and irrelevancies from the past.

Go back to part one of this book and read the sections assigned to both your parents. Learn what their relationship expectations were and what their relating styles are.

Then decide that your goal over a long term is to find out everything you don't know about your relationship with them—to express feelings and ideas you've been afraid to bring up and to face bravely whatever grievances there might be on their part against you (hard as it might be to believe). The goal is to express love between you, free from hidden fears, hurts, and resentments. This is possible in every case, no matter how much gore you find below the surface.

What were the conditions existing in their relationship when you were born? What changes occurred in their lives as a result of your arrival? What was going on inside you and them while you were growing up?

Avoid a threatening tone. Seeking truth is not the same as presenting the prosecution's cross-examination of a defendant. If you want the best results, don't threaten—communicate.

You may wonder why you have to go back and start with parents or family members if you've been independent and living on your own for five, ten, or forty years and you've already got a life full of partners, lovers, friends, etc.

Parents are the real source of the mirage-monster syndrome. If you start at the real source, there will be a real healing. Real healing means real relationships. If you're communicating honestly with family members, you can try the same experiments with everyone else in your life and watch the results.

We spend our lives aping our parents in some ways, escaping them in others. A lot we can overcome—a lot we have to accept. Whoever guided you during those early years left an indelible stamp on you and provided you with a model for relating that you often strive to reject, yet seek to recreate.

Is it simply that if you come from a happy home you are more likely to seek out and accept intimacy? Are you cynical and practical, shy, romantic, married, single, heterosexual, homosexual? Where does it all start? If they were constantly at each other's throats, will you tend to shun close relationships? Was your father accessible or off in the distance? Were the men in your family hard or easy to deal with? Were the family members intelligent, racist? Did they really welcome you when you arrived?

It's strange, but the mere mention of childhood pushes such buttons. When you start thinking about things your mother said to your father, things he did to her, why suddenly, right in the middle of such thoughts, you'll fall asleep, get a headache, or get ravenously hungry—without knowing why.

Did they determine it *all*?

It doesn't matter what belief system you hold. Our parents have created a towering set of structures we have to deal with if we are ever to have real fruitful relationships. And you can trace everything back to those early relationships and read it all in the horoscope—those things we are *really* saying and thinking while we think we're saying and thinking something else entirely; the tricks we play on ourselves, one another; those little recordings that run madly through the mind while you are looking into someone's eyes or holding the phone to your ear and pretending to listen; the things people do and say as a way of grasping for security in the mind-squooshing games of relationships

—it all goes back to the family, because they're the first ones you tried your horoscope on.

Patterns do keep appearing. Although most of the big issues do come up for everybody at some time or other during life, certain, specific ones do indeed occur more frequently and have a greater affinity for some people than for others, according to Zodiacal Sign, of course.

But is it all random?

Does the stork open its beak to yawn at four P.M. on May 15 and you just happen to drop into a chimney at the corner of Elm and Maple to become the hapless puppet of Doris and Charley Whatchamacallit? Is there a giant cosmic game plan? Are there souls? Are our parents our parents for a purpose we can but dimly grasp? Do babies up there draw lots to who goes where, or is there after all some purposeful order to parent-child relationships? How much of it is made in Heaven?

No matter how true astrology is, when we're alone with ourselves in the bathroom or driving down the freeway, when we're with our thoughts and feelings, we don't think so much about the Moon or Libra or Sagittarius. The only reality we have to refer to is the home we came from. And when all else fails, when astrology breaks down and cannot give you the answer you need, by all means *blame your mother*.

· You've got to get through that stage. You cannot move ahead until you come to terms with the rage and anger you feel toward your parents for all the distortions they've laid on you. You've got to pass through it and embrace them totally on the other side of it. If you're ever to get to the love that exists beneath, you've got to pass through your anger and frustration. Early history determines your views on relationships and thus all the relationships you form.

Chapter Fifteen

MADE IN HEAVEN

When we go to a wedding these days, some of us find ourselves sitting in the back pew, shredding Kleenex and gouging our cheeks, thinking, "Look at them. So in love. I hate them both!" But before we kill ourselves in the bathroom of the church, we should really wait and talk to the happy couple eighteen months from now and hear what they have to say about each other, because time has a way of altering our perceptions.

We make gods and goddesses out of people, then are horrified to learn they've got hair growing out of their nose—or worse. We meet people and immediately start praying they're going to give us what we've never had—love, money, recognition. Anything we feel we don't have, these people seem to have plenty of. So we try to merge with them to get this elusive thing. It proves to be false, of course. Sooner or later we feel the emptiness again, and that shining, golden figure starts to turn a little green around the edges. The "savior" has as many holes as Swiss cheese, and before we know it all we can see is the holes, giant flaws that mirror back to us the emptiness of our own fantasies. What we are doing of course is projecting our own negativity onto other people, believing we can get rid of the Number One Major Problem in our lives just by throwing someone out the window. Of course it is wise not to get hooked on people at all, or at least resist judgment about someone's "divinity" until we see our favorite Adonis chain-smoking Camels, or our darling Venus getting fatter and fatter.

But we can't help it. We're driven into fantasy by a sense of deprivation we can bear for only so long. And then along comes a person eating an ice cream cone the very flavor we've been dying for. Lower your head and recite the Koran all you want, but eventually we all have to admit our need for human companionship. And then we're hooked. The person who is the source of our pleasure is also the source of our pain—the pain of the fear of withdrawal of pleasure. This person then gains overwhelming control over us.

So what do we do? To achieve appropriate distance, we'll find ourselves either on top of people, trying to crawl into their skin, utterly merging with them, or pushing them away for our own sanity. Sometimes we punish ourselves through relationships. If we pursue a wish we don't really believe we deserve to have fulfilled, we then live in a constant state of anxiety over rejection and will actually be relieved when it finally happens. If we think someone is going to fail us, then he or she will, because we'll set up a set of expectations that can never be met. So sooner or later the fatal flaw we've been waiting for will appear. We'll get someone dependent on us, hook 'em when they start to be free, reject 'em when they show us their need.

If *dependence* is our great fear, then naturally the universe will send us someone who's dependent on us or someone we're madly dependent on. Or because we are scared of dependence, we'll set up a relationship with someone we can't really count on, someone whose existence will prove to be socially embarrassing because they symbolize a part of ourselves we'd rather *not* be associated with.

When dependency issues become overwhelming or distortions threaten a relationship, self-reliance is the key to success. It's what makes widows start over in Florida, and divorced men join a health club and look great. It's the life force within us all, the drive to take action, be in control of our lives, walk without those goddamn crutches. It's the reason the doctors can throw up their hands, shrug and say, "It's terminal," and then the patient not only gets off the life-support machine, but sends the doctors a card from Tibet six months later. Self-reliance is all the stuff we'd like help with but know we have to do on our own.

Sometimes people can help us best by throwing us out of a moving car and telling us to get home on our own. It's a lonely path. Everybody wants to be taken care of. Strangely, through we'll waver and wobble and act helpless, at the last minute we'll surprise ourselves with our resilience. Though we may feel sometimes half of us has been ripped away when our fantasies fail us, the power of self-generation is amazing. And in the end, it's what prepares us best for real relationships with real people.

So, here we are. Maybe we're a little closer to a happier relationship life than we were at the start of this book. Naturally, if we didn't have any problems or curiosity about relationships, I wouldn't have written this book and you wouldn't have read it. The book is probably as much therapy for me as it is information for you. Actually, even we are having a relationship. You, the Readers, and I, the Author. I have some insights that may help you to heal and improve your interactions with others, and in return you are paying some money for the book. And if you've carefully read all twelve sections of part one of this book, then you should readily be able to determine where I fit in astrologically

Every contact between two people is a relationship, and every relationship is an outgrowth of the influences of the early family life. Those influences can be measured through the astrological wheel. I write the book "because" of my childhood and "because" of my horoscope; you buy and read it because of yours. Somehow in the great scheme of things we have found each other. At this distance, of course, we're both safe.

Ah, but in closer relationships, when greater cooperation and compromise are needed, when control issues arise, when emotions enter, how well do we both do then, dear readers? There's no reason at this point to give you a detailed account of my personal history in relationships. But in those relationships where I can be fulfilled, I have found great fulfillment. And in those relationships where distortions have not yet been eradicated, I have met grief.

Aha! So, Mr. How-to-have-a-good-relationship has grief, does he? So much for transformations from ideal to real!

Not so.

All right, so I don't have all the answers. I never said I did. I am a student of relationships. I never said I had already graduated.

Well, now where are we? Are we puppets being jiggled around the stage of life by our parents' string-pulling? Are we robots responding by remote control to the subliminal hum of planetary commands? If so, then we cannot hope for more than endless repetition of ancient calcified patterns or childish instinctive responses. Then we are doomed by our early, innocent love for our parents, condemned by our horoscopes.

There is no known way to separate early environmental conditioning from astrological observation. The possible connections between them will always stimulate vigorous philosophical speculation, but no way can the two be separated. Your horoscope and your parents are one; they are aspects of yourself you must accept. Period.

Who decided what family you were to go into or what astrological sign you were to be, I don't know. Childish magical thinking about the forces of destiny relieves our tensions temporarily but inevitably we are forced back onto the path of leading our own lives. Psychological therapies, religion and spiritual explanations about the origin and purpose of existence, furnish us with a faith that expands our capacity to understand and forgive.

But no method of coming to terms with self is of any value unless it shows up in our lives as permanent practical improvement. People don't want enlightenment unless there's gratification attached to it. And that can only happen if our explanations of why we are who we are correspond to a deep, organic, emotional, transformational release of the past.

And that involves the factor of ourselves. Each of us has a mind capable of solving every problem that is put before us, and a spirited will to put those solutions into everyday life. It has to be so, since every problem we have is a creation of our own minds. Our parents and our horoscopes are "realities" we cannot escape, but it is only our distorted perception and fear of communication that prevent us from a resolution of all paradoxes presented by them.

The horoscope (as well as our position in our families) symbolizes not at all what *is* but what *was* a long time ago. The satisfactory resolution of the issues raised by those "realities" will free us to live in the present, free us from enslavement to a repetition of past tendencies that dog us throughout life.

We can't change what was. Until a time machine is invented that will take us back into the past to alter it, we'll have to content ourselves with making some hard choices here in the present if we want to change the future.

Assuming you're in the market for someone who is available, in business or personal life, for example, you need to be on your toes, eyes wide open, ears free of wax, and nose in full operation in the very first meeting. A couple of hundred pages ago we talked about the conditions of that first meeting and how crucial they were to the foundation of any future relationship.

By now you have a lot more astrological information about yourself and anyone you meet for business or personal reasons than you had while reading the introductory chapters. Knowing someone's astrological coordinates will give you a new dimension of their relating style and requirements, conscious and unconscious needs for a full-grown relationship. You can see how you're being idealized by someone, how you turn them into a monster, and what the real issues behind the relationship might be.

In addition to that, always notice the conditions of the first meeting. Where were you? Why were you there? Who brought you together? What were your first impressions—surprise, excitement, disappointment? Be honest. What was the first conversation about? How did the first meeting end—who left first and why? How did you feel during the meeting and afterwards?

If you're brave and honest with your assessment of this first encounter, you will be able to measure the true level of someone's availability and appropriateness, as well as the foundation, structure, and probable outcome of the relationship.

If you open your eyes at the beginning, you'll be able to recognize the game of repetition as well. Many of our patterns are habitual, so that we do them instantly and automatically, without the slightest awareness. We act hostile and defensive or weak and babylike. We're competitive, controlling; we sexualize. The games and roles we engage in when we meet people set up a pattern for the relationship, and then, when other people respond to the cues we've given them, we get angry or hurt or disappointed.

Recognizing this behavior takes discipline. It's work to stretch your awareness, wake up your snoozing consciousness, and train those lazy muscles away from their old patterns.

When somebody pushes a button that sends you to the moon fueled by your own rage, this, too, can be an example of repetition. You've been attracted to someone for mirage reasons, then go up in flames when the mirage becomes a monster. If you get stuck in people's monsters, you probably have trouble communicating with the Great Source Monster—Family—and you have to go back there and start at square one.

Recognition of repetition is not a solution. For one thing, just because you notice a trait is not necessarily a reason to stamp it out. *The goal, of course, is to enhance the growth and development of patterns that make you and other people happy and to strive to eliminate those patterns that do not.* Don't expect to have a great revelation, hang your crutches on the altar, and dance away delirious and whole. You're involving yourself in a process. Healing is possible for everybody. A realistic assessment of how extensive the childhood damage was and the arrangement of the horoscope patterns will indicate the relative simplicity or complexity of the issues involved, and thus the relationships you'll tend to form to work on those issues. Simpler stories have simpler resolutions. Some people's road is longer and rockier than others, so the sooner we all get started, the better—and recognizing the patterns of repetition will keep you moving forward.

But on the other end of a relationship—at what point does one pull the plug? Facing the failure of a relationship to work takes courage on both people's parts, and as much cooperation to effect a satisfactory separation as it does a union.

If mutual goals are too widely different and interests so disparate that there are no common grounds to hold it together, then the politics of separation have to be dealt with. How you separate is crucial, because whatever new relationship you take up with is often a sly continuation of the one you left off, so it always pays to negotiate an appropriate separation.

How can you tell if a relationship is really over or some issue has been touched that you simply cannot deal with and are running away? Some people are so terrified of facing the aloneness that follows the release of a relationship that they'll hang on forever to something that doesn't exist anymore. Other people run the minute there's trouble and fill their lives with one faceless replacement after another, because it's too painful to go back to the source and heal it there.

A separation should involve both people. The one who leaves is often acting out the unexpressed wishes of the "abandoned," probably more passive partner. So to determine whether a relationship is alive or not takes both people to own up to their passions and anxieties. Separation is not a solution for conflict (contrary to what many Geminis will say), but when it is staring you in the face, deal with it.

The miracles we outlined for each of the twelve Signs really belong to everybody, and the most productive relationships involve the mutual mastering of them all. We will list them one final time:

> Dedication (clarity)
> Loving
> Intimacy (sharing feeling)
> Communication
> Manifestation (business)
> Confrontation
> Letting go (spirituality)
> Experimentation
> Depth (success)
> Openness (wisdom)
> Mystery

If you believe that relationships bring trouble and conflict and pose impossible choices, then your horoscope will indicate that fact with conflicting aspects and angles between the planets. If you don't know your astrological chart, just take a look at your life. If you see relationships as bad, you'll find yourself getting lost in the mirages, eaten by monsters. Though we think we're fleeing childhood, we are actually like sleepwalkers who have climbed out of our cribs and wander through the night, dreaming our adult life but never living it. And no matter how potentially thrilling or blissful a new contact may be, we'll wring every drop of tragedy out of it and turn it into a tear-jerker movie.

If, however, you see relationships basically as positive, life-affirming experiences, your horoscope will reflect it and your life will reflect love and trust as well.

True, I've seen some wretched orphans find great happiness in marriage, and many horoscopes with promise have also been wasted. So don't ever think you have it all figured out. Just when you've decided you can cope with loneliness, a flower pot falls out of a window with a gorgeous person sitting in it and lets you know just what you've been missing.

It's astounding how we draw the people we need exactly when we need them. Whoever is in charge of pairing people up, up there in Heaven, is doing a fabulous job. It's all so perfect. We get the ones we are supposed to get exactly when we're supposed to get them. "Supposed to" maybe not in the sense that the angels pick two people up by the scruff of the neck, throw them down in a house together, and say, "Here. Relate."

But we all have an inner guide. It's measured in the horoscope. The family nurtures it. But it's in us all. I stagger in contemplation of the perfection of it. I cringe; I weep with joy to behold astrology, its truth, and how it blends with the family to produce me. I scream in terror at the sight of the scary monsters; I'm still working on the miracles.

Every relationship we have comes at a time when certain planets are lining up and "bringing" certain people to us. That person represents a whole set of values, strengths, and weaknesses that it's obviously time for us to embrace. Heaven describes perfectly what is going on here on Earth. To view the majestic, impassive way the solar system whirls and tumbles us around in its vast automatic washer-dryer fills me with wonder, awe, and dread.

May we all be granted the healthy, loving relationship we all deserve. But praying for it is not enough. You've got to work on yourself, experience yourself, know where you're alive, face where you're dead, and learn how to leave the past behind without burying it a half hour before it dies. You summon people not by voodoo but by the sheer force of your inner needs.

Are some people destined to meet other people? Is there someone out there for everybody? Are some people written down for happiness and others slated for disappointment? It's there in the horoscope—all our relationship needs. Our patterns are made in Heaven, as is the potential for interpreting our past and living in our present and creating our future. Within the horoscope the family story is told. Within the astrological chart, as well, are the drive and will of every person to become a loving being.

But we get accustomed to deprivation, we accept a lack of fulfillment, and we live with repression, frustration, as if human sorrow were the only thing made in Heaven.

We live in the desert, trekking onward with parched lips, allowing ourselves two drops of water that we've got stored in our canteens, before we crash down in the sand and curl up in the shelter of a dune. Then we come upon an oasis: water everywhere, fountains splashing, sunlight glinting on wet bodies, everything green and tropical. Is it a mirage?

Love comes to us all. We all get a turn, no matter what our horoscope says, no matter what kind of family we come from. We have to know how to recognize it, seize it, ride it for all it's worth, and handle it, but it comes to us all.

Cynics, chuckle all you want to. Shake your heads and feel sorry for me. But I've been to the oasis. And it's real enough for me. You don't come upon one very often, but when you do, when you make real contact with a real person, music starts blasting out of every window in your soul. When you've experienced another person's inner core, been ignited by it, you're alive. And when you've been experienced, seen, touched, felt, and known, you want to live and live and live again. When you've been touched by another human being with love, it's natural to want to hold on.

That's when the trouble starts. Because when you want something more, you get something more—namely, the monsters. When you touch love, you don't want to think about monsters. But behind the innocent attractions we have for one another, complex forces are at play. And some of them are very scary. They all represent our very human and very flawed attempt to taste love.

At that point the mirage is dead, but the relationship is

just beginning, because relationships don't really ever end. Once you know someone, you can never unknow them. You may split up, go your separate ways, or one of you may die. But relationships do not ever end. They only change form. What final form they take is up to you.